Sons of the Conqueror

SONS OF THE CONQUEROR

Descendants of Norman Ancestry

LESLIE G. PINE,

B.A. London;
Barrister-at-Law, Inner Temple, F.J.I.,
F.S.A. Scot., F.R.S.A., F.R.G.S., F.R.A.S.

CHARLES E. TUTTLE COMPANY
Rutland, Vermont & Tokyo, Japan

Representatives
Continental Europe: BOXERBOOKS, INC., *Zurich*
British Isles: PRENTICE-HALL INTERNATIONAL, INC., *London*
Australasia: PAUL FLESCH & CO., PTY. LTD., *Melbourne*
Canada: M. G. HURTIG LTD., *Edmonton*

Published by the Charles E. Tuttle Company, Inc.
of Rutland, Vermont & Tokyo, Japan
with editorial offices at
Suido 1-chome, 2–6, Bunkyo-ku, Tokyo, Japan

Library of Congress Catalog Card No. 71-172001

International Standard Book No. 0-8048-0972-0

First edition, 1973

PRINTED IN JAPAN

Table of Contents

Preface

THIS is the third book in which I have written about the Normans and the Norman Conquest. I have always been interested in the subject and when I returned to take up the management of *Burke's Peerage* and other works after the war, I found that the claim to Norman ancestry was one with which any editor of the *Peerage* would have to reckon. More so still, if he proposed, as I did, to edit the work much more critically than had been done before. I therefore gave particular attention to the genealogical aspect of the Conquest.

In 1946 when I left the Royal Air Force and undertook the editing of the Burke volumes, unexpected difficulties were encountered. Nothing had been done to keep the books up to date; the rate and number of changes in the years 1939–45 had been far greater than in corresponding years of peace; there was no expert pre-war staff available, and staff had to be obtained and trained. Nor could my time be devoted to genealogy alone, for *pari passu* with the Burke volumes, there was also to be revived the Shaw's Standard Reference Series, work on the first of which was begun in 1946 at the same time as on the *Peerage. The Author's & Writer's Who's Who* (Shaw) appeared in 1948;

the first postwar *Burke's Peerage* appeared in 1949 after $2\frac{3}{4}$ years work. The new *Peerage* caused a great sensation. It was the 99th edition and many who knew it from prewar had not expected it to reappear. In addition, a very great effort of revision had been made and in place of myths and legends there were now credible pedigrees.

After this, work was begun on a new edition of *Burke's Landed Gentry* and here again a fresh critical approach was made. For the sake of the record, I shall mention that at the same time there was projected an entirely new work, *The International Year Book and Statesmen's Who's Who*. The first edition of the latter appeared in 1953 and it has gone healthily each year since. I edited the first eight editions, and planned the ninth.

The 15th edition of *Burke's Landed Gentry* came out in 1952, and again it received a vast amount of attention in the press. It was followed in 1953 by the 100th and Coronation edition of *Burke's Peerage*.

Those seven years, 1946–53, were a time of great labor, some anxieties, mainly of a mechanical production nature, and innumerable difficulties, but all the same a period of much happiness in achievement. As regards the books which I edited, I have the satisfaction that they are still being produced, and produced on lines which I laid down during my more than 14 years, from 1946 to 1960, of executive editorship.

During these years, 1946–53, I found time to write several books, *Trace Your Ancestors, The Middle Sea, History of Mediterranean, The Story of Heraldry, The House of Wavell* and *The Golden Book of the Coronation*. The last named was written for the *Daily Mail*. When it was commissioned, I was told that the requirement was for a book which would still be kept after the Coronation. Judging by the price which the rarely available copies command, the order appears to have been met. *The Stuarts of Traquair* was my first book, printed in 1940 in the U.S.A., to support the claim of a friend to a dormant earldom. Here, too, the book is priced quite high at secondhand. During the war, while serving in Africa and Italy, I had written a short history of the Mediterranean which arose out of a series of lectures that I had given to my squadron and many other units. Later when serving in India, I took advantage of the libraries in the Secretariat in New Delhi and checked many details, also getting the manuscript typed. On my return home, the book was published by Edward Stanford (George Phillips) under the title, *The Middle Sea*. It is to be republished in a revised edition by Messrs. David & Charles Ltd., of Newton Abbot, Devon, England. I mention it in some detail here as it is one of my books which has nothing to do with genealogy. I was always interested in being a writer, and had written a great deal pre-war, which I destroyed in 1946 on my return, deciding then to make a fresh start as an author. In the result, my authorship was for many years canalized into genealogy, heraldry, peerage and allied subjects, a channel from which I am now emerging to write, as I originally intended, in more general literary forms.

The Coronation year, 1952–53, saw also the development of an enormous journalistic production on my part. I have no idea how much I was called upon to write for all sorts of newspapers, magazines and other organizations during that time, but it started a vast output of articles which has continued ever since, my own estimate in *Who's Who* of some 2,000 commissioned articles being certainly within the limits. In 1953 I had the pleasure of being called to the Bar at the Inner Temple, after six years as a student, reading for the Bar.

Of the three other works mentioned above, *Trace Your*

Ancestors was well received and has proved its use over many years by the publication of several new editions and reprints. It is now a paperback. The immediate genesis of the little book was a suggestion of John Pudney, who at that time was literary adviser to Messrs. Evans Bros. Ltd., but I had long felt the need of such a book, since I, who was working all day in matters of genealogy, found the existing textbooks very hard to understand, and therefore could sympathize with those who, ignorant of the subject, wished to learn about it.

The House of Wavell was a private family history which I felt deeply privileged in being asked to write. I had met the first Earl Wavell and his successor, the latter only a little while before his tragic death.

So far everything had gone well, with the kind co-operation of the various offices of arms. Now in 1952 with the publication of *The Story of Heraldry*, the first signs of trouble appeared. I was, as I am now, and always have been, a free writer unconstrained by allegiance to anything but the truth; unfettered by any scruple except that of good feelings. In this last named book I wrote of the history of heraldry as the science had developed in the English-speaking world. I pointed out that in England, as contrasted with Scotland, there was no real heraldic law. The two procedures by which the English heralds had sought to control the use of arms had failed to operate after the 18th century. There had been no Heralds' Visitations since 1686; the Court of Chivalry had not sat since 1735–37. In 1952 this was true but I added that I thought it unlikely that the court would be revived. If my remarks were correct, then there was nothing to prevent anyone in England or Wales from using arms which he had assumed for himself. Indeed the point was immediately taken and letters flowed in—from places as far apart as Finland and East Africa—thanking me for my help in clearing up armorial troubles. Clearly there would be others whose feelings would be the reverse of gratitude.

In 1952 also the new *Landed Gentry* contained an introductory section which I had devised, in which were four articles, on English, Welsh, Scottish and Irish genealogy, each written by a native of the country. The first I wrote, and in it I gave a list of the admitted Companions of the Conqueror, to which I added the name of Adelolf de Merc. A full account of the controversy over this is given in the present book in Notes 41 and 47. I need not do more here than mention it, except to say that like the cloud no bigger than a man's hand, it portended a downpour.

Some time in this period I was told by a former officer of arms, "you have done much good work, but you have made many enemies." I was to discover the truth of this. There were many persons who were upset by the removal or alteration of cherished items in their family histories in Burke. They relished their legends or myths, and often were quite content to hug known falsehoods to their bosoms. Then there were those whose blood had boiled at the thought that arms could be assumed at will. In other cases people had approached me with suggestions for publication which I as an executive felt unable to recommend; and finally one has to think of possible opponents among those whose contracts of employment it had been my lot to terminate.

In 1954 with the publication of *They Came with the Conqueror*, some critics came into the open. The book was a publishing success. It went into two hard-cover printings, an American edition was sold, and now 17 years later, it still sells, as a paperback. Out of more than 100 press notices, less than half a dozen were not such as to please both publisher and author. In fact, they may have pleased the publisher because I took up the few unfavorable reviews and thus the book gained even greater publicity. I know that following the controversy in *The Observer*, in May–June 1954, the proposal for an American edition was clinched.

The Observer review was written by the late Randolph Churchill in a style to which I took the greatest exception. I replied at equal length the following Sunday. I expected to be involved in a furious word war with Churchill but to my surprise the third Sunday a champion of a very different stamp appeared in Churchill's stead. This was Dermot Morrah, of *The Times*, and Arundel Herald Extraordinary (i.e., one of the extra heralds appointed by the College of Arms from time to time, especially in Coronation years). He began an attack upon the scholarly quality of my book. I felt sorry that he should have been engaged in such a controversy. So, before the close of it, did he, I think, for I am perfectly sure that he had no wish to attack me. In a subsequent letter which he wrote to a third party, an editor, who showed it to me, he wrote: "I entered *The Observer* correspondence at the request of an eminent person who thought that Randolph Churchill had been unjustly assailed, but who felt debarred by his official position from intervening himself."

There is much that is amusing in this account; the idea that Randolph Churchill could have been upset or even assailed, is not one likely to commend itself to those who witnessed his exploits in controversy. Even more amusing is the idea of the highly placed person who did not think it well to intervene. He was wise in his generation. No matter what his eminence, he would have got the same treatment as anyone else who I thought was being unfair to me. As to the identity of the highly placed, I have no doubts.

One interesting sequel to the views set forth in the earlier work, *The Story of Heraldry,* was the fact that in 1954–55 the Court of Chivalry was revived. In no other country in the world could such a thing have happened, for an institution to be revived after a dormancy of $2\frac{1}{4}$ centuries. The proceedings of the court have been set forth in several works, but the essential fact is that despite the sitting of the court, heraldic anarchy is still prevalent in England and Wales, where there cannot be less than 50,000 cases of use of arms which have never been registered in the College of Arms. In fact there is a very considerable growth all over the English-speaking world, not the least in England itself, of the type of suggestion that if you will send in your name you will receive a picture of your coat of arms. The court has not sat since 1954–55, and the reason is simply that the then Surrogate (or assistant to the Earl Marshal, the Duke of Norfolk) the Lord Goddard, Lord Chief Justice, in giving judgment for the court, in the test case then decided, certainly reaffirmed the court's existence and validity, but he also strongly urged those who might wish to have more frequent sittings of the court to obtain an Act of Parliament setting out the sanctions of the court. This has not been done, and it is not common sense to convene the court to deal with every little cricket or golf club which has designed its own arms.

The echoes of the controversy over *They Came with the Conqueror* are occasionally heard in the form of some canard, such as the one which came to me, from of all places, an American magazine, to the effect that I had introduced errors into Burke. This has never appeared in print, since it would be actionable. I do not argue about it, but merely point out that it is not only a lie but a silly one, since a man accused on the one hand of iconoclastic tendencies in his editing of Burke would not be remotely likely to include errors of the same order as those he was expunging.

My second book on the Normans was *Heirs of the Conqueror,* published in 1965, in time for the 1966 celebrations. Except that it mentions the genealogical consequences of the Norman Conquest, it is not a genealogical work, but a straight study of the Conquest and its consequences to the present day in every sphere of the national life. Whether it will have as long a life as my previous Norman genealogical study, could be a reflection on readers' interests. I think it is a better and much more interesting book.

The present book is an attempt to provide everyone, especially in America, with a study of the Conquest, and the records available, which will help the inquirer to discover his or her own Norman background, or the possibility of the same. It is not a directory of names of known Normans, although many hundreds of names are mentioned, and many of these must be borne by Americans, as by people in other English-speaking lands. I have made every effort to give the necessary cautions to those who may be inclined to jump to conclusions on the fact that they possess a Norman name.

From my correspondents all over the world I have had immense help, in their raising of questions and suggestions. From them I have learned nearly as much as I hope they have learned from me. If any readers desire to send in inquiries, I will certainly do my best to answer them.

L. G. PINE
Hall Lodge Cottage, Brettenham
nr. Ipswich, Suffolk, England

CHAPTER ONE

Why such interest in Norman ancestry?

THE student of English genealogy and of any genealogies derived from English sources, as in America, Canada, Australia, New Zealand or South Africa, must be impressed by the frequent appearance in English pedigrees of a claim, or more often, an outright assertion, that the earliest known ancestor "came over with William the Conqueror."

It is one of the facts with which all students of genealogy must reckon, that in every country there is a national myth, legend or tradition. The first of these is a story without basis in fact, such as the old Greek fable that the goddess Athene sprang fully adult from the head of Zeus; or the Japanese account of the origin of their royal line through an act of heavenly union. These are myths and fables, fairy tales, deserving to be described by that much misused word, fabulous. They should not be called legends, because a legend contains an element of fact. Sometimes the expression is used of "a wild legend," as when the family of Peveril of the Peak in Derbyshire was described as being sprung from a passing liaison of William the Conqueror. Sir Walter Scott opened his novel, *Peveril of the Peak,* with the story of this bastardy.

15

Even when I first read it, as a boy not yet in my teens, it struck me as right out of character. There is no real evidence for it. Whatever we may think of the Conqueror's character, sexual indulgence was not among his faults. One unkind critic of William, while conceding this and William's faithfulness to his wife, Matilda, put forward the suggestion that the Conqueror was undersexed, as he would never have denied himself anything that he wanted.

A tradition is an account handed down from father to son in a series of generations; or passed down in the form of what one might call collective memory. Formerly it was the habit among historians to dismiss tradition, and to contrast its untrustworthiness with the reliability of written records. The advantage of the latter over oral tradition consists in the fact that a document can be dated within certain limits, after which it may not be much altered. Tradition, contrariwise, is supposed to alter, magnifying or distorting with each generation. Documents are, however, written by human beings who may for various reasons err greatly as to facts. A tradition, if fairly sound in its appearance, may be worth more as evidence than a professedly historical account written by a prejudiced person. The vast fabric of *The British History* produced by Geoffrey of Monmouth is a piece of art now generally given up by historians. In comparison the traditions found in parts of the British Isles can be far more reliable.

Here, in the light of definitions set out above, we can examine the English obsession with Norman ancestry. It is advisable to study the traditions of the other races in the British Isles, in order to understand how they are distinguished from the English in respect of ancestral tradition. The Irish have long been famed for their

Milesian pedigrees, based on the tradition that their early settlers came from Spain, the leader of the tribes being the son of the king, Milesius, of that country. There is nothing inherently impossible in this story but it has been rendered ridiculous by the Noachian and even Adamic genealogies shown in books such as Hart's *Irish Pedigrees*. In these the Irish regal lines have been connected with the Biblical genealogies, but this was not of course part of the original Irish tradition. In every country in western Europe there was the tendency of the monastic chroniclers to try to connect the ancestry of their own royal house with the Old Testament genealogies. This was based on the assumption of complete literal acceptance of the narratives of the Old Testament, a belief which many centuries later led to Archbishop Ussher's chronology— still used in many English Bibles to provide the marginal dates, e.g., 4004 B.C. for the creation. Until less than 200 years ago, the Ussherian framework was generally accepted by the learned. Clearly the races of mankind were derived from the three sons of Noah—Shem, Ham and Japheth. It is not therefore surprising that the chroniclers of the Middle Ages should have linked their monarchies to the family trees of the Biblical worthies. We are able to find the sutures in these productions and having removed the Biblical portions we can get at the original tradition.

In the case of the Irish, their migration from Spain is supposed to have occurred about 1000 B.C. Why such a voyage should be thought impossible is not clear. Obviously the inhabitants of Ireland must have reached it by sea; the journeys of the Maoris in the much vaster reaches of the Pacific ought to give pause to the skeptic. In Ireland before the mission of St. Patrick, the only writing was the Ogam script, perhaps similar to the runic inscriptions of Scandinavia. With St. Patrick and the conversion to Christianity, monasteries were established and in the latter the writing of chronicles and other documents began. Allowing for a person who lived to-ward the end of the 5th century being able to remember the name of his father, his grandfather and possibly his great-grandfather, there is no really sound reason for doubting the Irish pedigrees back to the year 400. In referring to their pedigrees I mean, of course, those of the greatest men, the kings of the four main provinces— Ulster, Munster, Leinster and Connaught—and of the High King, the Ard Ri, of Ireland. In this way we can see that the famous Niall of the Nine Hostages was an historical personage, the High King, the ancestor of the great family of the O'Neills. He is said by tradition to have died in battle about A.D. 405 on the river Garonne in France. His title was evidently derived from his conquests and raids upon several nations.

It may be that the lists of royal progenitors of the various Irish lines, such as the O'Kellys, are reliable far beyond A.D. 400. They are simply lists of names, and why should anyone want to invent them?*

Tradition has the greater force when it occurs among unlettered peoples who are bound to rely upon their memories, since they cannot make notes; or in nations where instruction committed to memory is viewed as a matter of religious obligation, as among the ancient Jews who had a saying that a good disciple is like a well, he loses nothing.

The Irish pedigrees have pride of place among those of western Europe, since no others can approach a length of 1,500 years, except the Welsh. Here again when the

---

* Note 1. Irish pedigrees.

Biblical portion of the pedigrees has been removed, we meet something nearer reality. The Welsh traditions connect their greatest families with the distinguished men of the late Roman Empire in Britain. I do not think that any of these affiliations can be substantiated generation by generation, but it is true that several Welsh families have pedigrees traceable lineally for 1,000 years. A tradition which began a millenium ago has something to be said in its favor. Archaeological work in recent years has shown that the "many towered Camelot" was not simply the idealization of a Victorian poet, but that the setting for a 5th or 6th century Arthur did exist. If Welsh traditions far back in the Middle Ages seek to connect their pedigrees with a worthy who was contemporary with King Arthur, there seems no room for downright skepticism.*

The Highlanders of Scotland have many colorful traditions, but not of an age which compares with the Welsh or Irish. Few if any Highland chiefs have a traditional ancestry before the 11th century, and the majority are of much later date. Stories of the supernatural, of the second sight, and of encounters with monsters like the kelpy or water sprite, are not hoary legends descending from a remote time, but a feature of Highland life some 300–400 years ago. For instance, in the history of the clan Thomas (also named Thoms and MacThomas) there is a story, dated in the early 18th century, of a conflict between a chief of the clan and a kelpy. As scientific observers have been unable to explain the phenomenon known as the Loch Ness monster, perhaps more care should be given to the evaluation of the peculiar Highland traditions, not as with the Irish

---

* Note 2. Welsh history.

and Welsh, because of their length, as this they do not possess, but owing to the nature of the stories involved.

It may be observed in passing that in modern times a myth has been created in connection with the Scottish Highlanders. They have become identified with the Scots, so that Lowlanders and Highlanders alike are now confounded together. The kilt, the conception of clanship, the style of dress and the traditional weapons, the bagpipes and the customs of the Highland Gael have been bestowed upon all the inhabitants of Scotland. To see what a remarkable transmogrification this has been, we need only turn to the writings of Scotland's greatest man of letters, Sir Walter Scott (1771–1832). From his novels and poems it is abundantly clear that he regarded the Highlanders as a race distinct from the Lowlanders to whom he and his forbears belonged. Needless to add, he was not alone in his opinion, as all historical study bears it out. Yet it was partly due to Sir Walter that the identification of Scot with Highlander began. In the visit of George IV to Edinburgh in 1822—the first paid by a British sovereign since Charles II—it was Sir Walter who acted as a combination of manager of festivities and public relations officer. Under his guidance George IV appeared dressed in the Royal Stuart tartan and wearing not the trews but the kilt. Thus he was accepted at Holyrood Palace in the capacity of Chief of Chiefs, the father of the Scots nation. After the rebellion in 1745–46 had been put down, the severest measures had been taken by the British Government to prevent the revival of the trouble. The hereditable jurisdictions of the Highland chiefs were abolished so that they could no longer call out their clansmen in arms. The Highland dress was proscribed and it became an offense punishable in the last degree by transportation for seven years to wear the kilt. It was not until 1782 that this law was repealed. By then most of the knowledge of clan tartans had been lost with the deaths of those who had woven them. With the revival of interest in the Highlanders and the fillip given to the matter by King George's having worn the Stuart tartan, everything Highland became the rage. In older books about the Highlanders, writers refer to the Highland line, meaning the areas where the mountains approach the Lowlands. In modern clan maps of Scotland no distinction is made between Highland and Lowland. Lord Macaulay (died 1860) described the myth with scathing sarcasm. To show Bruce and Douglas in the kilt, he wrote, was like depicting George Washington in war dress and feathers, brandishing a tomahawk.*

I have devoted some space to the consideration of traditions among the Irish, Welsh and Scottish Highlanders, because it is thus easier to bring out the difference between such long-standing traditions and the beliefs about ancestry which prevail in England. To begin with, the same type of pedigree existed in England in pre-Conquest times as in other parts of the British Isles. In the *Anglo-Saxon Chronicle,* there is extant a pedigree of the Kings of Wessex who through Egbert (reigned *circa* 825) are the ancestors of Queen Elizabeth II. This pedigree just like its Welsh and Irish counterparts joins the traditional ancestry of the Wessex royal line to Noah. As the old English royal families all claimed to be Wodenborn, i.e., descended from their chief god, Woden (Odin), the Christian chronicler had the task of assimilating into the Biblical genealogy a pagan god. This did not appear to worry him overmuch; perhaps he had imbibed the ideas of Euhemerus who in the 3rd–4th century B.C.

---

* Note 3. Highland clans.

had taught that the old Greek gods were only divinized men. If he had read Livy, the chronicler would be familiar with the apotheosis of Romulus, the founder and first king of Rome, who became the god Quirinus.

At any rate, Woden was made to fit into the pedigree of the Wessex kings joined on to the descendants of Noah. Nor can the ingenuity of the chronicler be denied. In addition to the scriptural sons of Noah, he added one Hrathra, born in the Ark, from whom the Woden line descended. (In some versions the name is Sceaf.)

There is no reason to suppose that this pedigree was unique in Saxon England. Indeed the genealogies of the kingly houses of the period are composed on the same lines as those of the Irish princes. The Hrath just mentioned was in the thirteenth generation before Woden, and the string of names is undistinguished by any details as to their lives. Why should a round dozen names like this be made up? From Woden again to Cerdic, the first King of Wessex is another string of names, covering ten generations in all. From Woden descended the kings of Kent, East Anglia, Essex, Mercia, Lindsey, Deira, Bernicia and Wessex, these being the small kingdoms of the Heptarchy (a loose term) which eventually coalesced under the rule of Wessex, owing very largely to the Viking invasions. Because they were royal pedigrees they have been preserved in various references. The Wessex line suffered an eclipse at the Norman Conquest but was later reunited with the Norman dynasty when the Conqueror's son, Henry I, married Edith—Matilda —the daughter of Malcolm Canmore, King of Scotland, by his Queen Margaret, herself the granddaughter of Edmund II, Ironside, the famous fighting hero.*

---

* Note 4. English royal pedigrees.

What of the non-royal English pedigrees? Even the pedigrees of the greatest noble families have been scantily preserved. No man stood higher in England in four reigns than the great Earl Godwin. Married twice, first to a sister of Canute, then to Gytha, the daughter of the redoubtable Thorkils Sprakalegg, Godwin seems hardly to be the swineherd or at best the son of a small farmer which post-conquest legend has made him. In W. G. Searle's account there is a pedigree going back to Godwin's great-grandfather. The latter's name was Ethelric Egelric to whom are assigned seven sons. The eldest of these was the odious traitor, Edric Streona, who betrayed both King Edmund II and Canute, to meet his just deserts at the hands of the latter in 1017. Edric was married to Edith, a daughter of Ethelred II (the Unready). Another son of Ethelric Egelric was the father of Edric *Silvaticus* or the Forester (Edric the Wild) who has been assigned as the ancestor of the famous English family of Weld of Lulworth in Dorset. From this pedigree it would appear that the humble origin of the great Godwin is simply a later account, for if the family were married to royalty about the year 1000 they must have been far from lowly.

The house of Earl Godwin was not only connected by marriage with the royal lines of England and Denmark but also secured the English throne, though only for ten months. In dealing with the families of the Anglo-Saxon nobles, apart from the royal houses, Searle stated: "The genealogies of Anglo-Saxon noble families. . . are mostly very short and fragmentary. That they are not more complete is due to the circumstances that no history of any of these families exists. All that was possible was to put together such information as could be derived from the scattered notices of the members of these families found in the histories and charters; from the wills which contain references to them, and from their signatures appended to the charters." (*Anglo-Saxon Bishops, Kings and Nobles*, 1899, p. xi)

It seems very probable that the position of the great English nobles before the Conquest was too well established for them to need elaborate pedigrees. The flaunting of such is usually the sign of the parvenu; probably, too, the old English pedigrees were recited by the bards or skalds, and have therefore failed to be preserved. Searle remarks of the pedigree of the great Earl Leofric that it is one of the best which we possess. It goes back through five descents before Leofric, each name being that of an earl or great nobleman. Leofric was the husband of the famous Godiva of Coventry, and they were the parents of Alfgar, Earl of the East Angles, whose sons were Edwin and Morcar, earls of Mercia and Northumberland. Now here is a pedigree of eight generations whose names have been preserved owing to their having held high ranking positions. There is no sign of any sudden arrival at greatness. It is very unlikely that anything of the sort occurred in the case of the other noble families. Searle included the pedigree of the famous Hereward the Wake, "partly on account of the interest aroused by Kingsley's novel, *Hereward the Wake;* the references and the double line . . . will, it is hoped, prevent the supposition that the writer presents this pedigree as deserving the same amount of credibility as the pedigrees preceding it." (*op. cit.* p. xi)[*]

The caution exhibited by Searle seems unnecessary. Charles Kingsley to whose novel he refers went much further. He definitely identified the Leofric who is named

---

[*] Note 5. Hereward the Wake.

in old sources as Hereward's father, with Earl Leofric, husband of Godiva, and the head of the great house, the Leofricsons, the only rivals of the Godwinsons. He could not produce any more references for this affiliation than those quoted by Searle, but he reasoned that a man who was the leader of the last great stand in the Isle of Ely, the leader of the old English nobility (what was left of it), including several earls, was very unlikely to have been anything but an aristocrat himself. Perhaps a useful comparison and even more a contrast exists in the history of Sir William Wallace. When the Scots nobles had submitted to Edward I, a simple gentleman raised his countrymen to revolt, and for a time, like Hereward in England, was successful. Crushed in battle and eventually like Hereward, betrayed, Wallace met a fate far more terrible than the worst which conflicting accounts mete out to Hereward. By his death Wallace awoke in one of those Scots lords, who had fought for Edward, the sentiment of freedom. Robert Bruce, of the Norman line of Skelton, Yorkshire, England, took up the struggle on behalf of Scotland's freedom. The fact remains that during his lifetime, Wallace had no following among the nobles. The contrast in Hereward's stand in Ely is obvious; there would therefore seem some cogency in the theory that a leader of earls and lords was himself at least the son of an earl. Be that as it may, the dark uncertainty which tantalizes our curiosity over the pedigrees of the pre-Conquest nobles in England demonstrates that a great divide exists in the record of genealogy between the end of the 11th century and the beginning of the 12th. It was a period of vast change and settlement; not a sweeping away of old institutions but of their adaptation by a new governing class. At the close of his reign, when all re-bellion had long ceased, William decided to take stock of his new kingdom. The resultant *Domesday Book* of 1086 was not only the first systematic, official government survey of England, but the earliest of its kind in Europe. In a rough and ready way it was the first census. It could never have been undertaken, except in a country with the apparatus to perform the task, since the Normans certainly did not bring such a means with them. It has provided the learned with an inexhaustible mine of materials for argument. It is unlikely that the exact meaning of parts of the narrative will ever be known. Certain facts do stand out from a study of *Domesday*. Written 20 years following the battle of Hastings and a dozen years after the Conqueror had put down the last English rebellion, the great survey records very few English landowners—some 8 per cent of the whole. When their names do occur it is usually as holding from some foreign lord the ancestral lands which they had previously owned as their own. In church and state the Norman is master of the land. It is an England ruled by foreigners who speak a foreign tongue. Only a little less than a generation after Hastings, England, which the Old English kings had thought the center of the Empire of Britain, has become a province of Normandy, itself a province of France. A noble European kingdom has been struck down and held subject by a portion of continental Europe. When 500 years later Shakespeare wrote of an England which never did nor never shall lie at the proud feet of a conqueror, time's annealing power must have made him forget the Norman Conquest—though his qualifying expression, "while England to herself do rest but true," could truly go far to explain both the Danish and the Norman Conquest, in that this essential quality was missing in those two epochs.

The *Domesday* survey was practical and utilitarian.*
It had no concern with genealogy, but only with the
economic return to be expected from the land, and the
feudal dues which were owed to the Crown. Attempt
at continuous record of the landowners begins with the
first of the series in the Rolls of the Pipe in the latter part
of Henry I's reign and even then it is not until the time of
his grandson, Henry II (1154–89), that the Pipe Rolls
are continuous. It follows that the pedigrees of the
Norman settlers are little better than those of the English
whom they displaced. A gap of two generations between
1066 and 1130–35 (the last years of Henry I's reign)
followed by the troubled 19 years of King Stephen
(1135–54) does not afford the pedigree maker much more
than a few hints eked out by conjecture. When the
permanent narrative begins in the middle of the 12th
century two questions always arise. Was the man who was
a landowner in 1150 a grandson of the *Domesday* tenant?
In some instances we are able to ask, was the holder of
land in 1130 or so a son of the *Domesday* lord? Again, when
we come to the reign of Henry II are the landowners
always of foreign origin or did some of the older race get
back their possessions? In most of the old family histories
dating from the 12th century, the answer to both these
questions is simply that we do not know. Many of the new
foreign lords did not last. Thieves and murderers do not
always cherish sentiments of loyalty to each other. As
early as 1075 there had been a rebellion against William
in which two of the three leaders were foreigners—Ralph
Wader, half English and half Breton, and Roger, Earl of
Hereford. They involved Waltheof, who was married to

---

* Note 6. *Domesday Book*

the Conqueror's niece and was the last English nobleman to hold great position. Later, in the reigns of both William Rufus and Henry I there were rebellions on the part of Norman barons. Under the rule of Henry I, one of the greatest of the Normans was driven out of England. This was Robert of Belesme, the son of Roger de Montgomery, a powerful supporter of the Conqueror whose possessions on the Welsh border had been so great that the county of Montgomeryshire took its name from him. The rebellion and banishment of Robert of Belesme took place in 1102. At the same time another equally great noble, William, Earl of Cornwall and of Mortain, nephew of Bishop Odo, was also driven out of the realm. The later Montgomery family, of the Earls of Eglinton, descended from other scions of the original Roger.

It is thus clear that many Norman lords were dispossessed by their own kings. If they were ready to rebel even within the decade of Hastings, their loyalty was not likely to endure when the dangers of a general English rising had ceased.

Very few pedigrees in the male line can be traced to persons who were either at the battle of Hastings or who are known to have been living at the time. This applies just as much to Normans as to English. It requires a chapter to itself in which to deal with this aspect of the subject, especially as there are so many people now living who descend through female lines from Norman ancestors. The numbers of these latter have been enormously increased by the descendants, in legitimate lines, of the Norman kings. The Marquis de Ruvigny in the early part of the present century wrote six large volumes on the descendants of the Blood Royal of the Plantagenets. The number of persons listed in these books as being then alive amounts to some 36,000 and there is no reason to suppose that this is an exhaustive summary. It is in fact usually said that 100,000 people in Britain can deduce their descent from Edward III (1327–77) and so of course from William the Conqueror, Edward's ancestor. The numbers will be further swollen by descendants in America and elsewhere.

The psychological reason for the claim to alleged Norman descent so frequently heard among English people is, I think, derived from the existence of a species of snobbery. The desire to be one with the best people can be most adequately fulfilled if one descends from the conquerors. A somewhat ludicrous illustration of this occurs sometimes in the Channel Islands. Natives of these islands occasionally pride themselves as being the conquerors of England, which they affect to regard as their colony. Similarly, French writers like to think of England as their conquest, forgetful of the fact that as a direct result of the Norman Conquest, their own country was invaded and devastated by Englishmen on too many occasions almost for an historian to make a reckoning, and twice even nearly conquered.

The feeling of oneness with the higher strata of English society is the cause of the claim to Norman descent. As to its reality, much will be said in the present study. Suffice for the moment to mention that probably some 200 of the old county families in England can trace their ancestry to the 12th century. How many of these are of Norman origin it is well nigh impossible to state. Enough has been written above to show how very different is the traditional belief regarding ancestry among the other nations of these islands; and the reason for the failure to substantiate many English traditions being simply that the Conquest provided a break in continuity as far as family legend and tradition were concerned, with the very gradual rise of genealogical information among the new ruling class.

There are fashions in ancestor tracing. At certain times reaction against Norman forbears has set in. To claim English or Saxon ancestors became a fashion in the 17th and 18th centuries, partly for political reasons. In Richardson's novel, *Pamela*, the old gentleman, the family authority, refers to his family as older than the Conquest. Claims to ancient pre-Conquest descent are not infrequent now; they leave in respectful wonderment the genealogist who knows the history of those times, as to what people can bring themselves to believe.*

---

* Note 7. Attitudes toward the Normans.

CHAPTER TWO

The Norman influence
on England

THERE are four great events in the history of the English people before the present century. They are the settlement of the original Angles and Saxons in the Roman province of Britain in the 5th century; the conversion of the English to Christianity in the 7th century; the Conquest of England by the Normans 1066–72, and the change from Catholicism to Protestantism in the 16th century. It is fruitless to inquire which of the last three events had the greatest importance, but of the influence exerted upon England by the Norman Conquest there can be little exaggeration. The life of the English people was profoundly affected by the Conquest. It is true that the country remains England and the people English, as 1,000 years ago; but a country and a people very different from the way in which they would have developed without a Norman invasion.

Nowhere as much as in the sphere of genealogy is this the case, but in order to understand the reason we must know how Norman influence affected English life. In the first place we have the evidence of our own words, our speech, our writing. Let us look through any page of modern English speech, and we shall find at least half the words used are of foreign origin. We can recognize in most cases words derived directly from the classical languages, Latin and Greek; they entered English in the era of growing scientific knowledge from the 16th century onward. Other languages have known the same assimilation. There are, however, other borrowings many of which have come from the French or in a more or less disguised form from Latin through French. This is not surprising when it is considered that French was the language of the ruling classes for 300 years from William the Conqueror (1066–87) until Edward III (1327–77). Before 1066 a fairly small number of foreign words had come into English, all from Latin, through the usage in the Church, to express ideas and things for which no English equivalent could be found. A similar practice has prevailed in modern Christian missionary work in African primitive communities. With the settlement of the Normans in England there was not unnaturally a vast influx of new words, either French or Gallicized Latin.* The political and social framework of the country experienced many changes. Contrary to the popular and still prevailing opinion, the English at the time of the Conquest possessed an elaborate and country-wide organization. They had considerably more culture than the Normans and a well-equipped chancellory. They had a body of law. The Normans for all their expertise as conquerors, for all their savage brutality, could not change the essentials of the system which they found. They imposed upon it their own authority, changed its language and altered pieces here and there. The Witanagemot was renamed the Great Council (*Magnum Concilium*), and in the course of centuries it was considerably enlarged until

---

* Note 8. Use of French in England.

its writs of summons took in the class of person who was to form the House of Commons. The debates and proceedings of the Council were much the same as those of the Witan, but conducted in Norman French, not in English. Both bodies in their original composition were assemblies of great landowners, for feudalism existed in England before Hastings. The Normans greatly extended the system, in a very consistent manner. Before 1066 there were small districts which knew no lord from whom they "held" their land. After 1066 there were no such free holdings. Before and after William the Conqueror, the king owned his lands of ancient demesne—probably coeval with the settlement of the original English kingdoms. After that date, by the accepted theory of feudalism the king owned all the land in England, and let it out to great tenants, they in turn to their sub-tenants. One of the consequences of the Conquest was the debasing of the free smallholders and their addition to the numbers of the serfs. There were of course serfs in pre-Conquest England, but their numbers were increased by the fact that the imposition of a new ruling class necessitated the progressive down-grading of the whole strata of English society until the poorest freeholders were merged with the existing servile class. Slaves as such did begin to disappear from the life of England; it has to be remembered that the slave trade from Bristol to Ireland was still going on after the Conquest, and that it certainly was not invented by the Normans. While slavery went out in the century following the Conquest, the large mass of former small or free holders became a servile section of the community—in short the villeins of medieval society. They were not slaves in the sense that they could be bought and sold, like the wretches whom the English had shipped into Ireland, but they were not free to move from their land, without the lord's permission, and they owed many services to the lord. It was not until the ravages of the Black Death that the villein class began to lose its chains. If ever the slogan of the 19th and 20th centuries had any meaning—workers unite, you have nothing to lose but your chains—it was in the period after Hastings—from the 11th to the 14th century. Any idea of the Normans, ecclesiastics or otherwise, being a kindly, considerate folk deserves the name of myth.

The English governmental system was adapted by the conquerors to their own use, but the apparatus which they found was developed by them, not abolished. Thus in every county—itself a unit which they found existing before their arrival, at least over most of England—the Norman official was the sheriff or shire reeve. Many of the incoming lords were known as counts, on the continental model. Within a short time, probably a very short time, these counts were called earls, after the English style. The latter term had already superseded the older name of alderman, which had formerly denoted the nobles. Alderman survived and survives as the description of the senior councillor of a town. There had always been lords and ladies in Anglo-Saxon England, meaning the loaf warden and the loaf giver, but when the title of earl came to be used, in imitation of the Norse jarl, the wife of the earl had no distinguishing title. She was the earl's lady, just as he was her lord. Consequently we have the apparent anomaly of the earl and his countess, but the count was never domiciled in the ranks of English nobility. Great earls there had been in England in the reigns of Canute (1016–35), and of Edward the Confessor (1042–66); in fact, one of the main contributory cause of the Conquest was the independence of these earls. Had the northern earls, Edwin and Morcar, stood by their brother-in-law, King Harold II, the Norman might never have fastened his yoke on England.

With regard to the other, and ecclesiastical, sphere of government, there was undoubtedly a great change in the condition of the English church. How far it was in a poor state in the 11th century is open to criticism. It is customary to say that the Conquest brought the church into touch with the reforms initiated from Rome, by Hildebrand, later Pope Gregory VII, and by the Cluniac monastic movement. It did not of course change the faith or practice of the Church of England, except in so far as there was an attempt to make clerical celibacy the rule, and certainly more monasteries were founded. As to the hierarchy, by the end of the Conqueror's reign, hardly more than one high appointment was filled by an Englishman. The process was more gradual than might have been expected. Stigand, Archbishop of Canterbury, was not deprived until 1070, which is surprising in view of his having received the pallium—the symbol of archiepiscopal dignity—from an anti-pope. However, despite the papal support which William had sought and obtained, he showed himself very much opposed to papal interference in the affairs of the Church in England. In his rebuttal of papal claims to fealty and the like, it is interesting to observe that William refused what he thought excessive claims, on the ground that his predecessors had not accepted them. He based his refusal on the procedure of the Old English kings.

The Normans brought with them neither law nor literature. The lack of the former they remedied by developing English law. The law courts evolved from the regal court but the shire and the hundred court remained. At first the exigencies of the feudal system brought into being a large number of baronial courts, courts of the manor, which must have been instruments of harshness and tyranny. It was only by gradual development over 200 years that royal justice got the better of the local courts. In England there grew up the system of two forms of law—Common Law and Equity—an arrangement which has been bestowed on all legal systems derived from England. When Common Law rules and procedures could not deal with a case, the aggrieved person applied to the Crown, and the chancellor of the king would hear the appeal and administer what amounted to natural justice. Separate courts of Common Law and of Equity arose. They were often opposed to each other, and not until the reforms of 1873–76 in England were they merged.

With reference to literature, the Norman Conquest interrupted the course of English literature. The English possessed a considerable literature, mostly, though not all, in the West Saxon dialect. There still exist 30,000 lines of Old English poetry, of which the poems, *Beowulf*, and *The Dream of the Rood*, are the most famous.* In historical writing much progress had been made. The *Anglo-Saxon Chronicle* begun some 200 years before 1066, and continued until 1154, started as dryly as most annals but reached a standard of excellent prose, especially when describing the vile treachery of Edric Streona, or the ungentlemanly conduct of William the Conqueror in ordering the compilation of the *Domesday Book*. Translations of various works are found, including Boethius' *de Consolatione Philosophiae* or the *Cura Pastoralis* of St. Gregory. Translations of at least some books of the Bible were made. There were sermons, moral treatises, and romances from the old classical world. This abundant literature came to

---

* Note 9. Old English poetry.

an end, except for the continuation of the *Chronicle* at Peterborough, because such writing as there was, was in Latin. The charters and formal documents of the pre-Conquest kings usually had been in English. William's first charter to the Londoners was in English, the oldest document preserved by the City of London regarding itself. It was not until considerably after the Conquest that literary works, albeit of no very high quality, began to appear again in English. They showed foreign influence, especially in so far as stories of King Arthur and his Round Table appeared in English. That Arthur should be exhibited as an English hero—he who had spent his life fighting against the lords of the White Horse, the pagan English—was certainly a remarkable metamorphosis. Perhaps he is the first example of that strange phenomenon, the adopted Englishman, the man who ought to have been an Englishman! Not for 300 years did English recover as a literary language. Then the formal rules of West Saxon grammar were gone, Geoffrey Chaucer wrote in the east-midland dialect and did much to fix it as the literary language for succeeding ages. John Langland in *Piers Plowman* used a much rougher language, much less easy to understand, but full of force and vigor. John Gower wrote easily in Latin, French and English, giving proof in this trilingual achievement of the translation from the two other tongues into the vernacular.

No department of the national life was more affected by the Norman interference than that of building. They had conquered in England, as they did in so many other countries, by virtue of being highly efficient soldiers.* Castles arose all over England, simple structures at first,

---

* Note 10. Norman military ability.

designed to give some protection to the new lord. They were the motte and bailey castles, made of wood on a mound, surrounded by a ditch. Once the Conquest was completed, these simple structures gave way to more elaborate buildings, especially in the royal castles. Examples are the Tower of London, Lewes Castle, Dover, Durham and the powerful forts on the Welsh border. The English had not been without fortifications before the Conquest. The policy of Alfred the Great and his succesors had been to contain the Danes by means of fortified burghs and many of the subsequent Norman castles must have been built on earlier foundations.

Much the same is true of church building. The Old English churches which have survived—some 300 in number—are small, and this has given the impression that Saxon churches were only small ones. They are of course in stone, or they would not have survived 1,000 years. Most of the Saxon churches may have been built in wood, but it is now well known that many of the glorious cathedrals which grace England, as a legacy from the Middle Ages, had pre-Conquest foundations and were preceded by Saxon buildings as at Hexham and York. Still the Normans did set out to make larger and more imposing places of worship. As they usually pulled down the large Saxon minsters, we are left with small churches only, which convey a wrong impression. Much of the Norman work was itself later altered and enriched. Westminster Abbey though raised by the Confessor was inspired by a Norman edifice. It was almost entirely rebuilt by Henry III so that only the foundations of the 1065–66 building remain. Many Norman church buildings seem to have been akin to the Norman military structures, reminiscent of Sir Walter Scott's remark anent Durham Cathedral, as "half house of God, half castle 'gainst the Scot."

The most important influence of the Normans came through the fact that the new King of England was also Duke of Normandy, and in the latter capacity, a vassal of the King of France. Because of this dual position the affairs of France and England were embroiled for some 500 years from the Conquest with consequences of immense suffering for both countries, especially for France. In the end the dynastic struggles between the two monarchies were transformed into national quarrels so that both English and French became mutual enemies in each other's eyes.

Who then were these immensely influential people, the Normans, who diverted the course of English history and must have contributed a powerful strain to English genealogy?

CHAPTER THREE

Who were the Normans?

"THE Normans of the 11th century were men of Scandinavian descent who had cast away every outward trace of the language, manners and feelings which made them kindred to Englishmen, and had adopted instead the language, manners and feelings of Latin France." (E.A. Freeman, *Norman Conquest,* Vol. 1, p. 149, edition of 1870)

In brief the Normans were part of the great dispersion of the Vikings in the 9th and 10th centuries. The explanation of this sudden arising by the peoples of Scandinavia is even more uncertain than the meaning of the term Viking, variously defined as "sea-warrior," "creek dweller," or "sea-roving." Hilaire Belloc thought that the conquests of Charlemagne over the heathen Saxons had had the effect of stirring the northern savages to retributive action.* This seems unlikely for it would imply a feeling of racial solidarity with the pagans of Germany on the part of the admittedly closely related tribes in Scandinavia. It seems much more likely that we have here a genuine case of economic causes in operation. The Scandinavian lands have never been able to support a

---

* Note 11. Hilaire Belloc.

large population and by the end of the 8th century economic necessity in Norway and Denmark may well have
thrust the warriors onto the warpath, to get what spoil
they could in western Europe. That this is the real cause
of the Viking descents which cover a period of 200 years
is evidenced by the fact that however much devastation
the Vikings committed, they tried to settle in every land
reached by their vessels. How successful they were in
Iceland and in eastern England is a matter of history.

Of spoliation and ruin they were indeed the instruments. They proved a besom of destruction to all the
countries which had to endure their presence. No good
was ever said of them by any who wrote of their invasions.
Modern historians have discovered that they possessed a
culture of their own, though they had no literature and no
knowledge of writing beyond the signs in their runic
inscriptions. The opinion held of them by Christians is
summed up in the English prayer: "From the fury of the
Northmen, Good Lord deliver us." Cruel, faithless,
rapacious and destructive of everything civilized, is the
description of the Vikings which has come down to us
from their victims.

The countries which were invaded by the Vikings were
Ireland, Scotland with its islands, England, France and
Germany; Russia, and Iceland, Greenland and America.
Their seaborne operations extended over the great
Russian rivers, through the Mediterranean, over the
Atlantic and the Arctic. In the course of their voyages
they reached America about the year 1000 under a chief
named Eric the Red. Cutting through the dense jungle of
argument about the Viking discovery of North America,
it is not difficult to discern the facts. There was a Viking
colonization of Iceland in the 10th century and voyages
to Greenland, where a settlement lasted for hundreds of

years. The passage thence to Canada would not present much difficulty to sea rovers who had dared the northern ocean from Norway. In fact the Norsemen did try to settle part of the mainland of North America but the settlement was not permanent.

The Vikings were pagans. They did not become converted to Christianity until the Church had existed for 1,000 years. The Scandinavian peninsula was little known to the Romans who regarded the navigation of the North Sea as fraught with terror. Readers of Tacitus in his *Germania* can perceive how veiled in obscurity were the lands north of the Baltic Sea. Little increase in knowledge had taken place in the period of 700 years between the publication of *Germania* and the beginning of the Viking raids on England in 787. The western Europeans were to gain their knowledge of the Scandinavian entry to world history in the most painful fashion.

In a short survey of the Norse or Viking invasions, we may begin with Ireland. Converted in the 5th century to Christianity, Ireland became a center of civilized life in the Dark Ages. Monasteries arose throughout the land, in which learning and the peaceful arts flourished. To Ireland there came scholars from other lands. From Ireland went forth many missionaries who labored to convert the heathen. One of the few Greek scholars in the West in the early Middle Ages was Scotus Erigena, John the Scot from Ireland, who has a large place in the history of philosophy. All this brilliant advance which earned for Ireland the title of the land of saints and scholars was crushed by the fierce northern men. Their conduct in Ireland was typical of their doings in other lands. First, there were desultory raids in the nature of probes to spy out the richness of the land. Then followed the seizure of a vantage point, like an island or estuary where they could base their ships. The most dangerous stage in the Viking assault on a territory was their abandonment of the practice of raiding in summer, and when they took up the habit of wintering in a place. Then they had formed the project of colonizing that country. When this happened they tended to bring some of their womenfolk with them. In Ireland, by the middle of the 9th century, they had succeeded in controlling half the country. Eventually their power declined but they kept control of the ports, Dublin and Waterford especially. It was not until 1014 at the battle of Clontarf that the High King, Brian Boru, ancestor of the O'Briens, succeeded in inflicting a great defeat on the Vikings and preventing them from overrunning the whole of Ireland.

Scotland lost most of her islands to the Northmen for centuries, indeed not until the 15th century was the Viking control overcome. Even to this day in the Shetlands the Scot is viewed as something of a foreigner. In at least one case, that of the Cloustons of Clouston in the Orkneys, a Viking family has held land for 900 years.

In England the Vikings made their first appearance at the end of the 8th century, but these were only sporadic raids. The Bretwalda, Egbert of Wessex (*circa* 825), defeated them, but after his death they renewed their attacks and wintered for the first time in 851 at the Island of Thanet just off the Kentish coast, thus following the same course as in their Irish operations. In fact the Vikings appear to have had a well thought out strategy. When they invaded England they were favored by the internal conditions of the country. The times of the Heptarchy meant the temporary ascendancy of one of the English kingdoms; Kent, Northumbria and Mercia, between 597 and 800, all held in turn the position of overlord and their rulers styled themselves Bretwalda or

Ruler of the Britons. With the long reign of King Offa of Mercia (757–796), that country, which roughly corresponded to what are now termed the midlands of England, reached its peak of power. Offa had treated with Charlemagne as an equal but after his death, Mercia rapidly declined and Wessex took its place just as Mercia had replaced Northumbria. The course of English history before the Viking invasions thus resembles that of Ireland, but whereas the Irish system of High Kingship never developed into a full scale nationwide monarchy, the royal House of Wessex did evolve into the ruling dynasty of England. With the exception of the Danish kings of England, and of Harold, William I and II, Henry I and William of Orange, all the sovereigns since Egbert have descended from him.

The consolidation of England was due to the Vikings. In this sense it is true, as modern Danes often maintain, that their ancestors made England a kingdom. The military skill behind the Viking incursions presupposes in the leaders a sound intelligence service. By attacking England when the north and center had been so weakened that they had come under the overlordship of Wessex, the Danes ensured that they could settle in the northeast of the country. Naturally they did not remain content with this area, but tried to conquer Wessex as well. Everyone knows the grim struggle waged by Egbert's successors, and in particular by King Alfred against the Danes. There were phases of good and bad fortune and in 878 King Alfred was caught off his guard by a winter campaign, one of the enemy's favorite tricks. His army was beaten and dispersed, he himself compelled to hide in the famous Isle of Athelney in Somerset. This is the time to which belong the stories of his life in a peasant's hut, the burning of the cakes, and of his venturing into the Danish camp disguised as a minstrel to learn their secrets. These stories are traditional and do not appear in literature until some 300 years after the time of Alfred. If they are not true in substance, why should a chronicler writing in Normanized England bother to record them, being, as they are, to the glory of a king of the conquered English?

Alfred emerged from the Somersetshire marshes to reform his armies and lead them to victory at Ethandune (Edington), probably in Wiltshire. The Danes were shut up in their camp and compelled to accept Alfred's terms. Their leader Guthrum agreed to be baptized. Indeed he kept his word and lived in peace henceforth with Alfred, nor did he take part with other Vikings in the later wars against Wessex. In the remaining 20 years of his life Alfred—the only English king to be given the title of Great—received the loyalty of other Christian kings and princes in Britain. In the extreme north of England, the Scyldings submitted to him, and from them descended the Scottish family of Swinton. Mercia gave him allegiance, his daughter Ethelfleda being married to the sub-king, and the Welsh princes commended themselves to him. As for the Danes who were settled down in the northeast side of England, they acknowledged a vague supremacy on Alfred's part, but they kept their own customary law. Hence this part of England was known as the Danelaw. It straggled down into the midlands and the extent of Danish influence may be gauged by the fact that so English a town as Derby bears a Scandinavian name, this having replaced the former English name of Northweorthig.

Alfred's achievement was outstanding. He is one of the very few characters in English history of whom it can truly be said that he saved England. Under his direct rule he held only the small kingdom of Wessex, which until toward the latter part of his reign (886) was bounded on the north by the river Thames. He did obtain the accession of London by a campaign—a great asset—but his main work had been done in stopping the Danes from taking over all England, and in making possible the future advance. He left behind him a well-organized kingdom, having found time, energy and resources to institute an educational program.

In the reigns of Alfred's son, Edward the Elder (Edward I before the Conquest who died in 924), and of his grandson, Athelstan, the recovery of the rest of England proceeded, particularly of the midlands. Athelstan was the first to call himself King of England, and retrospectively the same title is given to his predecessors back to Egbert, who thus becomes nominally the first King of England. Elizabeth II is his 63rd successor. Athelstan also used the style *Rex totius Britanniae* and the Greek *Basileus,* from which it can be seen that from very early times the role of England as the nucleus of an empire was clearly understood.

The course of English history in the 10th century is marked by a steady growth in the English state and in the strength of its monarchy, with a cessation from Viking ravages, and a development in civilization. The cruel and wicked murder of Edward the Martyr (Edward II of pre-Conquest reckoning), at Corfe Castle in 978, brought England's progress to a halt. Edward was succeeded by his half brother, a boy of 10, the notorious Ethelred the Unready or Evil Counsel (Ethelred II). Edward appears to have been the victim of a conspiracy on the part of some nobles who were opposed to him, and which was powerfully aided by his stepmother who wanted the throne for her own son. It was generally thought that the murder was the worst crime committed among the English peoples since their first coming to Britain. Nothing was done to bring the murderers to justice from which it is obvious that they were abetted and urged on by a person in the highest place, Elfrida, the Queen Mother, Edward's stepmother.

From the accession of Ethelred in 978 nothing went right for the English kingdom. He reigned until 1016 when he died in London on 23 April (St. George's day, although St. George had not then become the patron saint of England). The name Ethelred means "noble counsel" and the adjective which always accompanies it in historical works, "unready," is of course ironical, and also an incorrect rendering since it should be "evil counsel" or "no counsel." However the name is interpreted, it is certain that Ethelred made every possible mistake in dealing with the Danes who renewed their onslaught on a scale reminiscent of the previous century. Ethelred's method of meeting the troubles was to pay money to the Danes to leave him in peace. This shameful practice produced the word Danegeld as a permanent addition to the language. Unable to meet his foes fairly and squarely in battle, Ethelred resorted to violence and murder which did not even achieve its object. For one venture into spasmodic brutality, Ethelred organized a murder hunt against Danes living among the English. This was the notorious murder of St. Brice's day (13 November 1002). How far the killings extended it is impossible to estimate, but unluckily for England among the slain was Gunnhild, the sister of Sweyn, King of Denmark. With their usual excellent intelligence service the Danes had correctly estimated the weakness of the

English kingdom in the weakness of its head. The murder of Gunnhild and other Danes only added an incentive to lead the Danes to an attack on England.

Sweyn's campaign against Ethelred was completely successful. Ethelred was driven to seek refuge in Normandy. In 1013 the Witan, or Council of the Wise, the forerunner of the present English Privy Council or Great Council, offered the Crown to Sweyn. The Danish objective had been won, and on the throne of Alfred and the other great princes of the house of Wessex was seated a heathen Viking.

Ethelred was recalled by the Witan who had soon found Sweyn an unacceptable master. He promised to rule better in the future. How he would have fared we do not know, for in the midst of renewed warfare with the Danes, Ethelred died. Sweyn had also died, and the English scene was now dominated by Ethelred's son, King Edmund II and Sweyn's son, Canute. Edmund bears the nickname of Ironside and is aptly described by Charles Kingsley as the last man of Cerdic's race worthy of the name. He and Canute fought a series of campaigns across the length and breadth of England. Edmund could have won a decisive battle at Ashingdon in Essex between the rivers Thames and Crouch, but was betrayed at the decisive moment by Edric Streona, an English quisling. This man's motives are hard to follow, since he betrayed both Edmund and the Danes in turn. Even more obscure is the seeming trust reposed in him after his treacheries. Perhaps his power was too great for him to be disowned. In due course he met his just deserts from Canute, a swift and resolute killer.

At last in 1016 an arrangement was made by which Edmund remained king, with the area of Wessex as his effective kingdom, the rest of England being left to

Canute. Scarcely had this composition taken place than Edmund died on St. Andrew's day, 30 November 1016. His end was mysterious and the obvious explanation was that he was murdered by orders of Canute. The Danish leader then persuaded the Witan to offer him the Crown of Wessex, and thus became King of all England. The brothers and sons of Edmund were set aside. One brother, Edwy, was murdered at Canute's direction, and supposedly on advice of Edric Streona. Edmund's two young sons, named Edwin and Edward were sent by Canute to the King of Sweden with a request that he should quietly do away with them. The Swedish monarch did not comply and sent the children on to the King of Hungary where they were well received. The elder child, Edwin, died in Hungary, but the younger, Edward, married a daughter of the brother of the Emperor Henry II (the Holy Roman Emperor). He was known as Edward the Exile and his children were "Margaret, Queen of the Scots, and the consecrated virgin, Christina, and the Atheling, Edgar" (thus a contemporary chronicler, Florence of Worcester, quoted in *English Historical Documents,* Vol. I, p. 286).*

Leaving for the moment this grandchild of Ethelred the Unready, let us consider his children by his second marriage, for Edmund Ironside was the child of his first marriage. In 1002 he married as his second wife, Emma, the daughter of Richard I, Duke of Normandy. This marriage came about as a result of one of Ethelred's acts of uninformed energy. We know nothing of the matter from English sources but according to Norman writers some quarrel had occurred between the English king and the Norman duke. Ethelred sent a fleet against Normandy

---

* Note 12. *English Historical Documents.*

with orders to burn and destroy the country. The raiders landed in the Cotentin peninsula but were completely defeated by Neal, the viscount of the district.* There must be some truth behind this story for it is known that Pope John XV intervened to put right unfriendly relations between the two countries. Such an affair is in accord with Ethelred's character; it is typical of him to waste his resources against Normandy when they should have been husbanded for use against the Danes. On another occasion Ethelred carried out a harrying of Cumberland, while neglecting the defense of Wessex, so an invasion of Normandy would be quite in keeping with his conduct.

The most important outcome of this quarrel with Normandy was that on its settlement Ethelred married the Norman Emma. Her brother was Richard II, the reigning Duke of Normandy. It was therefore natural for Ethelred when he fled from England to go to Normandy, to his brother-in-law's court. With him went his wife and his two sons by her, Alfred and Edward. This was in 1013 and on Ethelred's return to England his children were left in Normandy. They were then young boys of an age to absorb an upbringing in Norman ways. The connection of England with Normandy had begun. Ethelred's death in 1016 is only half a century from Hastings. From then on every turn of events led to the Norman domination.

---

* Note 13. Ethelred's invasion of Normandy.

CHAPTER FOUR

The Dukes of Normandy

FRANCE was distinguished from England and Ireland in the Viking age in that there was far more devastation and less settlement. It may be that Viking hosts who were unable to make a permanent colonization in England turned to the continent and indulged in wholesale raids there. Certain it is that only in northern France did the Vikings effect any large colonization. There they made so deep an impression that the country has ever since been called by their name, Northman's land or Normandy. The French king Charles the Simple, finding that he could not subdue the invaders, succeeded in making an arrangement with their leader, Rolf or Rollo usually named the Ganger, in 911. By the treaty of St. Claire sur Epte, Charles recognized Rollo's sovereignty over the country later called Normandy. Rollo and his men became Christians and Charles is supposed to have given Rollo his daughter Gisela in marriage. As Charles was then only 32, she would have been very young. Rollo was in any case provided with a wife. The Norman dukes for several generations manifested the Viking habit of keeping wives and mistresses at the same time.

Rollo's pedigree is interesting since it shows the high

descent of the Viking chiefs and their purely Scandinavian origin, whatever may have been the transfor-
mation of their descendants. We are fortunate in having
early Norse records in addition to those of the French
Norman chroniclers, and the former are more reliable
than the latter. The famous sagas give the early Norse
history and these were first edited by Snorre Sturleson,
an Icelander born in 1177. His book was called The
Story of the Kings of Norway (the *Heimskringla* or
world's circle).* Before Sturleson there was the writer of
the first Norse chronicle—Are Fode (Are the Wise or
Learned)—who produced a history of the settlement of
Iceland, and biographies of the kings of Norway, Denmark and England. Are was born about 1067 and drew
much of his information from the skalds, the bards of the
Scandinavians, who were the keepers of such historical
knowledge as was preserved. Between the 9th and 13th
centuries, 170 sagas were composed—the work of the
skalds. The descent of Rollo is traced from Fornjot, King
of Finland. His great-great-grandson was Thorri who had
two sons, Norr and Gorr. The latter emigrated westward.
Norr took Norway. Gorr, who settled in the Lofoten
Islands, had a son Sveithi, the Sea King. Then in succession, generation by generation come Halfden the Old,
Ivar, Earl of the Uplands, Eystein Glumra, the Noisy, to
Rögnvald, Earl of Moera (867), who supported King
Harold Fairhair in his attempt to unify Norway. This
Rögnvald has had his name Gallicized to Reginald. He
married Hilda, the daughter of Rolf Nefia, and had issue
two sons, Thorer and Rolf or Rollo the Ganger. Despite
his father's support for King Harold Fairhair, Rollo was
a Viking pirate and after forays in the Baltic he put into

---

* Note 14. Norse sagas.

Oslo fiord and pillaged the king's lands. For this he was banished from Norway and sailed to the Hebrides. His nickname was earned because he was too big for a horse to carry him and therefore had to walk. He was quite probably a big man, but as the only horses available in his homeland were small breeds about the size of ponies, we need not credit him with a giant's stature.

From this point in Rollo's story, the chronicler is Dudo, Dean of St. Quentin. After many adventures and going to England where he seems to have been with Guthrum (at that time Alfred's friend), Rollo went to France, where he committed the usual Viking ravages. In 886 he was in the Seine Valley (this date is more likely to be accurate than the normally given 876). In 890 he captured Bayeux. Among the defenders was Count Berenger de Senlis who was killed. His daughter Popa or Papie was married to Rollo in what is termed by some genealogical historians as a marriage *à la Danoise*. In plain Biblical English, she was his concubine or mistress. It is useless to look in the records of the Norman dukes for the ordinary details of marriage. Of the seven dukes from Rollo to William the Conqueror, at least three, including William himself, were bastards, and simultaneous marriages (or concubinage along with the possession of a lawful wife) were the practice of the first six dukes.

Rollo received the name of Robert at his baptism, when he submitted to the French king, and was then styled the Patrician of Normandy, an interesting survival of old Roman usage; the style of duke did not come into use for the Norman chiefs until two reigns later. Some Anglo-Danes now settled in the new territory; how many it is impossible to say. One of the governing factors in the size of the Norse settlements was the capacity of the ships which carried the Vikings. From remains of such vessels and from references in old records it appears that the average ship's crew was 30–40. In one instance we are told that 12,000 men were carried in 250 ships, an average of 48. Allowing for a preliminary settlement under Rollo and the arrival of fresh contingents who had learned of his good fortune, the figure of 20,000 would perhaps represent the highest number of Scandinavian settlers in Normandy. We have no means of knowing the size of the population into which they settled but it must have been sufficient to absorb them fairly quickly. Only in the Bayeux area did they retain their speech 150 years after Rollo had settled.*

In 927 Rollo died, having nominated his son by Popa, William Longsword, as his successor in 925. Rollo was buried in the sacristy of Notre Dame at Rouen, the coffin being later removed to the chapel of St. Romanus.

William Longsword, the second duke, did homage to the French king in 927 for his duchy. In general the Norman dukes were faithful to their liege lord, the French monarch, until at least the time of the Norman Conquest. William Longsword enlarged his dominions, also overrunning Brittany. He annexed the Cotentin, the Channel Islands and the Avranchin. He took Sprota, a Breton, as his mistress. He was bilingual, in French and Norse, whereas his father Rollo (Robert I) spoke only Norse. He had been brought up by Botho, a Viking, and his own son by Sprota, Richard, was sent to Bayeux to be educated by Botho and was taught to be bilingual. Bayeux was the center of the Norse-speaking population. "Probably this was because that from ancient times a Saxon colony had existed at Bayeux, the Saxon tongue prevailed there, and the immigrant Norwegians and

---

* Note 15. Lord Lytton's novel, *Harold*.

Danes gravitated naturally to the place where their language was understood." (Onslow, *The Dukes of Normandy and their Origin*, p. 51, where the word Saxon must refer to some Scandinavian lingua franca and not to any form of Old English.*) In William I's later years some Danes settled in the Cotentin. Like his father he was styled Patrician of Normandy, though both he and Rollo are called Dukes of Normandy in most accounts. He married Liutgarda, the daughter of Herbert, Count of Vermandois, by whom he had no issue. The dukes were in the habit of forming useful marriage alliances so that by the time of the Conquest they had connections along the whole western European seaboard.

William Longsword was murdered on the island of Picquigny in the Somme, on 17 December 942, at the instigation of Arnulf of Flanders. He was succeeded by his bastard son, Richard I, *Sanspeur*, the Fearless, a child ten years old. He was technically the first duke, though usually reckoned as the third. He was educated by Bernard the Dane, by Botho and Oslac. He took a mistress, Gunnor, and had many children by her, though he also married Emma, the daughter of Hugh the Great, Duke of Burgundy, Count of Paris, and Duke of France.

The name of Bernard the Dane indicates a person who bore a Christian and non-Scandinavian name, and was styled the Dane to distinguish him from other Bernards. He is described as very Scandinavian in outlook; he left a son Torf and a grandson Thorold, who was said to have been the ancestor of many of the noble families of Normandy and of England—especially of the houses of Harcourt and Beaumont. Richard I is supposed to have introduced feudalism into Normandy and there were

---

* Note 16. Earl of Onslow's work

between 100 and 120 fiefs in the dukedom at that time. He died in 996. He had become formally duke in 945 in a ceremony at Epte in which there was a shadowy acknowledgment of the French king as suzerain. He was succeeded by his eldest son by his mistress whom he is supposed to have married after the death of Emma.

Richard II, the Good, was married three times, his first wife being Judith, daughter of Conan, Duke of Brittany, by whom he had, among other children, two sons, Richard and Robert, both of whom succeeded him. Of his time Onslow (*op. cit.* p. 95) remarks: "Heathenism was dead; Norse may have lingered in some of the remote villages of the Cotentin or near Bayeux." In this connection it may be noted that the dukes all bear French Christian names, and by the time of the Conquest the Scandinavian names have disappeared among their followers.

Our main interest in Richard II is that his sister, Emma, was married to Ethelred II and that the latter sought refuge in Normandy during the Viking invasions, leaving his two sons to be educated there. When Emma became Ethelred's queen, "troops of impecunious young Normans followed Emma to England, and soon began to inveigle themselves into English estates and profitable posts. During the 64 years between the arrival of Emma and that of her great nephew, the Conqueror, this process continued to grow, and the result contributed to the rapid conquest of a great country by a small and comparatively insignificant state." (Onslow, *op. cit.* p. 103) As to the possibilities of Norman ancestry being traced to this period in England, more will be said later.

Richard II died in 1027 and was succeeded by his eldest son, Richard III, who died in 1028, leaving no legitimate issue. He had a bastard son, Nicholas, who became Abbot of St. Ouen, and who attended the Conqueror's funeral. Richard was succeeded by his brother, Robert II, the 6th duke, known as the Devil and the Magnificent, who died in 1035 at Nicea in Bithynia while returning from a pilgrimage to Jerusalem. He had had a bastard son by his mistress Arlotta, a tanner's daughter of Falaise, whom he had seen washing clothes in a ditch. The son was William the Conqueror, first of Maine, then of England, 7th duke of Normandy. At his death, his father willed that the boy, then aged about eight, should succeed him. This his father's friends enabled him to do, despite the opposition of William, Count of Arques, a son of Duke Richard II by his second marriage, and the boy William grew up to a vigorous manhood. Overcoming all opposition within and without his duchy, William by 1050 was able to marry Matilda, the daughter of Baldwin, Count of Flanders. There was trouble because they were said to be within the bounds of consanguinity proscribed by the Church in its rules of marriage. It took some years before the matter was regularized by the skill of Lanfranc, Prior of Bec, an Italian who had attached himself to William's service. The Normans had become the great champions of the Church. Already, as in the case of Duke Robert II, they were undertaking pilgrimages to the Holy Land. In the next generation after the Conqueror's time, the Normans would be the leaders in the First Crusade. By adhering to the Church the Normans adroitly advanced their own interests. The interconnection of church and state was all important in the events leading up to Hastings.

Before passing on to the narrative of the Conquest, it is as well to deal with two persons whose names have been mentioned above. Arlotta married Harlevin, the Seigneur de Conteville, and by him had issue:

1. Odo, the celebrated ecclesiastic and soldier, Bishop of Bayeux, Earl of Kent, who died in the First Crusade at the siege of Antioch.
2. Robert, Count of Mortain.
3. Adelaide, or Judith, who married Earl Waltheof, the last of the Old English nobility to hold high place. They had an only daughter, Matilda, Countess of Huntingdon, who took as her second husband, David I, King of Scotland.

These names are likely to recur in our narrative.

The second individual whose importance it is hard to exaggerate is Emma, the wife of Ethelred II. After the latter's death she married Canute (Cnut) in 1017. He appears to have had a handfast union with an English-woman, Elfgifu of Northampton, by whom he had a son Harold, afterward King of England (Harold I to be distinguished from Harold II who was slain at Hastings). By Emma, Canute had a son Hardicanute, also king after him. Canute died in 1035 and Emma in 1052. Her relations with her sons by Ethelred appear to have been far from friendly. She is a shadowy figure but a Norman woman who was wife of two kings and mother of two others must have exerted some influence on affairs.

CHAPTER FIVE

The Norman Conquest of England

PHASE ONE

The end of the Danish Domination

In retrospect, the half century between the accession of Canute and the coronation of William the Conqueror appears to be marked with all the signs of a predetermined fate. England seems to resemble the gallant Turnus in his conflict with Aeneas in the last book of the *Aeneid*. Try as he may, Turnus cannot win, for he has the gods against him. *Sic Turno, quacumque viam virtute petivit, Successum dea dira negat.* (Virgil, *Aeneid,* Bk. xii)

The Normans are seen approaching on the national horizon inexorably while the victim's struggles to avert her fate only serve to render her subjugation more certain.

The Norman Conquest of England does present to the theological student a moral problem, or another facet of the age-old dilemma of the book of Job. Why does evil prevail? The historians whose unthinking conscience allows them to justify the Norman Conquest, could as easily justify the Nazi subjugation of Europe. Had Nazi Germany triumphed in 1945, they would undoubtedly have found good reasons to see, in German rule of the continent, the hand of Providence, working for the good of humanity.

Leaving these considerations, we can study the 50 years of the pre-Conquest period step by step, in order to see how the Norman connection with England grew, and yet how fortuitous it really was.

From 1016 to 1042 England was ruled by Danish kings, first by Canute, then in turn by his two sons, Harold I (Harefoot) and Hardicanute. Between the father and the sons there was the greatest contrast. Canute reigned until 1035. He had become a Christian and a devout son of the Catholic Church. Monasteries and churches which had been ruined or destroyed in the Danish wars were rebuilt and new ones founded; saints' days were promulgated with the force of law, and a code of laws written in a definitely Christian spirit was drawn up. In the earlier part of his reign Canute was a swift and efficient disposer of his enemies. If exile or promotion to a post in some other country did not seem likely to remove the obnoxious individual, then Canute had him killed, Edric Streona being only one such person. As his dominions became more settled, Canute's use of violence lessened. His rule in England proved popular and within a few years of his accession to the English throne he was able to dismiss his foreign guards and to replace his Danish advisers by English ones.

Canute was the first ruler of England to control territories outside it. If we except the short period from his death in 1035 to William I's accession in 1066, the monarchs of England from the time of Canute until now have always possessed within their dominions lands outside England.

Canute's title was that of King of Englishmen, Danes,

Norwegians and some of the Swedes. He was certainly King of England and of Denmark, and intermittently of Norway. It is often said that Canute was the ruler of an Anglo-Scandinavian empire, but this is hardly borne out by the disposition of his dominions at his death. More important, for the first time England was ruled by a conqueror, it is true a conqueror who very quickly adapted himself to the way of life of the English. He became an English king and England was the center from which he administered his empire. In Norway he had to fight for supremacy and succeeded in overthrowing the king of that country, the future St. Olaf who was later killed by his own people. In 1027 Canute felt sure enough of his position in England and in the empire to go to Rome for the coronation of Conrad, the Holy Roman Emperor. The journey was also a pilgrimage of devotion and of penitence. From the emperor and from other princes he secured useful trading concessions for English merchants. From the Pope he obtained a reduction in the charges which were made on English archbishops when they went to Rome to receive the pallium, the sign of archiepiscopal dignity. He was careful to let his English subjects know of what he had done for them when he returned from claiming his Danish kingdom, and wrote letters from Rome to apprise them of his doings.

Canute brought the Scandinavian lands into the community of Europe. They began to be Christian and to share in the Latin civilization. Unfortunately this able ruler was troubled by weakness over women. He had married Emma, the widow of his father's half-hearted rival, Ethelred the Unready, and by her had a legitimate son, Hardicanute, who at the time of Canute's death was ruling in Denmark. Canute meant Hardicanute to succeed him in Denmark and in England, but in 1035 Norway was undergoing one of the recurrent rebellions against Canute's rule. Hardicanute was therefore unable to leave Denmark to take possession of the English throne which the Witan was apparently ready to offer to him. Queen Emma, and Earl Godwin, one of the principal men in the realm, proposed the election of Hardicanute as king although absent. The Earl Leofric of Mercia, who with Siward of Northumbria formed the counterpoise to Godwin, put forward the idea of a regency in which he was supported by London and much of the country north of the Thames. Meanwhile, another son of Canute, Harold Harefoot, took his place in politics. This man was the son of Elfgifu, mentioned above, and was a bastard, being the result of his parents' handfast or Danish marriage (a "common-law marriage" in modern English), or in plain words the son of Canute's mistress. The Leofrican idea of a regency was accepted and Harold became the regent in 1036. Elfgifu appears to have been a woman of strong character. She had been Canute's representative in the north of England and later in Norway. It soon became clear that she was using the idea of regency as a cover for the advancement of her son Harold to be king, instead of her rival's child. No doubt she had regarded Emma of Normandy as her displacer in Canute's affections, or, if he really loved Elfgifu and had merely married Emma as an act of policy, then the woman's natural feelings would be even more exacerbated when she saw her own son likely to be set aside by Hardicanute. Whatever the background of feminine intrigue, by the summer of 1036 Elfgifu had brought many of the English leaders to take an oath of loyalty to Harold as king. Thus he became King Harold I of England, king of the whole country by 1037. That personal hatreds had been active in the substitution of one ruler for another was evident when Queen Emma was driven out of England, this being her second experience of exile. Before she left the realm, she received a visit from her elder son, by Ethelred, Alfred, who along with his brother Edward had been reared in Normandy. We know nothing of this young man's character but it seems not unreasonable to suppose that he was not actuated solely by desire to see his maternal parent in coming to England. He must have known fairly well the conditions in the country. With a certain amount of dissension as to the acceptance by the English of one or other son of Canute, might there not be the possibility of revival for the house of Wessex of which Alfred was the Atheling or heir apparent?

This is only conjecture. One of the most irritating features in the history of the Conquest is that while we have on the whole a good narrative of what happened, we do not know the reasons for many of the events. This is so with one of the key happenings in the Conquest, the visit paid by Harold Godwinson to Normandy.

In the case of the Atheling Alfred we know that when he reached England he was seized or captured by Earl Godwin. His followers were dispersed and some of them killed. The Atheling was put on board ship—was it intended to send him back to Normandy?—and then blinded. He was taken to Ely where he died of his injuries.

Was Godwin responsible for his death? This is one of the problems of the time. The famous historian E. A. Freeman in his *History of the Norman Conquest* after a long examination of the matter acquits Godwin of the crime. A modern historian, Sir Frank Stenton, thinks that he was responsible, or at least acquiescent in the murder.* The outrage took place while Alfred was out of Godwin's custody but even so he could have given the order. The best that could be said for him is that possibly some over-zealous followers of his decided, as with King John's treatment of his nephew Arthur in Shakespeare, to take their leader's nod or apparent sign as sufficient warrant to break into the bloody house of life. Godwin had shown the most violent antipathy to the Atheling and the subsequent outrage would be a quite natural result of the earlier rough treatment. Perhaps most important, much contemporary opinion considered Godwin guilty. Hardi-canute did; so did Alfred's brother, Edward, later King and Confessor, and so did the Normans, though they had the strongest reasons for hostility to the house of Godwin.

Earlier something has been said of Godwin's ancestry. The man himself, whatever his origins, is sufficiently remarkable for his achievements to be worthy of careful study. It is a profound pity that in the histories of these great persons of earlier times, we have not been provided with a few letters, memoranda, or even short diaries, so copiously produced by everyone since the 18th century. We are told by contemporary chroniclers that Godwin's counsel was as if one had opened the oracles of God. In four reigns he was one of the leading politicians in England—the reigns of Canute, of Canute's two sons, and of Edward the Confessor—and he secured for his family the succession to the throne. What was his guiding motive? Ambition, it would seem, at first for himself, then for his family. Not all the early accounts condemn him, which is the more surprising considering the Norman hostility to the Godwinsons. Some writers speak of his

---

* Note 17. Historians of the Conquest.

ability and his services to the state, even of his benignity to Edward the Confessor.

It seems that Godwin, having made his career under the Danish Canute, had decided that the best thing for him, and therefore no doubt for England, was the continuance of the Danish royal line. This may have been the reason for the initial rough handling of the Atheling and even for his blinding. If the Danish kings were to be integrated into the realm, there could not be room for a revived house of Wessex. If this is the correct interpretation, Godwin had seriously overreached himself. By 1040 the trouble between Denmark and Norway was resolved, and Hardicanute with a fleet of more than 60 warships prepared to invade England. There could have been a civil war but Harold I died before his half brother reached England. He was buried in Westminster.

The crown was then offered to Hardicanute in Flanders where his mother had taken refuge. He accepted, and reigned until 1042. The quality of Canute's sons was poor. Harold I had been distinguished for fleetness of foot, hence his nickname, but nothing else of any positive kind can be recorded about him. His half brother was savage and revengeful. By his orders Harold's body was dug up, beheaded and thrown into the Thames. When the body was washed ashore on the Strand, the Danes of London reinterred it in a burial place of their own, the name of which is preserved in the church of St. Clement Danes. One of Hardicanute's contemporaries said of him that he did nothing worthy of a king in his two years' rule. He did, however, try to clear up the matter of the Atheling Alfred's death. After he had settled down in England he prosecuted Godwin and Lyfing, Bishop of Worcester, on the ground of their being responsible for Alfred's death. It was only with great difficulty that

Godwin was able to clear himself, by making expensive presents to Hardicanute and by taking a very solemn oath that he had had nothing to do with the Atheling's blinding.

Even when Hardicanute was appeased in this manner, he still evidently thought that he should show benevolence toward Edward, Alfred's brother. He appears to have regarded Edward as his heir and treated him kindly. There may have been something unhealthy in the composition of both Harold I and Hardicanute for they were only in their twenties when they died. Canute himself did not reach 50. Hardicanute died at a wedding feast on 8 June 1042. There was no other candidate for the throne and the Atheling Edward was at hand. He was chosen as king even before Hardicanute was buried.

If, as seems most probable, Godwin did not wish for an English restoration, he was here presented with the arrival on the throne of a person bound to be opposed to him. Edward appears never to have believed that Godwin was innocent of Alfred's death and Godwin knew this. None the less Godwin, though temporarily under a cloud, was able to assert himself so that he remained a great power in the land. He did more. He became the king's greatest subject and eventually in 1052 succeeded in imposing his authority upon Edward.

So ends the first phase in the events leading to the Norman Conquest, the restoration of the house of Wessex, and the end of the line of Danish kings. It is often said by historians that the Norman Conquest brought England into touch with the full tide of western civilization and prevented her absorption into a Scandinavian empire. Apart from the hypothetical nature of this view, I do not think that the facts bear it out. For one thing, England, from its first conversion to the Christian faith, was part of Catholic Christendom. She could not have been anything else. In the 7th century when the conversion of England took place, the great split between the Latin western Church and the Greek eastern Church had not occurred. There were dissensions between West and East; there was a temporary lack of communion at times but the final break did not occur until 1054 when the Patriarch of Constantinople and the Pope of Rome exchanged anathemas (only withdrawn recently after 900 years!). In the far west, in the British Isles, there was a Celtic Christianity, particularly in Ireland, in Wales and the islands off the western coast of Scotland. This form of Christianity differed from that approved by Rome in such matters as the date of keeping Easter and of making the clerical tonsure. More important, in the Celtic churches the monastic establishments had more influence than the episcopal order. These churches were necessarily part of the main stock of western Christendom, had the same doctrines, priesthood, sacramental system and use of Latin as on the continent. Their divergencies from the Roman pattern were due to separation from the rest of Christendom. St. Patrick, the apostle of the Irish, was a Briton who had been carried off in a slave raid to Ireland. When he got away he received his theological instruction on the continent. The 5th century in which St. Patrick lived was the age of the breakdown of the Roman Empire in western Europe. There was a flourishing British church in the Roman province of Britain. It had produced the first martyr of Britain, St. Alban, the first British heretic, Pelagius, against whom St. Augustine fulminated, and there were at least three bishoprics in Britain in the 4th century. The venerable church of Glastonbury was credited as being the foundation of Joseph of Arimathea. All this hopeful development was swept away by the arrival of the pagan English tribes in the 5th century. In what was to become England, the Christian church disappeared. It survived in Wales where the hatred for the Saxons was so great that it extinguished Christian charity, even in the bishops. They refused to cooperate with the Roman missionaries under St. Augustine of Canterbury in taking the Gospel to the heathen English. St. Augustine is described as the Apostle of England, but half the English kingdoms at least were converted by the Celtic missionaries of Iona and of Ireland. Not until the Synod of Whitby in 663 did the Roman rules of keeping Easter, etc., prevail, but from then on all England was in full communion with the rest of the Latin Church. In the 9th and 10th centuries the influences of the purified Western monasticism spread to England as can be seen in the life of St. Dunstan, the monk of Glastonbury who became Archbishop of Canterbury. It is hard to see any reason that the same process should not have been repeated had William I lost the battle of Hastings. The revival of monastic life which derived from Cluny must have spread into England. The Catholic Church was universal in western Europe and all christened men belonged to it.

As for the merging of England in the group of Scandinavian nations, this seems unlikely unless some other Norse ruler had imitated Sweyn, Canute's father. Even then, something much more serious than military conquest must have occurred. It is true that Norse influences were felt in the renaming of places after the Viking settlements, and that many Norse words came into the language. When a less civilized people conquers a more cultured race it is unusual for the latter to adopt the customs and behaviour of the conquerors, unless they are more numerous. *Graecia capta ferum victorem cepit*—Greece captive took captive her savage conqueror. (Horace,

Epistularum Liber II, 1, 156) Just as Canute became a
Christian English king, so very many of the Norsemen
were converted. With the failure of the Danish line, the
movement for restoring the Old English kings triumphed.
There is not a sufficient factual basis for the belief that
but for the Norman Conquest, England would have been
a Scandinavian-dominated state.

P H A S E   T W O

The Reign of Edward the Confessor

AT his accession Edward was about 40 years of age. He
reigned from 1042 to the beginning of the year 1066. In
the 11th century this was a fairly good age for a king to
reach. William I was about 60 when he died.

Everything turned upon the character of Edward.*
Although his mother was Norman and he had been reared
in Normandy and had a preference for Norman ways, he
was still an English king and could not have been without
some sense of responsibility for his realm. He strove to
live at peace with other lands and succeeded, except for
trouble with Grufydd, the Welsh prince. The King of
Denmark was intending to invade England (Canute's
empire had broken up after the death of Hardicanute)
but was drowned before he could sail.

The character of Edward seems to have baffled the
historians, even those like Lingard and Belloc, who were
Catholics. All of them seem to regard him as colorless and
his reign as a kind of interim period, a species of preparation for the arrival of William. This was certainly
not the view of contemporaries in England. When they

---

* Note 18. Lives of the Confessor.

thought of a power menacing the land they looked north to Viking lands, not south to Normandy. Why should they? The greatest warrior of the north, after Sweyn and Canute, was Harold Hardrada of Norway. He was looking around for lands to conquer, and might well seek to emulate Canute. I think that the failure to understand Edward is due to the inability to realize that here was a man consciously and deliberately trying to become a saint. It was natural enough for Protestant or unbelieving historians to fail to understand, but strange for Catholics to have misunderstood. All that Lingard, a Catholic priest, can say of Edward is: "precluded by circumstances from every rational hope of obtaining the crown, he had solaced the hours of banishment with the pleasures of the chase, and the exercises of religion: and he brought with him to the throne those habits of moderation and tranquillity which he had acquired in a private station. He was a good, rather than a great, king. To preserve peace, and promote religion, to enforce the ancient laws and to diminish the burthens of his people, were the chief objects of his government: but he possessed not that energy of mind, nor that ferocity of disposition, which perhaps, were necessary to command the respect, and to repress the violence, of the lawless nobles by whom he was surrounded." (*History of England*, by John Lingard, D. D., Vol. 1, pp. 399–400, edition 1825) The same writer coolly observes in narrating Edward's marriage to Godwin's daughter, Edith, that "he disclosed to (her) that he had bound himself to a life of continence; but he offered, on the condition that he should observe his vow, to place her by his side upon the throne." (p. 404) In other words, Edward deliberately refrained from any attempt to beget an heir to his throne. The nominal marriage took place in 1044, so that had it been con-

summated, there could have been a son to succeed
Edward 20 years later. Had such an heir existed there
could not have been any question of succession by
William the Conqueror. Yet almost all writers have
passed over Edward's deliberate childlessness as if it were
a factor of no importance. Possibly only Charles Kingsley
in his references to the Confessor in his work of fiction,
Hereward the Wake, has glanced at the subject when he
makes one of his characters refer to the king as one too
holy to leave behind him an heir. Even then this reference
is probably inspired by Kingsley's passionate belief in
married love, and dislike of celibacy and not by an
insight into the importance of Edward's chastity as a
factor in the Norman Conquest. The man had made a
vow to the Blessed Virgin of lifelong continence, often one
of the stages in the development of a saint.

When Lingard comes to the end of Edward's reign he
gives the usual summing up of the king's character. He
was a good king who labored for his people's weal and
studied their happiness. Not a word about this exemplary
monarch's failure to provide an heir! The realm is left
without an undisputed succession and the historian makes
no comment. I cite Lingard more than anyone else
because I would have expected that he, as a Catholic
priest, would have paid some attention to the matter.
Even the subject of Edward's title, of the Confessor, is
dismissed as a surname presumably as being of the same
nature as William I's, "the Conqueror," or Henry I's
"Beauclerk." "The surname of the 'Confessor' was given
to him from the bull of his canonization, issued by
Alexander III, about a century after his decease."
(Lingard, *op. cit.* p. 434) The rabid Roman Catholic,
Belloc, does not enter into even this explanation. Viewing
the Norman Conquest as a good thing, he was perhaps too

eager to get to the Norman kings, and so passed over Edward's reign as quickly as possible.

In a note* I have given full details as to the term Confessor when applied to Edward. In the early ages of the Church, e.g., in the time of St. Cyprian, *circa* A.D. 250, a confessor was a man or woman who had confessed the name of Christ, and had been willing to die for Him, but had not been put to death. These confessors were in some sense living martyrs, and were greatly admired in the Church. Their intercession was often sought by those who had fallen away from the faith in times of persecution. When the Roman Empire was officially converted to the Christian faith, martyrdom ceased and with it confessorship in the sense just given. There were martyrs from time to time in the centuries between Constantine the Great (died 337) and 1066, men like St. Boniface, the Apostle of Germany, but these were the victims of semi-savages, not of the civilized state. The term "confessor" then began to be used "to designate those men of remarkable virtue and knowledge who confessed the faith of Christ before the world by practice of the most heroic virtue." (*Catholic Encyclopedia*, 1908, *sub* Confessor)

Edward then was a latter-day Confessor. Whereas the early confessors had been men and women, martyrs in will but not in deed, he underwent a daily martyrdom, in contact with the world, while wishing and striving to live the Christian life.

Having completely misunderstood the essential object in Edward's character—the aim of his own sanctification, an aim common enough in the *Acta Sanctorum* but in this instance complicated by the saint's tenure of a throne—

---

* Note 19. The title of Confessor.

it is not surprising that the majority of writers have misrepresented him. We are treated to the picture of a tall, slim, white-bearded person, rather venerable but weak in mind and body. We are then told that his recreations were in the field with his hounds and his hawks. A day in the saddle; a day in the hunting field. Strenuous now, much more strenuous nine centuries ago. In the 11th century there was no riding to a meet along nicely made roads, no handing one's horse to a groom and going home by car. The quarry was not the fox, but the red deer, the boar or the wolf, and the chase would be over rough country, with an equally rough ride back to a hunting lodge, e.g., the original Windsor, or the king's lodge near the Welsh border which was burned by Prince Grufydd. The picture of the physical weakling does not accord with the strenuous follower of field sports. As to mental feebleness, although Edward did not make war, he was ready to assume arms and to meet an attack, and one of his characteristics, according to contemporary chroniclers, was a royal rage. We have two instances of the latter. Count Eustace of Boulogne (the father of Godfrey de Bouillon who captured Jerusalem in 1099) was returning from a visit to Edward, when some quarrel occurred between his retinue and the men of Dover. Edward ordered Godwin, as Earl of Wessex, to harry Dover in reprisal. When Godwin refused, Edward called out the fyrd from all England. With an army at his back, the king was able to give Godwin five days in which to leave England. The earl's exile was shared by his sons, and even Queen Edith was sent into a convent. Then again, when the northern men turned against Tostig, their earl, one of Godwin's sons of whom Edward was very fond, the king wanted Harold to harry Northumberland with fire and sword.

When the king was established on the throne he decidedly punished his mother Emma. From a council held at Gloucester, Edward, with the three greatest of his lords, Godwin, Leofric and Siward, hastened to Winchester where Emma was living, seized her treasures, and carried off crops and cattle from her dowry lands. All sorts of stories were current about the Queen's misdoings, even of treason against Edward and of being an accomplice in Alfred's death. After this rough lesson, Emma was allowed to live on at Winchester and to receive the fruits of her dowry lands. There she lived until her death in 1052. There is no doubt that the normal relationship between mother and son never existed between Emma and Edward.

Enough has been said of the latter to show that he was not the colorless weakling of coventional histories. It was his misfortune to be a saint upon a throne, rarely if ever a successful combination. Plato sighed for kings to become philosophers, or philosophers kings,* but when 600 years later the philosopher king, Marcus Aurelius, became emperor of Rome, it was hardly a golden age which he inaugurated. He was not oversuccessful in prosecuting warfare against the northern barbarians, his choice of colleagues was far from good, and his philosophic principles did not prevent scandal in his household, persecution of Christians, and finally the succession to the throne of a monster of depravity and vicious cruelty, his son Commodus. In a sympathetic narrative by Walter Pater, *Marius the Epicurean,* the unfortunate consequences of Aurelius's very virtues are well brought out.† Similarly in France when a royal saint was king—Louis

---

* Note 20. Plato.
† Note 21. Marcus Aurelius.

VII—the French armies were singularly unsuccessful in the Crusades and the king himself died in his last effort in Africa.

In English history the saintly king has been noted for misfortune. Edward was indeed much luckier than his successors in the same genre. Henry III lived a most devout life, with especial zeal for the Confessor, whose Abbey at Westminster he rebuilt. He was not a successful king. Henry VI was near to sanctity and after a very unhappy reign was murdered in the Tower of London; yet his foundations of Eton College and of King's College, Cambridge, have long outlived the sanguinary machinations of his enemies. Charles I, the only person ever to be canonized in the Church of England since the Reformation, ended on the block. One would hardly like to call Richard II saintly, yet his devotion to the Confessor extended to impaling his coat of arms with the alleged arms of Edward. He embellished Westminster Abbey and had decidedly artistic tendencies which were not shared by his nobles, who eventually dethroned him.

Edward's life ended in peace, nor did he suffer like some of his successors. Actuated as he was by the quest for saintliness, he did not entirely neglect the subject of his successor. In 1051 the quarrel between Godwin and the king ended in the former's exile. From the beginning of his reign the king had favored his Norman friends, naturally enough considering that he had lived with them for 27 years, from the age of 13. During Godwin's exile, Duke William of Normandy came over to England (according to some accounts) to visit his cousin (William was the son of Robert, the nephew of Emma).* This was in the winter of 1051 or in 1052. According to the Norman

* Note 22. Duke William's visit to England in 1051.

writers it was during this visit that Edward promised William the succession to the throne. We shall never know if he did so. If Edward did make such a promise he was going far beyond his authority as king. Under the Old English monarchy, succession to the throne did not go by primogeniture from father to son. Succession always went to an atheling of Cerdic's blood—a circumstance telling against Harold II—but the son of a king was often disregarded as too young or simply as not suitable, and a brother of the late sovereign would succeed. This was so when Alfred the Great succeeded his brother; the latter left children whose descendants never aspired to the throne.

The English crown was elective, in the gift of the Witan or Council, and ultimately by the free consent of the people. The English monarchy did not become hereditary in the sense in which we understand it (cf. the English formula, the king never dies, or the king is dead long live the king) until after 1485. Even now the principle of election retains a place in the Coronation ritual* when the Archbishop of Canterbury asks all those present in the Abbey if they will have the new sovereign as their king or queen. At the coronation of William I this question was no formality.

Edward had, then, no authority to promise William the succession to the throne. At best he could only have commended William to the Witan. The wily Norman may well have extorted some sort of promise of commendation. When he returned to Normandy, any hope of succession to the English crown must have seemed remote. Nor did events in the next five years (1052–57) lend any encouragement to his wishes.

---

* Note 23. Election of British monarch.

For in 1052 Godwin returned with a fleet and army. Again Edward gathered his host but the army, although large, was unwilling to fight against Godwin's men. The other leaders, Leofric and Siward, preferred the return of Godwin to a possible civil war which might present Harold Hardrada with a chance to invade England. Godwin's banishment was rescinded, and he and his family returned to wealth and honors. Within seven months of his return Godwin died. The manner of his death illustrates the king's undying distrust and suspicion over his brother's death. One day at the royal table, conversation turned to Alfred's death when Godwin, probably in exasperation, took bread and said as he swallowed it, "may this bread choke me if I had anything to do with the Atheling's death." It did choke him, and a few days later he died without regaining the power of speech. To the Confessor this must have seemed the judgment of God.

Edward's dislike of Godwin did not extend to his family. Tostig he loved and made Earl of Northumberland on Siward's death. His relations with Harold were always friendly. Now the problem of the succession became acute. After ten years of childless marriage, there were clearly not going to be heirs of Edward's body. Thoughts turned to the children of Edward's elder half brother, Edmund II, Ironside. The elder boy, Edwin, had died young and childless. The younger, Edward the Exile, married to a kinswoman of the Emperor, had been reared in Hungary and was living in Germany. He must have been even less English than Edward himself. The Bishop of Worcester was to go to Germany to bring the Exile home. In due course Edward, the Exile, nephew of the Confessor, arrived in London, in 1057 with his wife Agatha and his children,

Edgar, Margaret and Christina. "The people who received him with lively demonstrations of joy, were plunged into mourning by his sudden death (at the age of 41). There is something mysterious in this prince's fate. It was natural that Edward should be anxious to embrace a nephew who, like himself and for the same reason, had spent the better portion of his days in banishment and whom the English monarch had now chosen for the purpose of perpetuating on the throne the race of Cerdic. Yet from the hour of his arrival to that of his death, the prince was by some contrivance kept at a distance from the king: a circumstance which will almost justify a suspicion that he was deemed by Harold a dangerous obstacle to the success of his future projects." (Lingard, *op. cit.* p. 424) Thus the attempt to secure the continuance of the house of Wessex had failed. Although the son of the Exile, Edgar the Atheling, was the only surviving male of the house of Cerdic, next to the king, he was not regarded as heir to the throne. The tradition or custom of choosing the most suitable male still prevailed, but now there was no one of the royal line to prefer before Edgar, and he was deemed too young.

What then was the position after 1057? The most powerful man in England was Earl Harold, who had succeeded to more than his father's power and position. He was Earl of Wessex, his brother Tostig held the earldom of Northumbria, his sister was queen, and his own status resembled that of the king's chief minister. There was only one source of trouble—the Welsh Prince Grufydd, who won the first rounds in his contest with Edward and Harold. At length Harold by a skilful invasion of Wales shut up Grufydd in Snowdonia, while by a combined seaborne operation, Tostig cut off supplies from abroad. In the end, Grufydd was starved out and his own people brought his head to Harold. This was in 1063. The realm of England was united under Edward's rule, and the prestige of Harold stood high, after the complete overthrow of the Welsh, whose country had been thoroughly devastated.

As no other person had any blood claim to the throne except the Atheling, the choice, in the view of many English folk, appeared to be Harold. His claim to be king had no more blood support than William's. The Norman was the bastard great-nephew of Edward's mother; Harold's sister was Edward's queen, and in addition he had a connection through his mother with the Danish kings. Godwin's wife Gytha was the sister of Ulf, the brother-in-law of Canute. Neither claim had any real force, but given the fact that the Witan could bestow the crown, Harold was in a far better position than William, being on the spot in England ready to take advantage of Edward's approaching end.

It seemed that Harold had everything in his favor, and then occurred one of those events in the Conquest which are inexplicable. Harold went to Normandy and while there swore an oath of fealty to William. This is the story of the Bayeux Tapestry and of the Norman chroniclers who add that Harold was sent by Edward to offer the crown to William or rather to confirm the offer which had already been made. Some chroniclers state that he went to ask for the release of two members of his family, Haco and Wulfnoth, whom Edward had required from Godwin as hostages for his good faith. The third story which appears much more likely is that Harold had intended a cruise in the channel and had been blown on to the shores of the Count of Ponthieu, a vassal of Duke William.

Harold was roughly treated by Count Guy, and William

was able to appear in the guise of his liberator. Once Harold was at the Norman court, although he was treated with deference and respect, it was soon made plain to him that he would not be allowed to return to England unless he became William's vassal, i.e., unless he swore to support and aid the latter in his ascent to the English throne. A good deal which is purely conjectural has been made of the scenes in the Bayeux Tapestry. Harold is shown embarking at Bosham with hawks and hounds, as though intending a visit to France; on his return he is supposed to look downcast before Edward, etc.*

Whatever the explanation, two things are certain, Harold was in Normandy, probably in 1064, and took an oath in William's favor. This oath was made over the bones of the saints, thus rendering it more solemn and binding. The most sanctifying oaths were taken and readily broken in the Middle Ages but when things began to go wrong for the forsworn he probably felt a super-stitious terror and assuredly his followers felt it before he did.

William allowed Harold to return and, strange as this would seem to a 20th-century dictator who had got a dangerous rival in his grip, there was sound sense in the maneuver. Probably William felt that Harold would break his oath, and that he would then be able to pro-claim him as a perjurer. William was well in with the Church and knew that the spiritual power would back him against such a person, especially as the English Church, though doctrinally sound, was inclined to sit somewhat loose to papal authority.

Within two years of Harold's return, King Edward sickened and died. In the later years of his reign, his

---

* Note 24. Bayeux Tapestry.

mind had been occupied with the building of his abbey at Westminster on the model of the great churches which he had seen in Normandy. Originally Edward had made a vow to go on pilgrimage to Jerusalem, but his magnates would not hear of it. When the matter was referred to the Pope, he agreed to release him from his vow on condition that he built an abbey in honor of St. Peter. As surely the Pope would have absolved the king from his oath of chastity had he been requested to do so.* Edward was unable to attend the consecration of the abbey on Holy Innocents' Day, 28 December 1065. He died on 5 January 1066. As he lay dying his mind was troubled by visions in which he saw some of his former friends in Normandy. They lamented the state of England and when the king asked:

"Will there ever be a day when He remembers
The English and sustains their honour?"

he was answered in an allegory which he told to his hearers, and which was from early times interpreted as meaning that there would be three reigns without right. After these three reigns, of Harold II, William I and William II, the marriage of Henry I with Matilda, the heiress of Edmund Ironside and of Alfred the Great, would restore the rights of the house of Cerdic.†

Perhaps in the last hours when he was so gravely troubled, Edward realized the appalling suffering which his attainment of sanctity would bring upon his country. His was indeed a Saint's Tragedy, to borrow the title of Charles Kingsley's play about Elizabeth of Hungary.

Toward the close Edward gave his voice in the election of Earl Harold. Never did one king follow another

---

* Note 25. Edward's building of Westminster Abbey.
† Note 26. The king's death bed vision.

more quickly. On 6 January Edward was buried in his new abbey and Harold was crowned on the same day, possibly not in the Abbey but at Old St. Paul's. The Atheling was passed over, *quia puer tanto honori minus idoneus videbatur,* says a chronicler. His youth made him unsuitable.* After all, he could have been little more than a child when his father died in 1057. After Hastings, the Witan in London did indeed offer him the crown, but his most nominal of reigns lasted barely a month. When William in his progress of devastation around London reached Berkhampstead, Edgar formed one of the deputation which came to offer William the crown. As Freeman remarked: "Thither came Edgar, a king deposed before he was full king." Edgar must have been a singularly unimpressive and inoffensive person for William always treated him with kindness. For a time he was in William's retinue and was actually given a large estate as compensation for loss of the kingdom. Then he fled to Scotland where his sister Margaret married the Scots king, Malcolm III. Queensferry near Edinburgh is named after her and she was later to be canonized as Saint Margaret. One of her daughters, Matilda, married Henry I and thus the blood of the Old English line mingled with that of the Norman conquerors and enabled Queen Elizabeth II to be styled today the 63rd sovereign from Egbert of Wessex, her ancestor. Edgar's other sister, Christina, became a nun, the common refuge of oppressed women in those times. The rest of the Atheling's life may be soon told. After William had asserted his supremacy over the Scots king, Edgar went to France, where the king, who had become alarmed at the increased power of his Norman vassal, allowed him to harry the

---

* Note 27. Reference to the Atheling.

duchy of Normandy. Eventually an agreement was made by which the Atheling was permitted to leave for Italy with some 200 knights. He took part in the First Crusade and died peacefully about 1120 when he was around 70 years of age. He must have been a good fighting soldier to survive the Crusade, in which many thousands perished, but either he did not possess the qualities of leadership needed to regain England's throne, or he was too much a stranger to the bulk of the people to act as a leader in their desperate strait after Hastings. This estimate is hardly fair to the Atheling, for only a man of great character and abilities, aided by good fortune, could have stood up against the clear brain and relentless will of the Conqueror.

Did Edgar leave any descendants? Had there been any they must surely have prided themselves on descent from a long line of kings. On the other hand, nearly all Harold's children simply disappear from history, and so it may have been with the Atheling's.

PHASE THREE

The Struggle

ONCE William had heard of Harold's accession he lost no time in preparing for action. As a matter of form he sent embassies to Harold to require him to honor his oath, and to denounce him as a perjurer and usurper when he refused. Then William secured the assent of his barons, many of whom were persuaded to give aid in the form of money and supplies, rather than to take arms themselves. This is a very important fact to be borne in mind by all who think that their ancestors were at the battle of Hastings. It is not the high command which lands on the beaches on D-day; still less the contractors, the munitions makers or the civilian administrators. Many families of genuine Norman descent like the Curzons cannot show an ancestor present at Hastings field.

Then William began the building of a fleet to transport his army. Since his own duchy could hardly supply enough men for the enterprise, he appealed for volunteers and obtained them from all over western Europe. His master stroke in diplomacy was to secure the support of the Emperor and the Pope. In the papal court at Rome he put his case while Harold's went by default, though there were cardinals who denounced the expedition as a war of aggression. The English Church was not in high favor at Rome, perhaps because it had its own customs, such as a married clergy, and perhaps because it was slow in paying Peter's Pence. Moreover Stigand, Archbishop of Canterbury, had made the mistake of receiving his pallium from one who was later declared an anti-pope. The power behind the papal throne in several reigns was the ambitious Hildebrand, afterward to become Pope Gregory VII. William was able to obtain the Pope's blessing, a ring with a hair of St. Peter and a flag, the papal gonfalon blessed by the pontiff. One source and one only makes Harold to have been excommunicated, but even without the extreme sentence having been pronounced against him, his cause would suffer in popular estimation, while William's would gain from the papal attitude. So much did William succeed in setting forth his case, that 900 years later, popular histories of England can be found in which the Englishman, Harold, is referred to as a perjured usurper.

William had the advantage in that he possessed peace with his neighbors along the whole channel coast. Some years previously he had conquered and annexed Maine and beaten the Bretons. The Count of Flanders was allied to him by marriage, and the King of France was his good overlord. Harold on the contrary had to contend with a war on two fronts. His accession was welcomed in the south of England, but in the north he had to use all his diplomacy to secure support for his regime. He had had, previous to his accession, to acquiesce in the banishment of his own brother, Tostig, when the Northumbrians had rejected him as their earl. He now married Aldyth, the daughter of Earl Alfgar, the head of the house of Leofric. Aldyth was the widow of Grufydd of Wales, and her brothers were the Earls Edwin and Morcar, so important in the story of the Conquest.

Thus Harold removed the internal danger but he could not prevent the malevolence of Tostig, who considered that his brother ought to have supported his return to his earldom with force, as indeed Edward the king had desired. Tostig betook himself to the king of Norway, Harold Hardrada, and plotted with him to invade England. Tostig had previously visited William in Normandy; William was his brother-in-law, since Tostig in the time of Godwin's exile had married Judith, the daughter of the Count of Flanders. William therefore knew that another foe beside himself had been raised up for Harold. What provision he had made in his calculations to deal with Hardrada we do not know; possibly he reasoned only that to cope with a second invasion would be beyond Harold's power, but that he would so weaken Hardrada as to render the latter of small importance. Something even beyond his calculations did happen. Tostig's preliminary attempts at piracy around the English southern and eastern coasts were beaten off with heavy loss. At length with a small fleet he met the Norwegian king with a large armament, 300 ships. They disembarked their men, defeated Edwin and Morcar in a hard-fought action at Fulton, in Yorkshire, after which the two earls and the people of York made an agreement with Hardrada, who then intended to march south for the conquest of all England. Meanwhile, Harold, with fleet and army all prepared, awaited the Normans in the south. The wind blew from the north, favorably for Hardrada and unfavorably for William. Harold was compelled to let his fyrdsmen go, to get in their harvest. The fleet put back to London. Then came the news from the north of the Viking landing. At once Harold with his huscarls or picked professional troops set out for York, gathering levies on the way. On 24 September, the Vikings were drawn up at Stamford Bridge to receive the hostages of the Yorkshiremen. Instead, there issued from the gates of York on 25 September a large army led by King Harold. After a fierce struggle all day the Vikings were completely defeated. Hardrada and Tostig were both killed and the Viking menace was over.

While Harold was resting at York, a messenger who had ridden night and day, rushed into the hall and announced that William had landed in Sussex. During the night of 27–28 September, when the wind had suddenly changed and begun to blow from the south, William had sailed, and made his landing unopposed at Pevensey, three days after the battle at Stamford Bridge. He had had prayers said for the change of wind, and he landed unopposed on the southern shore, to find it devoid of defenders, though at that time he did not know of Harold's march to meet the Vikings. Thus the element of chance, if we care to give it that name, as with Turnus in his contest with Aeneas, comes on the scene. It is not the last time that chance will intervene in William's favor.

When Harold learned of the Norman landing, he moved south with a speed astonishing in a non-mechanical age. He could not have learned of William's arrival before 30 September, yet in two weeks or less—say thirteen days—he returned from York to London, a distance of 190 miles, regrouped and enlarged his forces and marched them 50 miles to Hastings to give battle to William on 14 October.

The circumstances of this world-famous battle are well known. After a very hard conflict on a clear October day, after eight to nine hours of daylight, beginning at 9 a.m., and continuing until darkness, and the great forest of the Weald, ended the conflict—the Normans won. King Harold and his two brothers, Gurth and Leofwine, lay dead with the flower of their army, and that included the nobility of Wessex.

What were the numbers of men engaged on both sides? This is a strictly relevant subject for inquiry in view of the claims to an ancestor at Hastings.* In older days—when I was a boy—the numbers of the Normans were usually given at 60,000. This estimate must be wildly out. Very few medieval writers, or for that matter those of classical or Biblical works, could estimate the numbers of an army or a crowd. It seems to me, however, that we have now gone to the opposite extreme. No less a military authority than Field Marshal Viscount Montgomery says categorically: "The English force totaled 6,000 to 7,000 men, about the same as the Normans." (*A History of Warfare*, 1968, p. 163) In the same passage in which he makes this statement he describes the ridge at Battle occupied by the English army as being 700 yards long; each man is allotted about two feet of the line. This gives the number

---

* Note 28. Numbers at Hastings.

of men in the front rank as 1,050, the depth being al-
together 10 or 12 ranks. Clearly this gives us 10,000 to
12,000 men—all combatants without reckoning the usual
number of auxiliaries or camp followers, inevitable in
almost any army. Montgomery's views of the numbers are
reinforced by other military authorities, such as Lt. Col.
Charles H. Lemmon (*The Field of Hastings,* 1964). Here
it is said that the calculations of the Norman numbers
were made by General James on a basis of 696 ships, the
number given by Wace, and the lowest given by any
chronicler. On this it is reckoned that there could have
been nine men with horses on a ship, or 25 men without
horses per ship. This gives a figure of 11,000 to cross the
channel, and allowing for detachments for various duties
would reduce the numbers in the line at Hastings to about
8,000. Behind Colonel Lemmon are such formidable army
historians as the late Lt. Col. Alfred H. Burne and Major
Gen. J. F. C. Fuller. It may seem temerarious to challenge
such authorities but I think that in this case it must be
done. There are two considerations. One is the nature of
the ground held by Harold. On Montgomery's own
calculations this gives a figure well in excess of his own
estimate of 7,000. Secondly, the essence of the battle was
for William to break Harold's line, and for Harold to
maintain an unbroken front. A dense mass of men on the
English side is what we should expect from the shield wall
formation which had been developed in the Danish wars.
It was not until late in the day that William by dint of
simulated flight succeeded in breaking the defense and
getting his horsemen onto the hill. Even then the English
fought on and the battle could have been drawn had not
the duke's stratagem in ordering his archers to shoot
upward resulted in the fatal wound to Harold. It seems
difficult to believe that a battle fought so grimly, with the

defeated army losing all its leaders, and fighting on into the October twilight, could have been waged for long with such small numbers. The numbers of men per ship (minus horses) is smaller than that allowed for the Vikings (Hardrada had between 12,000 and 14,000 men by that reckoning), and probably further reinforcements came over while Harold was away in the north. Armies in those days were little burdened by supplies as they tended to live off the country and William set his troops to a very vigorous foraging in Sussex.

Whatever the truth of this side of the battle, there is no shadow of doubt that it was decisive. It altered the course of English history. It thereby altered the course of world history. Few battles are really decisive but Hastings was one of the few.

After the battle William rested for some days and then began to march toward London. He showed clemency to any place which received him in peace; ferocious treatment to any who resisted. Canterbury submitted and William camped there for a month owing to some illness, possibly dysentry, which he had contracted. During this time he sent messengers to the Confessor's widow at Winchester asking for the submission of the old capital. It was given. Then on 1 December he resumed his march toward London. He left a swathe of destruction in his wake. At Southwark he burned the buildings after a fight. He crossed the Thames at Wallingford, having marched along the south bank to Silchester. Turning north across the Thames he marched eastward to Berkhampstead, thus making a circle round London and isolating the city.

Meanwhile in London, the surviving leaders, Edwin and Morcar and Stigand, were talking around the person of the poor young Atheling. They had proclaimed him king and if they had made a fierce resolution to uphold his cause they could have provided the necessary unity which would in the end have shaken off the Normans. The strength of will was lacking to these half-hearted leaders. The magnates set out from London to offer William the crown. He received them in his camp and after some slight pretense at doubt as to accepting the offer, William was able to say that the only authority in the kingdom which could legally proffer the crown to him, had done so. The date of the coronation was fixed for Christmas Day, and the place to be Westminster Abbey. The march was resumed toward London and William made no effort to check any ravages committed by his soldiers, although he did not order devastation, or spoliation. It was part of his deliberate policy to let the people know that they were conquered. Another indication of even greater importance was the building of strong points or castles at strategic places. In the march on London, a detachment of the Norman army went forward to fortify a position near the city, to serve as a base. The wooden pre-fabricated castles which the Conqueror had set up in the neighborhood of Hastings were very soon to be spread throughout the land. At first they were the motte and bailey castles where a mound was thrown up, surrounded by a moat and with a wooden structure on the top. Within the Conqueror's reign, many of these were converted into stone castles. The mounds at Berkhampstead and Bishop's Stortford with their ruins remind us of the original early Conquest erections which were later rebuilt in more lasting form.

William was crowned on Christmas Day, 1066. Within the year England had had three kings. At the ceremony there occurred the famous incident in which the great shout of assent from the English people to William's election as king was mistaken by the Normans outside the Abbey as an attempt on the king's life, whereupon they started to burn the neighboring houses. William was left alone in the church with the ministering ecclesiastics.

Eventually when William, duly chosen, consecrated and crowned as king of the English, went out of the Abbey, he witnessed a scene the like of which had never been known at the coronation of any of his predecessors: flames and fighting, tumult and commotion, his native and his newly acquired subjects in conflict. It was a bad omen for the future. Both Harold and William had appealed to the judgment of heaven. William's victory poses a serious moral problem. How could God have allowed William's cause to prosper when it involved an act of plain aggression upon an innocent people? Even the future pope, Hildebrand, admitted that he had been criticized for unleashing a war of naked conquest upon a peaceful nation. No amount of casuistry can justify the Norman Conquest. If, as I am inclined to think, Harold had in some way, by forced promise or oath, or even by express command of Edward, agreed to support William's succession to the throne, this could not bind the Witan or the English people who would never have freely chosen William as their king. The only solution to the moral problem is that, as with many other incidents, the Norman Conquest was permitted by God, tolerated by Him, perhaps because our old English ancestors had allowed themselves to drift into a state of moral indifference, a permissive society, which by the working of a natural law brings with it its own consequences and retributions.

The Conquest did not end with William's coronation. It was a severe and bloody struggle which did not finish until 1072. In the course of this long, drawn-out conflict untold misery and a great amount of dimly recorded suffering were inflicted upon the English. Whereas William had been naturally hard and brutal, resistance to his will made him ever harsher, and the cupidity of his followers, ever eager for fresh lands at the expense of the English, drove him from cruelty to cruelty.

At first William behaved as an English king duly elected. True, the estates of all who fought for Harold were confiscated, on the ground that since Harold was a usurper, his supporters were traitors against William. Even when the lands of an Englishman were returned to him, it was made clear that the land was no longer his own. It belonged to William and when he returned it to the previous owner, he regranted the property. In addition there was always a Norman overlord. The feudal system, not unknown in England before the Conquest, was now to become complete and all-embracing.

In the two years after Hastings, we do not hear of much fighting as William was an effective king of the southeast of the country, an area extending roughly from the Wash to Southampton Water. Within the southern counties and in East Anglia he was able to find plenty of forfeited lands with which to reward his followers. In March 1067 he felt able to visit Normandy, taking with him the great lords, Edwin, Morcar, Waltheof, Stigand and Edgar Atheling. He left as rulers in his absence William FitzOsbern, Earl of Herefordshire, and his half brother, Odo, whom he had made Earl of Kent. He knew well that these regents could be relied on to oppress the English and to goad them into rebellion. Sure enough revolts broke out in both Herefordshire and Kent. In the latter county suppression was easy but on the Welsh border of Herefordshire, rebellion spread like a forest fire.

William knew well that while he had been acknowledged as king by the whole of England, his effective
authority did not extend beyond the southeast. In the
next five years he set out to conquer all England. In the
spring of 1068 Exeter and the west of England, including
Cornwall, was subdued. Some of King Harold's sons had
gone to Dublin and with Viking help from there had made
piratical descents on the Somersetshire coast. Actions of
this kind had no value, and were not even coordinated
with rebellions in other parts of England. There was no
concerted movement against William and no national
leader until it was too late. He was always able to act with
full force against one adversary at a time.

He kept Easter 1068 at Winchester. His queen, Matilda, was brought to England and was crowned at Westminster on Whitsunday. After this Edwin and Morcar
rebelled but soon submitted when they heard of the
capture of Warwick by William. Technically William
now controlled the midlands of England. Edgar Atheling,
meanwhile, with his mother and sisters managed to escape
to Scotland with some of the northern nobles such as
Gospatric and the Sheriff Maereswegen. Here too a
powerful movement could have been organized against
the Normans but due to the vacillations of the English
leaders, the Scottish King Malcolm Canmore was not
pressed into service.

William confiscated much land in Leicestershire. At
Nottingham he built a castle which was entrusted to a
Norman named Peverel or William Peverel. York sub-
mitted to William who put up a castle there with a strong
garrison, one of the commanders being William Malet.
The Bishop of Durham, Ethelwine, also submitted to
William, and Malcolm of Scotland rendered him homage.
Soon afterward a vast revolt broke out. A force of about

1,000 men under Robert de Comines which took possession of Durham was destroyed except for one wounded survivor. The Northumbrians then rose in revolt against the York garrison, while Swend, King of Denmark, dispatched a fleet of 240 ships to the English coasts. William was hunting in the Forest of Dean when he heard of this latest danger.

York was captured and the Norman garrison destroyed, Waltheof having displayed prodigies of valor. William's main concern was with the Danes whom he bought off and they now disappear from English history. This accomplished, William dealt with the north. In a winter campaign of 1069–70 he devastated Yorkshire and the northern counties, killing humans and animals alike. Where he did not kill with sword or rope, he used starvation, driving off the farm animals, and seizing or destroying food stores. In January 1070 he had reached the north of England and then in February in very severe weather he turned south from York to Chester and so on down to Winchester. By 1070 he had won the whole realm of England. He had one remaining mighty antagonist to reckon with—Hereward the Wake, who in the Camp of Refuge in the Fens of Ely headed the last gathering of the English nobles and for two years defied the power of William. In 1072 even Hereward was overcome and forced by treachery on the part of the Ely monks to flee into the forests where he maintained a guerrilla resistance against the Normans. At length he too submitted to William, and the stories of his end are confused, although the heroic tale which makes him die, a man of war to the last, in a ring of a dozen Norman corpses, has extreme probability.

So closed William's Conquest of England. No doubt there were many local insurrections which lacked a chronicler. The last Englishman to hold high place, Waltheof, was implicated in a conspiracy in 1075 and put to death in 1076.

With Wales and Scotland the Conqueror was careful to maintain the overlordship which had been possessed by his English predecessors. He did not attempt to conquer Scotland but exacted homage from Malcolm Canmore and prevented the Scottish kingdom from becoming a base for operations against him. In Wales the Conqueror's policy was one of duplicity and wrong dealing. At that time Wales was ruled by more than one dynasty, it having been the fate of the country to be governed by a strong prince for some time, in unity, and then to have been allowed to relapse into disunity on his death, when his realm was divided equally among his sons. William received the homage of the Welsh princes, but instead of carrying out his obligations as overlord, he allowed his nobles to invade Wales and seize what lands they could. In north Wales the attempt failed, but in the south large tracts were taken over by the Normans. Three great earldoms—Chester, Hereford and Gloucester—were established along the borders and those Welsh men who had rejoiced in the fall of Harold found that they had in his place a much more dangerous adversary. The Norman influence on the whole of Britain was to be important, though less far reaching than on England itself. Ireland also was to be brought within the Anglo-Norman sphere, and the terms of the papal bull which authorized Henry II to invade Ireland are akin to the motives which inspired the papacy to bless William's expedition against England.*

In his conquered kingdom, William was determined to

---

* Note 29. Papal Bull on Ireland.

have everything systematic and in order. *The Domesday Book* of 1086 was the first rough-and-ready census of England, and no record similar to it can be found in any other western nation at the time. The preparation of this great work must have owed much to the English chancellory, which the Conqueror took over. In the same way he had used the English military organization for his own purposes. He had always called out the English fyrd in all his wars. He used English soldiers in his wars in France, in the reconquest of Maine, and in the later struggles with the King of France.

Domesday Book is the sufficient proof 20 years after the Conquest that the bulk of English land was held by persons who had come from the continent. Very few English or Danish names appear in the list of the *Domesday* owners of land. The bearing of this on matters of pedigree is obvious. Before going to the lines of Norman descent, it would be as well to say something about claims to ancestry in England before the Norman Conquest.

English pre-Conquest Pedigrees

ENOUGH has been written about the scanty remains of the pre-Conquest noble pedigrees to demonstrate the extreme unlikelihood of many living persons being able to prove such a descent. As many people still persist in saying that their family is of Anglo-Saxon origin—usually on the basis that they have Anglo-Saxon surnames, very often derived from place names—the necessary cautions cannot be too often repeated.

Not only are 1,200-year-old Saxon forbears confidently claimed but I have twice heard claims or suggestions of descent from pre-Saxon ancestors. It was once put to me that Pettifer is from pedifer or iron foot, the appropriate name for a Roman centurion whose descendants are supposed to have lived in Roman London right on through Saxon times. This idea was not suggested by a Pettifer, but by an interested stranger. It is amusing but I hope that it is not taken seriously.

That, however, is exactly what did happen with the pedigree of the Coultharts. In the *Dictionary of the Commoners* by John Bernard Burke in 1846 appeared a pedigree of Coulthart of Coulthart and Collyn in which the ancestry of John Ross Coulthart, a banker of Ashton under Lyme, was traced back to Coulthartus, a Roman lieutenant who fought under the famous general Agricola in the battle of Mons Graupius mentioned by the Roman historian Tacitus. The amazing thing about this nonsense is that it was accepted not only by Burke but also by John Gough Nichols, a celebrated antiquary and producer of *The Herald and Genealogist;* and by Joseph Foster, in other respects a careful genealogist. Not until 1865 when a pamphlet was published on the subject by a future Lord Lyon, George Burnett, did the fantastic fiction receive its death blow.*

One of the most notable Welsh pedigrees is that of Lloyd Davis of Whittington which is traced from Tudor Trevor, a great Welsh lord who died in 948. There are about a dozen known Welsh pedigrees which can be traced for a millenium and it seems a little unreasonable after such an achievement to try to go back yet another 1,000 years. Yet the originally submitted pedigree of Lloyd Davis when it came to *Burke's Landed Gentry* would have made the family history coeval with the landing of Julius Caesar.

---

* Note 30. Coulthart of Coulthart.

Viscount St. Davids' pedigree appeared in pre-1949 peerages as derived from Maximus, a Roman Emperor, and from Vortigern, King of Kent, in the 5th century A.D. The family have now to be contented with a mere 900 years.

Coming to the Saxon or pre-Conquest ancestry, the most interesting is that of Arden. No less a critic than the famous myth slayer, J. H. Round, wrote of the Arden family that it enjoyed "a distinction perhaps unique. For it had not only a clear descent from Aelfwine, sheriff of Warwickshire in days before the Conquest, but even held, of the great possessions of which *Domesday Book* shows us its ancestor as lord, some manors which had been his before the Normans landed, at least as late as the days of Queen Elizabeth". (i.e., Elizabeth I) The representation of this splendid family still exists, not only in England but also in Australia. It is very appropriate that to this unique family belonged the mother of William Shakespeare, Mary Arden. She was the daughter and heiress of Robert Arden of Wilmcote and Snitterfield from 1501 to 1556. She married John Shakespeare, bailiff of Stratford-on-Avon.

After Arden whose pedigree is unique because it is proven generation by generation, there are two others, one more in England, the other in Scotland, where there is every reason apart from complete documentary proof to accept the pedigree as pre-Conquest.

The English family of Berkeley from which derive the Scottish Barclays* is traced from a staller or chamberlain of Edward the Confessor, named Eadnoth, who transferred his allegiance to William the Conqueror, fighting for whom he died in 1068. The authorities for the affiliation

---

* Note 31. The ancestry of Barclay.

of the succeeding line to Eadnoth include E. A. Freeman and are given in full in the *Complete Peerage,* Vol. II, p. 124. According to these accounts Eadnoth was father of Harding, a substantial merchant of Bristol whose son Robert FitzHardinge (note the early assumption by the English of foreign Christian names and the Norman patronymic Fitz) had the distinction within a century of the Conquest of being granted the lands of a dispossessed Norman lord. The latter, Roger de Berkeley, had taken King Stephen's side in the civil war between him and the rightful heir to the throne, Matilda, the daughter of Henry I. Matilda and her son, Henry II, gave to Robert FitzHardinge the lands of Berkeley and of Berkeley Hernesse, because he had been faithful to their cause. Even as remarkable was the marriage of Maurice de Berkeley (Robert's eldest son) with Alice the daughter of Roger de Berkeley, the former and ousted possessor of Berkeley. In this way the English and Norman races were united, and in the fourth generation the despised English had secured baronial status and founded one of the greatest noble houses in medieval England, still represented in the British peerage by Baroness Berkeley.

The famous Scottish family of Swinton of that ilk (i. e., Swinton of Swinton, who take their surname from their property) descend in a proven line from Liulf, of Bamburgh, and of Swinton, sheriff of the Northumbrians, who was the first subject in Scotland whose ownership of land can be proved by contemporary writings still in existence. Among the Coldingham writs in the possession of the Dean and Chapter of Durham is a charter granted by King Edgar (of Scotland) about 1098, in which Liulf is mentioned as holding Swinton before that date. Swinton is in Berwickshire.

It was once more the great critical genealogist, J. H.

Round, who suggested the further ancestry behind Liulf. The latter was the son of an Edulf, and Round suggested that this Edulf was identical with an Edulf who was nicknamed Rus, and who murdered Walcher, Bishop of Durham, on 14 May 1080. The reasons for the identification were given in a note to the account of the Swintons in the *Landed Gentry*. "No other Edulf is known who could have founded an Anglo-Saxon line of hereditary *vicecomites* so soon after the Norman Conquest. Liulf, son of Edulf, and the early 12th-century Bamburgh family would have had a difficult time in administering turbulent Northumberland had they not belonged to the popular old Bamburgh house, which had already slain three alien administrators. Like Edulf Rus they had interests in Scottish Bernicia and the bulk of their lands (held in chief of the crown) lay in the heart of Bamburgh-shire, between the ancient earls' stronghold and the lands restored to the earls' Dunbar descendants." Given support from such quarters we may reasonably conclude that the Swintons are of very ancient English stock. In fact, tracing back from Edulf Rus we are able to reach the middle of the 9th century. To quote again from the opening of the pedigree in the *Landed Gentry*: "Prior to the Norman Conquest the Edulfing family ruled Bernicia (the district between Tyne and Forth) from the great rock fortress of Bamburgh on the Northumbrian coast. After the downfall of the Northumbrian kingdom in 878 [i. e., because of the Viking invasions—L. G. P.], the chief power north of the Tyne came into the hands of Edulf or Eadwulf, Lord of Bamburgh, who ruled Bernicia, cut off from the rest of Christian England by the Danes. Edulf accepted the overlordship of King Alfred the Great" about 886 and his grandson was appointed by King Edred in 953 as Earl of Northumbria. This process of the development from being an independent ruler via the state of an underking to that of an earl is another illustration of the way in which the Christian princes in England accepted the house of Wessex as the ruling dynasty, and thus helped on the evolution of that house into the royal house of England.

The rest of the early pedigree of the Swintons is of great interest partly because it illustrates the manners of those times (e.g., Aldred killed Thurbrand Hold in 1018, who had killed his father in 1016, and was in turn killed by Thurbrand's son while hunting at Risewood, 1038; or, this, Edulf, Earl of Northumberland, was killed at court by order of King Hardicanute in 1041), and also because many persons are able to claim descent from these hard-living notables. The Edulfings intermarried with the Scots royal house, including a marriage with Shakespeare's King Duncan whose cousin Macbeth killed him and took the throne, reigning for 17 years until in 1057 he was slain by Duncan's son Malcolm III, Malcolm Canmore or Great Head, who married the English Atheling's sister.

Anyone who has a royal descent from the Plantagenets —there are literally thousands of such descents known in the English speaking world—has a Norman ancestry, a descent from the house of Wessex, and from the Scottish kings.

Another scion of the earlier ancestry of the Swintons was Gospatric, the Earl of Northumberland from 1067 to 1072 when he was divested of the post by William. He then took service with the Scottish king by whom he was made Earl of Dunbar. The style of earl was not used until the time of his great-great-grandson about 1174, but the position of the head of the family was that of an earl. The 9th of the line, Patrick Dunbar, was also styled Earl of

March. The family lasted in Scotland as far as the main line was concerned until 1434 when King James I of Scotland seized the 12th earl's estates and declared them forfeited to the crown. The cause of this action was the excessive power of the Dunbars who by holding the great fortress of the same name were commonly said to hold the keys of Scotland in their girdles. The last earl fled to England where he was received with lands and honor by Henry IV. The Marquess of Bute represents the family; some families of Dunbar, notably of Mochrum, descend from cadet lines of the house, before the exile of its head from Scotland.

I have given some considerable space to these pre-Conquest lines because, as can be seen from above, they are usually mingled with Norman families. One more case, that of the Wilberforce or Wilberfoss family, may be mentioned as they claim descent from a soldier who was supposed to have been present at both Stamford Bridge and Hastings. I do not know the basis of this tradition.

CHAPTER SIX

The Normans in their Homeland

The method used in this book

FROM the preceding chapters I hope that the reader has now a clear idea of the course of the Norman Conquest, and of the difficulties in establishing a Norman descent. I propose to deal in succession with the following, (1) the Norman families known to have lived in Normandy at the time of the Conquest and who had become ancestors of families in England, (2) the Norman royal line, the ancestor of the present British royal line, and of innumerable non-royal scions, (3) the Normans actually known to have been present at Hastings, (4) the Norman-descended families in the present British aristocratic houses. These four constituents are basic and essential to any consideration as to sons of the Conqueror in America. To put the Normans across the Atlantic it was of course necessary to get them across the English Channel; across St. George's Channel to Ireland, and over the borders of Wales and Scotland. Although the Normans did not affect Wales, Scotland and Ireland as much as they did England, they certainly had great influence upon all three of these countries. In Ireland which was invaded by the Anglo-Normans 100 years after Hastings, the greatest Norman houses became truly Hibernian with the result that so chivalric a name as de Burgo turned into the common Irish Burke.

In the course of my narrative I shall give as many American pedigree examples as possible. I have been conversant with American genealogy for the past 30 years, since I edited the prewar *Burke's Landed Gentry* which had 500 pages of an American supplement giving 1,600 pedigrees of Americans of British descent.

Three cautions must be given to anyone who finds that he or she bears a surname identical with any Norman or other surname mentioned in this book: (1) The most important warning which can be imparted is with regard to the nature of surnames. Surnames as such were unknown in England at the time of the Conquest, that is, there were no second names which accompanied the baptismal name as they do in the 20th century. The royal house of Wessex had no surname. They were the line of Cerdic, the founder of their dynasty who was himself Woden-born, being descended like the rest of the Old English royalties from the gods. Of the three Edwards before the Conquest, each received what we should call a nickname or sobriquet. The case of the third Edward, the Confessor, has already been discussed; his two predecessors, of the same family, were Edward the Elder and Edward the Martyr. Before the Conquest there were three kings—Harold I (Harefoot), Harold Hardrada of Norway, and Harold II, Godwinson, distinguished, two of them, by nicknames, and the third having the appearance of a surname though it was not really so. Probably the family of Earl Godwin were referred to quite often as the Godwinsons but this need not have stuck as a surname. The sons of Harold II disappear from history but if they could have been traced, it is more than likely that their descendants in 300 or 400 years' time would have borne a different surname. Two sons of Tostig did settle in Scandinavia but I do not think that their family name was Godwinson.

Despite these facts few people realize how late, comparatively, is the appearance of the surname, and even now how in many parts of the world, particularly in Africa and in Asia, it has still not been adopted. Occasionally we come upon an instance of the absence of a surname even now in Europe. The great pianist Solomon appears in *Who's Who* with only one name.

Yet constantly assertions are made that a surname goes back to Norman or even Saxon times. A name like Bunting may well be of Saxon origin. The suffix 'ing' often denotes a tribe as with the Edulfings of the last chapter, but to possess such a surname now is no proof either that one is descended from such people or that there is a 900-year persistence of the name. One compiler of a pedigree which showed a respectable descent from the 14th century prefaced the account with a vague general statement of Saxon lineage. In fact he did more because he had drawn into the margin little pictures of Roman, Saxon and Norman ships in which presumably his composite lines of forbears had voyaged to this country.

In another instance an otherwise well-educated man wrote to inquire if the mother of William the Conqueror had been named Charlotte Skinner. The lady's real name was Arlotta, an unfortunately pronounced word only too well employed at Hastings by English soldiers with their accustomed healthy rudery. The idea that such a name as Charlotte Skinner could have existed in the 11th century demonstrates a state of mind that is far removed from historical understanding.

Sometimes success in genealogical research proves intoxicating. A good American pedigree, certified by the College of Arms, deduces the descent of the Hammon family from the 11th century in Normandy. The name Hamo was known in that country having been brought there as a forename by the Vikings who settled in Normandy. The form can be Hamo or Hamon. In course of time it became a baptismal instead of a mere forename, and as often occurred, was gradually adopted as a surname. It gave rise to the surnames of Hammond, Hammand, Hammant, Hamman and Hammon, with Haim, Haimes, Haymes and Hamon as variants. It is, I think it will be agreed, going too far to deduce the original name as having come from the ancient Egyptian god Amen Ra of Thebes, thus rendering a surname 7,000 years old.

Surnames were brought into England by the Normans, names such as Curzon, Haig (which soon spread to Scotland) and Tremlett. There is no reason to alter the view expressed by William Camden in *Remains Concerning Britain,* edition 1890, p. 114: "About the year of our Lord 1000 surnames began to be taken up in France . . . but not in England till about the time of the Conquest, or else a very little before, under King Edward the Confessor who was all Frenchified. And to this time do the Scottish men also refer the antiquity of their surnames, although Buchanan supposed that they were not in use in Scotland many years after. Yet in England certain it is, that as the better sort, even from the Conquest, by little and little took surnames, so they were not settled among the common people fully until about the time of King Edward II." This is a fair statement and anticipated most of the later studies on the subject. Camden lived from 1551–1623 and it was not until 1843 when Mark Anthony Lower published his *English Surnames: Essays on Family*

Nomenclature that anything more of value was written on the subject. Lower's work was a great advance on anything which had appeared after Camden but he was still capable of giving ridiculous derivations to some surnames. From this time can be dated the modern scientific study of surnames. It is now settled that all surnames fall into one of four classes: (a) patronymics like Williamson; (b) place names, such as Olney; (c) occupational names, e.g., Taylor, Fletcher, Warrener, and (d) nicknames like Strongitharm.* The period toward the end of the 13th century in England is that of the general adoption of surnames, and the end of the formative process for them. New surnames afterward came into England, but from other countries, where they had already been formed, as with the entry of French Huguenots.

Clearly the possession of a surname has little bearing on descent for not only were surnames late in adoption in the English-speaking world, but they were also until 200 years ago subject to a great deal of variation. It is still perfectly legal and in order in England for anyone to change his surname without process of law. Change by deed poll is a method which costs little and serves to register a change. The elaborate and expensive method of change of name or of taking additional names and arms by royal sign manual is used only when specifically required by the law, i.e., when under a will the beneficiary must take the name and arms of the testator in order to inherit the estate.†

Consequently as change of surname has always been a matter of personal preference, our ancestors had no hesitation in employing the alias now so generally

---

* Note 32. Surnames: sources of information.
† Note 33. Change of surname and legality thereof.

associated with something disreputable, or even criminal. Anyone browsing in documents or books of the 17th century is likely to come across many instances of the use of the alias by eminently respectable members of society.

Adoption of surname was often a matter of chance and therefore it is inadvisable to work on the basis that the identity of the surname necessarily denotes identity of family. In the very many cases of common names clearly it cannot, e.g., Attlee, which means "at or by the meadow," must have been borne by numerous families distinct from each other. This explains why the pedigree of Earl Attlee, the former Labor Prime Minister of Britain, is inextricably involved in the 18th century when many families of Attlee are found in Surrey. The only way in which the origin of a surname can be traced is by genealogical research and even then it is exceptional to be able to trace one's pedigree to the first bearer of the name.

(2) The second difficulty lies in the nature of the evidence on which a reliable pedigree can be constructed. There are many good American pedigrees which show all the generations from the first settler in the original thirteen colonies, but unless the place from which that settler came is known in England, it will entail a search resembling the proverbial finding of a needle in a haystack. In tracing pedigrees in England it can safely be said that most people can get back to 1700; quite a large number to 1600, but before that, to know one's ancestors they must have been property owners; not necessarily great landowners but simply people who would figure in property and tax returns, and so leave records of themselves. Such ancestors may be traced to 1500, perhaps earlier. Many of the old county families have been seated on their estates since the 12th century. During the Middle Ages some of the most useful records are those in connection with taxes, like the

inquisitio post mortem which resembled the modern estate or death duties and was charged on an estate before an heir could enter upon it. There is a gap in the English records between *Domesday Book* (1086) and the earliest of the *Pipe Rolls* in the reign of Henry I (1100–35), and between the latter and the records of the reign of Henry II (1154–89). So it is often quite impossible to prove that the *Domesday* tenant had descendants 100 years later in possession of his land.

A family history in point is that of the Okeovers of Okeover, a very ancient house now represented in the female line by Sir Ian Walker-Okeover, Bart., whose mother was an Okeover. The founder of the family was Ormus Helsweyn or Ormus de Acover (Okeover) who was living 1089–1158. He may have been the son of Eddulph the *Domesday Book* tenant. The names would seem to imply a native owner of the property of Okeover in Staffordshire.

Here, too, on the subject of names, we encounter a great difficulty, for soon after the Conquest, Christian names from abroad spread rapidly among the English. The older names were dropped quickly and their places taken by Norman or French baptismal names. In many lines of ancestry we may be dealing with people of English origin because by the time their history is recorded only foreign Christian names are found in their genealogies.* In the pedigrees of the FitzWilliams and the Berkeleys we can trace the origin of the family as English, but if the names of Godric and of Eadnoth, respectively, had been lost, we should have concluded that the family came from France. In the case of a family which has died out in Lancashire, England, the Claytons, the first name

---

* Note 34. Biscop genealogy.

on the pedigree was Leofwine, whose son was named Hugh. Here again the English origin could easily have been lost.

Then also care must be taken about the guides to be followed. In the proper place I shall have plenty to say about the Battle Abbey Roll, but suffice for the present to refer to the Duchess of Cleveland's book on the subject, in so far as the authoress stated that she had relied on the anonymous work which was published in Victoria's reign under the title, *The Norman People*. The criticism of the last-named book in the long-defunct magazine, *The Ancestor,* by J. H. Round (Vol. II, p. 165) is so penetrating that it ought to be read by anyone who thinks that his family is of Norman ancestry. As *The Ancestor* is accessible only rarely in secondhand book catalogues, it will be as well to give some notice here of its examination of the anonymous book. "There is certainly no work that can rival *The Norman People* in its appeal to claimants of Norman descent or in the vast number of families who will find their surnames within its covers." Round goes on to point out that the author had been perfectly right in many of his criticisms, especially in connection with the stories current in the last century in peerage books, but that he then went forward to fabricate genealogies of his own as unsubstantiated as those which he had ridiculed. He concluded that the peerage of England was almost entirely Norman. I should think that nothing could be further from the truth if, as the author meant, the male line descent was intended. In support of his contention he cited the dukes of Northumberland, the famous Percies. They are Percies only in the female line, and that at two or three removes. They are really Smithsons and the origin of that surname ought not to require very great etymological knowledge, but the author whose identity remained anonymous derived the Smithsons from a baronial family of Scalers or de Scallariis. There is no need for any elaborate refutation of such nonsense. He had only to see a name cast in a Norman or French form to perceive that it was of foreign origin, forgetting or ignoring that the medieval scribe rendered the personal names into a Latinized form so that good honest Smith became Faber. One of the main contentions was that about a third of the English people were of Norman blood, and another third of Scandinavian blood. This last argument is by no means disposed of, for it has recently been put to me by a Norwegian correspondent in New York who is determined that not only the people but even the language of England—probably the scenery too—shall have originated in Scandinavia. On this let Round make his usual forceful comment. "Among the families claimed by its author as 'Norman' are families which he himself deduces from Saintonge, Brittany and Toulouse. . . . As a matter of fact the Bretons and the Flemings were numerous in William's host, a fact to which we have been largely blinded by our use of the word 'Norman'. But even including all the populations re-presented among the invaders we can only reach the author's estimate by adopting every conceivable device to twist a name into a foreign shape, or to trace a house to a foreign stock. The real wonder is that there are any English left." To which it may be added that after all the Viking invasions and after the Norman Conquest, our country remains England, not Daneland or Norman-land. Its language bears the marks of influence from the Norse, and still more from the French, but remains lineally the same from *Beowulf* to Betjeman.

These considerations are by no means academic. In each generation despite the efforts of scholars and historians the old myths reappear. In 1966 there was celebrated the 9th centenary of the Norman Conquest, in itself a very strange thing for a country to celebrate its own subjugation. I was asked to give a lecture at Hastings on the battle and also to attend a lunch of the Pomeroy family (this is a genuine Norman line, to be dealt with in detail later). At the latter, which was attended by French and English guests as well as by family members, a lady remarked to me that at the time of the Conquest "they," meaning the English, "were not a nation, only a collection of tribes." This completely mistaken conception also received an airing in a B.B.C. television program about Harold and William. The national institutions no more began at the Norman Conquest than did the language. A distinctive national character has manifested itself from the days of King Alfred (died 899) to the present. During the 1966 celebrations many books were published about the Norman invasion and the fact emerged that in describing the pre-Conquest English the writers often succeeded in presenting a picture of their 20th century descendants. In the misrepresentation of the 11th century English, Hilaire Belloc took a considerable share. He was a writer of genius and a brilliant contributor to English literature, but that he ever really understood the English character is, I think, most unlikely. For one thing he was decidedly French in his outlook, being indeed of French blood, and for another he had neither liking or knowledge of the English Bible of 1611 which has worked itself into the writing of every author of note until the present century.

(3) The third important factor for the searcher to bear in mind is in the sphere of heraldry. It is unfortunately true that so many genealogists either do not know much of heraldry or profess not to understand it. Heraldry is

not a difficult science to master. Why should it be, seeing that it was devised as a means of rapid identification in warfare, for the most part by unlettered men? Indeed anyone of normal intelligence can learn the rudiments and essentials of the science in a few days and then go on as did our medieval predecessors to enlarge his knowledge every time he sees a fresh coat of arms. Now heraldry can be a great help in the study of genealogy, but it can also be a delusion and a snare. Originally and ideally the object of the science of heraldry is to identify the individual and usually as a member of a family or a group. It is a fact, however, that heraldry developed without any central or controlling organization so that every man did what he thought best to suit himself. This led to many alterations in the coats of arms borne by members of the same family and to the taking of the arms of another family. Sometimes the latter course was adopted when marriage took place to an heiress as with a member of the Pyne family who married the heiress of the Malets and settled at Curry and Shepton Mallet. He discarded his own coat of arms and adopted the escallops of the Malets. Again, in a particular county or district, armigerous persons might assume a variant of the arms of some great local magnate. This happened in Cheshire and such adoptions have often led to wrong conclusions as to blood connections which did not exist.

Thus heraldic identities or likenesses are not always indications of identity in pedigree. To which must be added that over the last 400 years many people have assumed arms merely because they bear the same name as an armigerous family. Not all Howards are members of the Duke of Norfolk's family.

Bearing these provisos in mind we can study the origin of many Norman names. The arrival of the Normans in England is dated between 1066 and 1204, the last date being the year in which King John was deprived of Normandy by the French. Up to that time, for 138 years, the kings of England had been also dukes of Normandy and in the latter capacity, vassals of the French king. Likewise their nobles had held land on both sides of the Channel. When the duchy was conquered by the French it became necessary for the nobles to decide on which side of the sea they wished to remain. One very great family, who do not appear to have taken any part in the Norman Conquest, decided in 1204 to throw in their lot with England. They were the Gorges, whose history takes up nearly four closely printed pages in the *Landed Gentry*. They derive their name from a place in the Cotentin peninsula of Normandy four miles north of Périers. They are traced to a Ralph de Gorges who lived in the latter part of the 11th century. The first from whom descent is proved in England is Thomas de Gorges who possessed that Norman fief when John lost Normandy. On coming to England he was made warden of the royal manor of Powerstock in Dorset by Henry III. He died in 1236 and from his time, in every generation since, the Gorges have been distinguished. The English representative, Howard Gorges, died recently. The family was much associated with the early settlements in America. Sir Ferdinando Gorges, who was Lord Proprietor of Maine, 1639–47, was an original member of the Council for New England, 1620. It is fitting that there should be a splendidly printed book on the Gorges by one of the American scions. This was produced by Raymond Gorges of Boston in 1944, titled, *The Story of a Family, through Eleven Centuries: A History of the Family of Gorges*. It is likely that there are more Americans of Norman descent than there are British, if only because, as in the case of

Gorges, the early colonization of America often came from families which have died out or become obscure in England.

The Gorges are not mentioned in a very exact and important work, *The Origins of Some Anglo-Norman Families* by the late Lewis C. Loyd (Harleian Society, 1951), but not less than 315 families are entered therein. I cannot comment on them all, but for the benefit of researchers, I give all the names in an appendix. The work is one of very deep scholarship, the conclusions of which can be relied upon. The book was edited by Sir Charles Clay, formerly librarian of the House of Lords, and by David C. Douglas, the greatest living authority on the Conquest period. Of the 315 families listed, 295 originated in one of the five departments of Normandy: Calvados, 95; Seine-Inférieure, 93; Manche, 50; Eure, 47; and Orne, 15. Although the title is *Anglo-Norman Families,* 16 are included from outside Normandy, including four from Brittany, three in the Somme area and three in the Pas-de-Calais.

Taking the letter A, we have some interesting examples of Norman names which have made history in the lands of their adoption.

Abernon, more easily known to English people from the place Stoke d'Abernon in Surrey. Incidentally the occurrence in England of two names for a place is an instance of the complaint of the psalmist that great men were wont to call their lands after their own names. The first part—Stoke—is the original name of the village, and D'Abernon indicates that Stoke was one of the holdings of the family. Roger de Abernon or Abernun is found in the *Domesday* as holding land in Surrey. The name comes from Abernon in Calvados, arr. Lisieux, can. Orbec. The family was not of great baronial status, and appears to have died out, though it is much more likely that the present representatives have been submerged under a change of name. The "de" form does not indicate as in continental lands a part of the name but is only a scribe's translation of "of". The interesting point in all the cases now being examined is that a Norman name has been brought to England, a ready-made surname and even conferred upon the land. Other examples of such use of a surname come from Stoke Mandeville in Essex, but while there are quite a few such instances in various parts of England, the usage is very common in the west country —Somerset, Dorset, Devonshire, etc.—where names like Sampford Peverel, Sampford Arundell, Curry Mallet, Upton Pyne, Combe Martin and many other places show the name of the incoming foreign lord affixed to the original, native name.

Two branches of the Aubigny (Albini) family occur, both taking their name from Saint Martin d'Aubigny in the Manche. One of these lines became Earls of Arundel, from the Conquest to the reign of Henry III (1217–72). The name has easily come into the forms of Daubeny, Daubney, Dabney, Dobney, etc. The other line received property at Cainhoe in Bedfordshire. There was in addition a further family of Aubigny which came to Leicestershire and which derived from a place in Normandy, Saint Aubin d'Aubigné in Ille et Vilaine, an illustration of the separate origin of families which bear the same surname.

Aumale or Albemarle, now an Anglicized name, came from Aumale in Seine-Inférieure. Continuing in the alphabet, Kingston Bagpuise is an old-sounding place name in Berkshire. It owes its second name to the family of Bachepuis, Bachepuz, or Bagpuz which hailed from Bacquepuits in Eure. In England they were under-tenants of the Ferrers, the Earls of Derby.

Bacon is a genuine Norman name coming from Le Molay, formerly le Molay-Bacon. According to Dr. Reaney the name does actually denote "a buttock, ham, side of bacon." It is definitely of Norman origin. Whether the Bacons, the premier baronets of England, the family to which belonged the famous Francis Bacon, were descended from this Norman line, is not known.

Bailleul or De Balliolio came from Bailleul-sur-Eaulne in Seine-Inférieure. They held lands in Sussex at Mayfield. The family of Balliol who provided two kings of Scotland, John and Edward (the latter reigned only a few months), came from another place called Balliol in the department of the Somme. With the Norman (and French) Balliols must not be confused a family of Baillieu (represented by Lord Baillieu) who came from Liège in Belgium. Here it is pertinent to remark that there are quite a large number of families which have settled in England from France, even from Normandy, but who most certainly did not come over with the Conqueror. One of the best-known of these is the family of Sir Laurence Olivier, now Lord Olivier, whose ancestry is traced in France to 1520 and whose forbears came to England in the Huguenot troubles. Yet another Bailleul Norman family originated independently from Bailleul-en-Gouffern in Orne, and held lands in Staffordshire and Shropshire.

The Bassets are identified with a family of Montreuil-au-Houlme in Orne. The surname is a nickname from old French, meaning "of low stature" (cf. basset hound) and Dr. Reaney quotes Ordericus Vitalis as saying that Henry II raised Ralph Basset from the lowest stock, *de ignobili stirpe ac de pulvere*. This does not agree with the fact that a Ralph Basset is mentioned in *Domesday*, that the Bassets held Montreuil in Orne, or with the pedigree in the

Landed Gentry for the Bassets of Tehidy, near Redruth, Cornwall, one of whom was justiciar to Henry I.

Roger de Beaumont, who was the holder of Sturminster Marshal in Dorset in 1086, took his surname from Beaumont le Roger in Eure. His descendants were the Counts of Meulan, the Earls of Leicester and the Earls of Warwick. The name is originally one (like Clifton) in England which could be given to many localities and therefore produced many families distinct in origin though having the same surname. The Beaumont peer and baronet now in the peerage books derive from the Frankish house of Brienne. According to Dr. Reaney, there were five places named Beaumont in Normandy. Variants of the name include Beumont, Beaman, Beamand, Belmont (a medieval form was Bellomont) and Bemment.

Another name frequently found in England and obviously of foreign origin is that of Beauchamp, but although there are two places so named in Calvados there is insufficient evidence to indicate the connection of the historic English peerage family with either. Dr. Reaney states that the *Domesday* family came from a place in La Manche. The name soon acquired an English pronunication, unlike Beaumont, hence the existence in England of two different spellings but having the same sound, i.e. Beauchamp and Beecham.

The well-known name Boyes, Boys, Boyse, Boice and Boyce is Norman, coming from Bois-Arnault in Eure. The family is not known to have settled in England before 1130 when Ernald de Bosco was tenant of Thorpe Arnold in Leicestershire, his lord being the Earl of Leicester.

The name Carteret is Norman, coming from a place so called in the Manche. This was situated on the coast near Cherbourg and Coutances. (Payne's *Armorial of Jersey* and Collins' *History of the House of Carteret*) The family have held for many centuries the seigneury of St. Ouen's, Jersey, Channel Islands, and one of them, Sir Philip de Carteret, was in 1166 the holder of as many as 13 or 14 knights' fees in Devonshire. In the war which resulted in King John losing Normandy, the Channel Islands remained firm in allegiance to the English crown, and the de Carterets were largely instrumental in keeping Jersey loyal to John and his successors.

Few names have gathered round them a more romantic attachment than that of Chandos. This is due to the exploits of the famous Sir John Chandos, so renowned in the wars of Edward III's reign. He came of a family seated at Radbourne in Derbyshire in the time of Henry III (1217–72). The *Domesday* Roger de Candos came from Candos in Eure and was an under-tenant of Hugh de Montfort in Suffolk.

Chesney comes from Le Quesnay in Seine Inf., Cheyney, Cheyne, Chainey, Cheeney, Chene, Chasney, Chasteney and Chestney are all forms of the name. The ultimate meaning of this surname is "oak grove."

Coleville, well-known in its English form of Colville, was brought from Colleville in Seine Inf. with Gilbert de Colavilla in 1086 as an under-tenant in Suffolk of Robert Malet.

Corcelle or Curcella is derived from Courseulles-sur-Mer in Calvados and Roger de Curcelle was a tenant-in-chief in Somerset. It would not be worth mentioning but for the attempt made at one time to connect the latter-day west country family of Churchill with a Norman Courcelle and thus obscure the easily explained etymology of their name.

The Courcys derive from Courcy in Calvados. Connected with this family is the story of the famous or infamous hat which the head of the family, the Lord Kingsale, is supposed to have the right to wear in the sovereign's presence. But for the fact that the family early acquired a peerage in Ireland, they would have remained completely obscure gentry. The famous John de Courcy who conquered the province of Ulster for the English crown in the reign of Henry II was not the ancestor of the Lords Kingsale. He came from the Norman lords of Courcy in Somerset, that is Stoke Courcy, or Stogursey, rendered famous by Bernard Shaw's little priest in *St. Joan,* but neither John de Courcy or the Courcys of Stoke are connected with the Irish peers.

Curzon, the name of the great Norman house, of which Viscount Scarsdale is the head, was brought from Notre Dame de Courson in Calvados. They held a property at West Lockinge in Berkshire under Henry de Ferrers, but their main seat has been for well over 850 years in Derbyshire.

The Ferrers who were the old Earls of Derby came from Ferrières-Saint Hilaire in Eure. Loyd remarks on the family: "The Norman branch of the family continued in the male line until the early years of the 16th century. The fact that Boscherville, Curzon and Livet, all of whom were Ferrers under-tenants of the old feofment in England, derived their names from places which were members of the barony of Ferrières in Normandy puts the identification beyond doubt." This line of the Earls of Derby died out in the reign of Edward I, but is now still represented in England by a landed gentry family. A very interesting line of descent has been sketched out for an Australian family which has settled in America. This was the family of the late John Villiers Farrow, the well-known film producer whose wife was Maureen O'Sullivan. John Farrow was born in Australia, served as a Lieutenant Cmdr. in the Canadian Navy in World War II, and received the C.B.E. Of his ancestry, the then Richmond Herald, now Sir Anthony Wagner, Garter King of Arms, wrote: "The pedigree of his family recorded in the College of Arms begins with Nicholas Ferrour, mentioned in 1500, but though a connected descent can at present be proved no further, a highly probable ancestry from a much earlier date can be indicated. Elias de Ferrers, whose origin is unknown, but who may have been akin to the Earls of Derby (see Ferrers of Baddeley Clinton in *Burke's Landed Gentry*) was party to a fine in Rudham, Norfolk, with his brother Eustace in 1208." From this Elias various persons of the Ferrour name in the same area of Norfolk are mentioned until we reach "Nicholas Ferrour, of Guist, mentioned in 1430, and may have been the father of the Nicholas with whom the proved pedigree begins."

Gamages is sprung from Gamaches in Eure. "It is stated in an inquest of 1251–52 that Godfrey de Gamages, a Norman, held Mansell Gamage, co. Hereford, of Walter de Lacy in the time of Richard I: that Matthew his elder son remained in Normandy at the separation, and that Godfrey gave Mansell Gamage to William, his younger son, whose son, another Godfrey, held it in 1251–52."

The Giffards, Earls of Buckingham, one of the most notable Norman familes and related to the Conqueror himself, derive from Longueville-la-Gifart (now Longueville-sur-Scire) in Seine Inf.

Grenville or Granville, from whom came the renowned Grenvilles of Devon (Sir Richard Grenville and the last fight of the *Revenge*), took their name from Grainville-la-Teinturière in Seine Inf. "In the Conqueror's reign Ralph de Granvilla witnessed a charter of Walter Giffard for the abbey of Cerisy-la-Forêt; and the family split into two branches, Norman and English, both under-tenants of Giffard."

The great Scottish family of Haig is of Norman origin and has achieved such immense status in history and romance that it deserves a special notice. It was of the Haigs that Thomas the Rhymer, Scotland's legendary poet, said, "Tide what may, Haig shall have Bemersyde." Lt.Col. Arthur Balfour Haig, the 28th laird of Bemersyde sold the estate in 1921, but it was then bought for the presentation to be made to Field Marshal Earl Haig, and given to him in recognition of his services in World War I. He became the 29th laird of Bemersyde, thus fulfilling the Rhymer's prophecy.

The first laird of Bemersyde was Peter de Haga. In Normandy La Hague (Haga, Hagua) was a district lying to the west of Cherbourg and was in the Middle Ages a rural deanery. The Cap-de-la-Hague, the north-westernmost point of Normandy, still preserves the name. Morville was a place only about 12 miles south of the limits of the deanery of La Hague. In Britain there is found a connection between Morevilles and Haigs, from the evidence of charters in Berwickshire, Scotland, and in Dorset, England. The two families, such near neighbors in Normandy, thus maintained their links when they came to colonize Britain. Like many nobles of the period 1100–1300 they possessed estates in both Scotland and England. This factor had great influence during the reign of Edward I, when the Scots were fighting for their independence. Many nobles held lands in both countries, which helps to explain why so often Scots lords gave allegiance to King Edward. When Bruce eventually triumphed these notables had to make their decision as to which kingdom they would support.

The name Hay (variants Haye, Hayes, Hays, Hey, Heyes, Heighes) was borne into England from La Haye-du-Puits in Manche.

Lovel is a name which according to Sir Walter Scott was much in use for the heroes of romances. The family which bore it in Norman times came from Ivry-la-Bataille in Eure. They were descended from the lords of Ivry also in Eure. The name comes from Anglo-French *lovel* "wolf cub," and is a diminutive of the Anglo-French *love*, "a wolf," (Latin *lupus*). William, Earl of Ivry, was called *Lupellus* to distinguish him from his father Robert, nicknamed *Lupus* from his violent temper.

Lucy comes from Lucé in Orne. The Malets, one of the very few families which can claim a member at Hastings, came from Granville-Sainte-Honorine in Seine Inf. The origin of their surname is variously explained as being from the French for "cursed," adopted from the Breton St. Malo of the 6th century or from connection with Martel, meaning "hammer."

The Mandevilles (Manvels, Manvilles and Manwells), who became very great lords in England as Earls of Essex, took their name from Manneville in Seine Inf. One of them, Geoffrey de Mandeville, had the distinction of being created Earl of Essex by both Stephen and Matilda during the wars between them. There were two other unconnected Mandeville familes, coming from Mandeville in Manche and Manneville-sur-Risle in Eure.

Marmion is from Fontenay-le-Marmion in Calvados. The name has been immortalized by Scott's poem. The Marmions held Scrivelsby in Lincolnshire where they were succeeded through the female line by the Dymokes, the head of whom is the sovereign's Champion.*†

Mohun is from Moyon in Manche. They were the holders of Dunster Castle in Somerset. Only two families

---

* Note 35. Queen's Champion.

† Note 36. Incidents of Grand Serjeanty.

have been possessed of Dunster since the Norman Conquest, the Mohuns and the Fownes-Luttrells.

Montfort must have been a fairly common name and would not have acquired its great celebrity but for Simon de Montfort to whom is ascribed the beginnings of a democratic Parliament. He came from abroad, his Father having been very active in the crusade against the Albigenses in the south of France. The *Domesday* tenant, Hugh de Montfort, was from Montfort-sur-Risle in Eure and is not claimed as the ancestor of the Montforts of 200 years later.

Montgomery was also an imported surname, derived from Saint Germain de Montgomery and Saint Foy de Montgomery in Calvados. In England the family became very powerful on the Welsh border where it gave its name to a county.

Mortimer, instead of being taken from the Dead Sea in some crusading adventure, is derived from Mortemer-sur-Eaulne in Seine Inf. Mowbray is from Montbrai in Manche.

The name of Neville comes from Néville in Seine Inf. The Nevilles are now represented in the British peerage by the Marquess of Abergavenny. Among the many historic characters in this great family the most famous is Richard Neville the Kingmaker, Earl of Salisbury and of Warwick, Baron Montacute and Baron Monthermer. He made and unmade kings, having had both Edward IV and Henry VI under his control. The Neville descent is another example of the mingling of English and Norman. Their male line descent combined the blood of the Scots kings with that of the Earls of Northumbria who were mentioned in connection with Swinton, and Robert FitzMaldred, the lord of Raby married Isabel, the sister and heiress of Henry de Neville. Their son Geoffrey de Neville took his mother's name and succeeded his father in 1242.

The Percy family takes its name from Percy-en-Auge in Calvados. It was founded in England by William de Percy, the *Domesday* tenant-in-chief and the under-tenant of Hugh, Earl of Chester. He was nicknamed Algernons, "William with the Whiskers," a Christian name borne by his descendants. His great-granddaughter Agnes de Percy married Joceline of Louvain, of Petworth, Sussex, the brother of Queen Adela, the second wife of Henry I. Their children took the name of Percy. The male line failed again in 1722 when the female line descendant, Algernon Seymour, 7th Duke of Somerset and 1st Earl of Northumberland of a new creation, succeeded. This duke's daughter married Sir Hugh Smithson who took the name of Percy and immolated his own name and arms on the altar of the twice removed Percy greatness.

Picot has differentiated into Picket, Pykett, Piggott, etc. A substantial under-tenant of the great Earl Roger of Montgomery, in Shropshire, was Picot de Say, from Sai in Orne. In the 16th century when huge roller pedigrees were the fashion, the original Norman Picot was depicted at the head of the family tree in armor and on horseback.

Pomeroy still represented in the peerage (through male succession) derives from La Pommeraye in Calvados. In 1086 the founder of the family in England, Ralf de Pomarai, was a great tenant-in-chief as well as holding other lands as an under-tenant of Robert Count of Mortain. Berry Pomeroy in Devon is named after this family. Viscount Harberton is the present head of the family. For a full account of this notable Norman house readers should consult John Prince's great work, *Worthies of Devon;* the article in *Burke's Peerage,* and a very good modern study, *The House of de la Pomerai,* by Edward B. Powley (1943) where the full descent is given generation by generation.

In the story of the Poynings family which took its name from the Sussex village of Poynings, it is not possible to demonstrate a Norman origin but there are strong indications that the family was Norman in origin and came from Martigny in Seine Inf. It was one of this family who in the reign of Henry VII was responsible for the famous Poynings law in Ireland by which an Act of the Irish Parliament had to be confirmed by the English Parliament before it could become law.

The famous line of the Sackvilles derives from Sauqeville in Seine Inf. The present Lord Sackville is the representative through the female line, being a Sackville-West. In 1166 William de Sauqeville held one knight's fee of the Giffards. A famous name is St. Clair, Sinclair as it has become. Its origin is from Saint-Clair-sur-Elle in Manche. The present representatives are the Earl of Caithness and the Lord Sinclair. As with so many of the greatest lords they held lands first in England and then some two generations later in Scotland. Some dozen other surnames of saints—St. Hilary, St. John (the well known English "Sinjohn") and St. Leger—all derive from place names in Normandy.

The Staffords certainly took their name from the English lands which they received but they were otherwise denominated de Tosny (or Toeny) in Eure. From one of the three brothers in this family at the time of the Conquest descend the Gresley baronets of Drakelowe. The original Norman name was abandoned in favor of the English place names of their estates.

The family of the premier earl in the peerage, the Earl of Shrewsbury, bears the surname of Talbot. There was a Norman in 1086 who was under-tenant of Hugh de Gournay in Essex, and another who held of Walter Giffard in Buckinghamshire. The names of these two under-tenants were Geoffrey and Richard Talebot, respectively. The name was not territorial, but the Talebots were under-tenants in Seine Inf.; they are definitely Norman, and so is their surname. "The exact connection of the family of the Earls of Shrewsbury with these Talbots has not at present been established by satisfactory evidence, though such a connection is in the highest degree probable." (Loyd, p. 100)

Tilly comes from Tilly-sur-Seulles in Calvados and in early 13th century, when the Tillys are mentioned, they are specifically described as being Normans, i.e., having held lands in Normandy. The Tracies, another well-known family, came from Manche, the surname being from Tracy-Bocage or Tracy-sur-Mer (in Calvados). One of them was numbered among the murderers of Thomas à Becket, hence the old saying "The Tracies have ever the wind in their faces" as a family curse.

The name Tremlett is a fairly good disguise for the Latin from *De Tribus Minetis,* itself the rendering of Les Trois Minettes in Calvados from which this family hails. It has been seated for many centuries in the west of England. The *minata* or *mineta* was a land measure.

Two deceptively English surnames are Vere and Vernon. They are both from Normandy. The former was assumed from Ver in Manche. In 1086 Aubrey de Ver held considerable fiefs in several English counties. He was the ancestor of the Earls of Oxford and by some unexplained process the family of de Vere has come to be taken as the ultimate in aristocratic association. Most people will recall Lady Vere de Vere in Tennyson's poem.

The Vernons derive from a place of that name in Eure.

Villiers-le-Ser in Calvados contributed the Villiers to England.

Warenne is from Varenne in Seine Inf., the French v becoming the English w, as also with the great house of Wavell, whose origin was at Vauville, a village which stands on the bay of the same name in the western portion of the Cherbourg peninsula. The seigneurs of Vauville were a younger branch of the barons of Briquebec, who like many others of the ruling caste in Normandy, were descended from the old Norse stock. A William de Vauville or Wavilla is mentioned in charters in both Normandy and England in the 11th century. In the reign of King John, Sir Richard de Vauville (Wauvill) settled in Sussex. It was at the close of the Middle Ages that they settled in the Isle of Wight. The first Earl Wavell was the British general who conquered Marshal Graziani and his massed Italian legions in Libya in 1940–41.

In studying the above cases and also those names which are given in the appendix to this chapter, I urge upon any and everyone the necessity of having every link in a pedigree proved before claiming that a family is Norman. Undoubtedly the many Norman names mentioned are found abundantly in the English-speaking world today, but there are so many adoptions of surnames for various reasons that only genealogical proof ought to be accepted. I have been told on good authority, though I have not proved it myself, that the Cornish family name of Beswetherick was changed from Williams 500 years ago; a much more recent change was that by which a family named Robinson adopted the old Norman name of Tremlett without a blood connection. Again, owing to changes of property, it can come about that a person bearing the name of an ancient family has no blood connection with it. A branch of the Carey or Carew family

from the west of England settled in Surrey, at Beddington, in the 14th century. By the 19th century, when the
Carews of Beddington ended, the "last of the line" had
only his surname in common with his predecessors. The
Earl of Lytton bears the surname of the ancient and
knightly family of that name, but he is not of the Lytton
blood as a close inspection of the lineage will reveal. Sir
William Lytton was succeeded by his great-nephew,
Lytton Strode who, upon inheriting the estate in 1704,
assumed the surname of Lytton. He died in 1710 without
issue and was succeeded by his first cousin on his mother's
side, William Robinson, who took the additional surname
of Lytton and so on.

These instances will show that identity of name does
not denote identity of relationship. No pedigree should
be put forward unless it can be proved in each generation. There cannot be gaps in a pedigree. The type of
statement which says that such or such a man was founder
of a family and that 10th in descent from him was, etc.,
has done immense harm. Quite often it is a lazy way of
writing a genuine pedigree but it can conceal or rather
reveal the failure to prove each generation in the ancestry.
A line of ten undistinguished rustics, "rude forefathers
of the hamlet," or a string of names in a Welsh or Irish
chief's pedigree, is often better proof of authenticity than
some labored document, the concoction of fraudulent
Elizabethan heralds, or of genealogical forgers in the 18th
or 19th century. The insistence of many searchers on
documentary proof instead of accepting a sound tradition has its amusing side. A lifetime of serious work, with
proper evaluation of all the kinds of evidence, can go
into a private family history, yet this work is not accepted
as evidence in an English court of law; whereas some
badly put together pedigree of the same family prepared,

possibly, by a venal herald of 300 years back, would be an official document of which a court would be able to take cognizance.

Fortunately the well-worked-out American pedigree is at least as good as anything of its kind in the world. There is no halfway house in American genealogy. It is either the most abysmal rubbish ever seen or the best-evidenced setting out of pedigrees to be encountered at the present day.

Note: As an example of rubbish I shall never forget the pedigree of an American which gave a perfectly good descent of ten generations of inhabitants of New England. At the beginning of this authentic genealogy was an impossible opening statement that the first ancestor had been a Capt. Harold Smith (shall we say) who had commanded a company of lancers for King Harold at Hastings. This was a complete fabrication by some unscrupulous genealogist who had foisted it upon the family.

Appendix

THE following surnames which occur in Loyd's work (beside those on which I have commented in this chapter), are of families known to have originated in Normandy.

Abetot, Abitot	Arguges
Acquigny, Akeney	Arques
Aincourt, Deincourt	Auberville
Aldrie	Auffay, Alfait
Amblie	Aukenvilla
Amundeville	Avilers
Angens	Avranches
Anisy	Baillon
Appeville	Baudemont (de Bosco)

Bavent, Badvent
Belmeis, Beunal
Berners
Bigot
Biset
Bohun
Bolebec
De Bordineio
Bosc-Rohard (Bois
	Rohard Borard)
Boscherville
Bosville
Braiboue, Braibof
Braouze, Braiosa
Broilg, Broy
De Buceio, Boceio
Busli, Builli, Bulli
Bygore
Cailli,
Calceis, Cauceis
Cambreis
Campeaux (de Campellis)
Camville, Cancille
Cantelou (Cantelupe)
Carleville
Caron
Castellon
Chamfleur
Champernowne
Chanfleur
Chaworth
Cherbourg
Chevercourt
Chiray
Clavilla
Clere, Clera
Clinton

Columbiers, Columbers
Colunces
Conteville, Cuncteville
Corbun
Cormeilles, de Cormellis
Costentin
Craon, Creux, de
	Credonico
Crasmesnil
La Cressimera
Cressy, Creissi
Crevequer, Crevecort,
	Crevecuir
Criketot
Cruel
Cuelai
Daivile, Vaivilla, Davidis
	Villa
Dive, Diva
Dol
Dumard, Dumant
Dun
Dunstanville
Envermou
Eschetot, Eshetot
Escois, Scohies
Esmalevilla, Malavilla,
	Smalavilla
Estouteville
Estre
Eu, Augurn, Ou, Count of
Eudo Dapifer
Evreux
Favecurt, Fanucurt,
	Fanencort
Favarches
de Feritate

Ferrers (of Bere Ferrers and Newton Ferrers, Devon)
Feugeres, de Fulgeriis
FitzOsbern
Floc
Folie
Foliat
Fontenay
Fraelvilla
Fresne
Fressenville
Friardel
Giron, Girunde
Gisors
Glanville
Glapion
Gournay
Grandcourt (Grancurt)
Grentemaisnil
Grincurt
Grinnosavilla
Givers, de Guerris
Hamo Dapifer
Harcourt
Helion
Hesdin
de Hispania (Hispaniensis, from Epaignes in Eure)
Le Hommet
Ivry
Keynes, Cahagnes
Laigle, L'Aigle (De Aquila)
Langetot

Lascy, Lacey
Laval
Lestre
Limesi
Lingieure
Livet
Locels
Longchamp, Longus Campus
Longvillers
Luvetot
Malet
Malory
Malquenci
Maminot
Marinni
Marston
Martel
Martigny
Martinwast
Massey, Maci, Masci
Matuen
Mauduit, Malduit
Mayenne, Meduana
Meiniers, de Maineriis (Maneriis)
Meinnil, Malgeri
Meisi
Milleville
Millieres, Milers
Miners, de Mineriis
Moels, Moles, Molis
Monceaux, Monceus, Mouncels (de Moncellis; there was more than one family

of this name from
various places in Nor-
mandy)
Montfichet
Montpinçon, Munpincon
Monville, Montvilla
Morers
Moreville
Muchegros (from
Missegros in Eure)
Nazanda
Neubourg, de Novo Burgo
Neufmarche, de Novo
 Mercato
Normanville
Nowers, Noers
Noyers, de Nueriis
Oglander, Orglandres
Orbec
Oseville
Pacy, Pasci, de Paceio
Pantulf
Patric
Pavilly
Paynel, Paganel
Pinkeny
Pierrepont, de Petroponto
Port (again two distinc-
tive families from the
same place in Calvados)
Portes
Portmort
Poteria
Praeres
Punchardon, de Ponte
 Cardonis

Quilli
Quincy
Raimes, Rames
Raineville, Reineville
 Reinerville
Reines, Raines, Rednes,
 Retnes
Reviers, Redvers
Ruddlan, Roelent
Ricarville, Ricardvile,
 Richardivilla
Rollos, Rullos
Ros
Rosei, de Roseto
Roumare
Roville
Ruili
Rumilly
Sachevilla
Saint Laurent
Saint Martin
Saint Ouen, de Sancto
 Audoeno
Saint Quintin
Saint Valery, de Sancto
 Walarico
Sainte Foy, de Sancto Fide
Saint Mere Eglisle
Salceit
De Sancto Cristofor
De Sancto Germano
De Sancto Manevo
De Sancto Planees
Sanderville, Salnerville
Sartilly
Saucy

Savenie, de Savigno

Scorchebofe

Scotney, Scoteni
(Scoteigny)

Scures

Sept Meules, de Septem
Molendinis,
Septem Molis

Sifrewast

Solney, Solennei, Sulignei

Spinevilla

Strabo

Steu, (William, son of)

Surdeval

Tahum

Taillebois

Taissel

Talbot

Tancarville

Tani

Terra Vasta, Terra
Guasta

Tesson, Taisson

Tibourvilla, Tedboldvilla

Tigerivilla

Todeni, Tosny

Toreigny

Tornai

Trailei, Tralgi

Tregoz, Tresgoz

Tuit

Turville

Umfranville

Valbadun

Valeines

Veilly

Veim, Vehim, Veyn

Venuz

Verdun

De Verleio

Vilers, Viliers

Waltervilla, Vatiervilla

Wancy, de Wanceio

Wasprey

Waspria

Wast

Many of the names given above will seem outlandish and far removed from any style of surname which we know today, but all are based on a careful study of the original sources. Some surnames have changed little through the centuries. Others must have been enormously altered, if they have survived at all. The habits of the medieval scribe must be taken into account. He had to cope with a preponderantly illiterate community. When he was writing a deed or some other document, he had to render what he heard as best he could, if the name sounded ever so strange, into a Latin which would be

intelligible. The only key to tracing the possible continuance of many of these apparently strange names is
for the present-day researcher to trace his genealogy
until he is able to discover the origin of his name.

CHAPTER SEVEN

The Norman Royal Line

NOT even Queen Elizabeth II can have a direct male line Norman ancestry. Nor for that matter had any of her predecessors after 1135 (the date of the death of Henry I, the youngest son of the Conqueror). The fervent belief of William of Poitiers, one of William's chaplains, that the Conqueror's grandsons would succeed him in England did not come about, in the way which the priest expected, i.e., in undisputed succession for several generations.* The Conqueror had several legitimate grandsons, of whom three are of importance in the history of England and Normandy. His eldest son, Robert, Duke of Normandy, had a son, William the Clito (a term used for a royal scion in the Old English monarchy), who died young while trying to assert his rights to the dukedom of Normandy. His youngest son, Henry I, left a very numerous progeny of bastard children but had only two legitimate issue. Of these the Atheling William, who appears to have been a cruel young savage, was drowned in the loss of the *White Ship* in 1120. Henry's daughter, Matilda, should have become Queen on her father's death, but

---

* Note 37. William of Poitiers.

her cousin, Stephen, Count of Blois, stole the Crown.
Matilda did succeed in asserting her rights, and eventually after 19 years of struggle (a period dubbed by
J. H. Round as the Anarchy), managed to convey them
to her son, afterward Henry II, the Conqueror's great-
grandson. King Stephen who precariously occupied the
throne from 1135–54 was the Conqueror's grandson,
being the son of William's daughter, Adela, by the Count
of Blois. Stephen was a usurper and the agreement
reached between him and Matilda precluded his son,
Eustace, who by an early death saved England from a
further disputed succession.

Thus the male line of William expired within two
generations. The divisions into dynasties in the history
books mark this clearly enough with the Norman kings
shown as distinct from their successors, the Plantagenets,
as they were from their predecessors, the 20 Saxon or
Old English kings. All succeeding sovereigns from 1135,
except possibly William III, have had a female line
Norman descent from William I; in the same way
Matilda and the Plantagenet dynasty which originated
in her womb were descendants in the female line from
Egbert and Alfred the Great. More than that, the
Tudors who succeeded the Plantagenets in 1485 de-
scended from the latter in the female line. The claim of
Henry Tudor, Earl of Pembroke, who became Henry
VII, was a decidedly tenuous affair. Even disallowing
Richard III as a usurper, there was still a young Planta-
genet heir who had a better claim to the throne than
Henry; to his misfortune, since it led to his being judicial-
ly murdered when Henry VII found it inconvenient to
keep him in prison.

The last of the Tudors, Elizabeth I, liked to sum-
marize in her heraldic achievements her many royal

lines of descent, including, through her male ancestry, her connections with the ancient princes of Wales, from Rhodri Mawr (844–78). When she died childless in 1603, she was succeeded by her cousin, James VI of Scotland, who became James I of England. In consequence the succeeding Stuart dynasty, in addition to its male line Scots descent, now claimed to represent the Tudor, Plantagenet, Norman and Old English lines.

On the expulsion of the Stuarts, they were succeeded by the House of Orange, in the person of William, Stadtholder of Holland, who became William III of England. His wife, Mary, was the elder daughter of the last male Stuart to reign, James II (in Scotland, James VII), but as William and Mary had no children, the next sovereign, Anne, James II's younger daughter, succeeded in 1702. She was the last Stuart monarch. The Stuart male line died out in exile, and Anne was succeeded in 1714 by a distant cousin, the German Elector of Hanover, who descended through a female line from James I. Most European royalties have had much more mixed blood than the peoples over whom they have reigned, but the Hanoverians, whatever Scottish antecedents they possessed, were completely Germanic in character. Never before their time had royalty been a closed caste in outlook and in practice in England, but for six reigns— from George I to Queen Victoria—the British sovereigns were married to royalties and Germanic royalties. Indeed it could be said that it was not until after the 1918 war that British royalty reverted to the older style of marriage in which alliances were made with the families of the British nobility. For Edward VII was married to Princess Alexandra of Denmark, and George V married his cousin, Princess Mary. After 1918 the disappearance from royal seats of so many monarchies, and the fact that the

German and Austrian houses had been among the nation's enemies, made it necessary for the British royal family to make a change in their matrimonial arrangements. Thus George VI, the Princess Mary, and the Duke of Gloucester married members of the British aristocracy.

In view of the above slight sketch of the make-up of the ancestry of the present Queen, it must be clear that her Norman descent is only to be made out through several female lines. The British royal family has for several generations summed up within itself the representation of all our dynasties (except the Danish kings) and it is always easy to select a particular strand, making that look like the main line. This was shown particularly at the time of the investiture of Prince Charles as Prince of Wales on 1 July 1969. He has at least three lines of descent from the man who for a short time in the 9th century united all Wales under his rule, Rhodri Mawr or the Great. Looking at such a tree one is apt to dwell on the Prince's Welsh forbears, especially if several generations in the pedigree are telescoped, e.g., five generations of Mortimers in the Middle Ages or the Hanoverian sovereigns from George I to William IV. The dominant strain in the Prince's ancestry is that of the continental Germanic lines. Owing to his grandfather, George VI's marriage with a Scots lady (Queen Elizabeth the Queen Mother), daughter of the then Earl of Strathmore, the German ancestry of the Queen was diluted. It was strengthened again, however, when she married her cousin, Philip Mountbatten, a member of the royal house of Greece, and through that of Denmark. The name of his family in the male line is Schleswig Holstein Sonderburg Glucksberg.

If then we seek for the descendants of the Norman

leader, we shall be right in looking to Elizabeth II, but it is an ancestry which she must share with a multitude of her subjects; and not only of her subjects, but of legions of persons of English or British descent throughout the United States. It is unnecessary to possess more than a moderate acquaintance with English history to know that from medieval times right up to 1714, English royalty married with the nobility, and the latter with the gentry; the gentry with the rest of the people. It is impossible to enumerate the number of people in the world today who can legitimately claim to be descended from William the Conqueror.

Sometimes the expression is heard: "a direct descendant of so and so." There is no call for the adjective. The only other kind of descent, apart from direct, is collateral. In other words, Queen Elizabeth I is not the ancestress of Queen Elizabeth II, since the former was childless, but she is properly described as collateral ancestress of the present Queen. However many changes of name may have occurred, however many female lines the descent has gone through, the person from whom one is physically descended is without any qualification one's ancestor.

It is well to remember that with each generation backward the number of our ancestors must double. Two parents; four grandparents; eight great-grandparents; sixteen great-great-grandparents. A real tableau of *seize quartiers!* We have only to think of this process going back over 30 generations to realize that at the time of the Norman Conquest England would have had a population as large as at present, if all lines of ancestry ran distinct and parallel. Of course they do not; in a large number of instances they crisscross, with the result that many, many persons have some ancestors in common.

Taking this fact in conjunction with that already mentioned—the lack of the continental-style system among the English royalty and nobility—it is clear that there must be many people who share with the reigning monarch a descent from William the Conqueror. Records are not wanting to demonstrate this. Early in the reign of Queen Victoria, Sir Bernard Burke, the son of John Burke who began the well-known publications which bear his name, brought out among his numerous works two large quarto volumes. These were called briefly, *Burke's Royal Descents,* but the full title, too lengthy for the spine of a volume, was the much more descriptive: *The Royal Families of England, Scotland and Wales, with their Descendants, Sovereigns and Subjects.* The books were published in 1851 and now, like most of the out-of-print Burke volumes, command a far higher price than when first produced. Volume I contains a sketch of English history to the reign of Henry VII, running to 197 pages, and is then concluded because the author says that "after his reign there is no regal source to which we can trace any existing families in this country except the Royal House itself." This is a somewhat cryptic utterance and did not deter the author from giving in the rest of Vol. 1 no less than 66 pages of royal descents from individual monarchs or from the various dynasties in Great Britain; nor did it constrain him in Vol. II, where in a larger book he gave in great detail 214 pedigrees of men and women whose descent is traced from English royalties. It is both time-consuming in its fascination, and instructive to all who are interested in Norman descent, to examine some of these pedigrees. Of course anyone whose genealogy was given in 1851 is now dead, but there is no reason to suppose that their marital prowess was less than that of their illustrious ancestry.

They must have left many descendants to carry on the gentle Norman blood, considerably diluted by other strains.

Take as an example the pedigree given for Charles Thomas Warde (Vol. II). His descent is deduced for 20 generations, inclusive from Edward I (1272–1307). This line is one of the more interesting specimens for it goes through royal or noble scions for the greater part of its length. In many pedigrees one encounters the dual or even threefold descent for the same person from the same king. The present Baillieu family, the head of which is a British peer, has double descent from Edward I. Some of these pedigrees are traced through Edward I's grandson, Edward III, of whose importance in this matter more later, but not all of them. A case of one-line descent from Edward I goes down to a John William Jodrell, of Yeardsley in Cheshire. The name of this family is associated with the now world-famous Jodrell Bank radio telescope, since some 600 years ago the family took its name from this place.

Several pedigrees are traced by Burke from Edmund Ironside (Edmund II) who died in 1016. His great-granddaughter, Matilda, married Henry I, and was thus the ancestress of the succeeding sovereigns. Descents do not in all such cases go through Edward III, but sometimes through his great-grandfather, Henry III, and his grandfather, Edward I. The Disneys (to whom the late Walt Disney was very probably connected) have a very involved descent from Henry II (1154–89). After about seven generations there are half a dozen lines of royal descent owing to double marriages and intermarriages.

Perhaps it may be thought that these are pedigrees of the exalted only, of earls and dukes. The names of many of the 1851 descendants are frequently common enough and their bearers often far removed from any immediate connection with nobility. Names like Clarke, Watts, Wynne, Graham, James, Lloyd, Price and Thomas are well known in both America and England.

Volumes of the nature of *Burke's Royal Descents* need to be used with care, for in the 120 years since they were prepared, genealogy has been scientifically studied. Research has overtaken pedigrees such as that of John Ross Coulthart, over which a decent veil ought to be drawn.

Some 60 years after Burke, the task of chronicling the royal descents was undertaken with a more critical apparatus by the Marquis de Ruvigny. In the early years of the present century he brought out six large blue volumes under the general title of *The Blood Royal of the Plantagenets*. These works contain some 40,000 names of persons living about 1910. Ruvigny estimated that not less than 100,000 descendants of the medieval English royalty could be found. Today there would obviously be many more.

Probably most royal descents go through King Edward III. A facetious quip calls him ancestor of the middle-class Englishman. That he was a man of fantastic prowess in the marriage bed (we are concerned here only with legitimate descents) it is unnecessary to postulate, though natural to assume. He had 12 legitimate children, six sons and six daughters, of whom one son and five daughters left no issue, and another son, the eldest, the famous Black Prince, had a legitimate son, King Richard II, who himself was childless. Still for a family of 12 to survive, almost all of them, to adult life was quite a phenomenon in the Middle Ages and much later. Out of the 10 survivors, for five to leave issue meant that within a few generations the descendants of Edward would be numbered in scores, possibly hundreds. The fact that he left four sons with descendants led to the Wars of the Roses, through the struggle of the houses of Lancaster and York, a struggle impossible to comprehend without genealogical tables. Another example of the very frequent crossing over of ancestral lines can be found in the detailed pedigrees of the present Prince of Wales. Some private works on this tree, worked out to 17 generations, contain as many as 12,000 names. Duplication of ancestry here can take two channels. As the Prince's parents are both the great-great-grandchildren of Queen Victoria, i.e., they are cousins, they have many modern royal lines in common. Secondly, through the Queen's remoter ancestors, and above all through her mother, large numbers of people of English and Scots descent have ties of affiliation with the Queen. Queen Elizabeth the Queen Mother is a daughter of the 14th Earl of Strathmore, the head of the ancient Scots family of Lyon. In the early part of the 19th century the then earl married an heiress in Durham, Miss Bowes. Her surnames he added to his own, as often happened in such unions; the Bowes arms with their pun or heraldic canting (bows), are quartered with the lion of Lyon. In most generations since then the heads of the Bowes-Lyon family have married English women, which has brought a number of relationships into being between ordinary English families (with ordinary ramifications in the U.S.A.) and the Prince of Wales. When one examines side by side the ancestry of Prince Philip and that of the Queen, the paradox emerges that he is more royal than she. Belonging as he does to the royal family of Denmark, with its tradition of intermarriage with families of the same status, his ancestry is more monarchical and princely than the Queen's. Hers, on the other hand, illustrates the essentially wide-spreading ramifications of the British royal house, and to the ordinary Mr. or Mrs. in search of pedigree is a much more comforting story and a much easier tree from which to have drawn a branch or sprig.

Edward III is a key figure in English genealogy. The stranger who visits London and who uses public transport is liable to find himself at times slightly bewildered by the railway lines within the capital. If he gets to Earl's Court or Clapham Junction, however, he will have reached a nodal point from which he can easily get anywhere else. So it is in genealogical inquiries when one reaches Edward III. He is in a crucial position. Not only is there a considerable satisfaction in having joined the ranks of royal descendants, but attainment brings with it the certainty that one can now claim descent from Edward's royal predecessors, back to William I, and his Norman ducal forbears; back to the Old English line, to the Counts of Provence and the Kings of Aragon, the Kings of Castile, the Kings of France, to Charlemagne, the Counts of Flanders, etc. Here indeed is a prize worth having. The steady ascent through a succession of plain misters, Smith, Brown, Jones and Robinson begins to widen out into a high plateau of nobility crowned at no great distance by the towering peaks of a range of truly monarchical splendor.

Nor has there been a lack of effort in American genealogy to attain these heights. When I was editing *Burke's Landed Gentry* in 1939, a large quantity of American pedigree forms was received for the 500-page supplement in that edition of family histories of Americans of British descent. By a careful sifting and winnowing down, the number of approximately 1,600 was reached, which were included in the volume. (The supplement was later published as a separate volume, under the heading *Distinguished Families of America*.) Among these were some notable Norman descents. In the Hill pedigree we have Samuel Hill, of Mason, Hillsborough County, New Hampshire, a soldier in the French and Indian wars, and in the American Revolution. In 1760 he married Sarah, the daughter of Capt. Ebenezer Cutler. She was the descendant of Sir Walter Baskerville, a Knight of the Bath, in 1501, of Eardisley, who died in 1505, and was the son of another Sir Walter Baskerville, also K.B., whose wife Katherine Devereux descended from King Edward I. Through this marriage the blood not only of the Norman kings but of a dozen regal lines entered the veins of the Hills. The representative in 1939 was Brig. Gen. the Hon. John Boynton Philip Clayton Hill, D.S.M., A.B., Attorney for Maryland and Member of Congress for the Third Maryland District. His wife was descended in the seventh generation from Charles Carroll of Carrollton, first senator of Maryland and one of the signatories of the Declaration of Independence. The Hill pedigree contains connections with notable English families having Norman blood, like the Grosvenors, Luttrells and Irbys, mingled with the Brownes of Hawkedon Parish, Suffolk, the ancestors of President Franklin Delano Roosevelt, which shows that the criss-crossing pattern of ancestral lines can bring Norman blood even into a family paternally of Dutch descent.

An ancient family in Sussex is that of the Bartlelots of Stopham (five miles from my former house). It must almost certainly be Norman, and is a baronetcy family from which is derived the line of a well-known writer and former British M.P., Vernon Bartlet. The Bartletts of Saint Louis, Missouri claim, I think reasonably, to be another case of the gradual modernization of Bartlelot into Bartlett.

Of one American descent the account given, from information supplied by the family, in *Burke* needs to be retold in full for the precise implications to be realized. "Mr. Hallowell is a descendant of the Hon. John Alden, who sailed on the *Mayflower* and a grandson of Francis Ricketson Slocum, sixth in descent from Rev. Peleg Slocum, of Portsmouth Township, Rhode Island (born there 17 June 1754), by Mary, dau. of Christopher Holder, of Providence, R.I., who married 12 August 1660, Mary, daughter of Richard Scott, by Katherine, daughter of the Rev. Francis Marbury of Alford, Lincs. by Bridget his wife, daughter of John Dryden of Canons Ashby, Elizabeth, daughter of Sir John Cope, by Bridget, daughter of Sir Edward Raleigh, of Farnborough, descended through the families of Grene, Talbot, Strange, of Blackmere, le Despencer from Gilbert de Clare, 7th Earl of Hertford, and 3rd Earl of Gloucester, who descended in direct male line from Geoffrey, natural son of Richard I, Duke of Normandy(943–996), grandson of Rollo, first Duke of the Normans, and ancestor of William the Conqueror." Here in a paragraph is the connected pedigree over 1,000 years which links the Norman duke with the modern American citizen.

As with the Roosevelt Norman connection, so too with the Wurts family Norman alliance. The Hon. John S. Wurts, a member of the Philadelphia Bar, and of the Bar of the Supreme Court of the United States, sometime commissioner for Puerto Rico, had a great-grandfather George Wurts, M.D., who on 1 April 1800 married Abigail, the daughter of Amos Pettit, by Esther Stout his wife, the last-named being descended through her mother from Col. St. Leger Codd, 11th in descent from Edward III. The son of this marriage, William Wurts, maintained the tradition, for his wife was descended through the families of Nobel and Highley, and of John Drake of Devonshire, England, and Dorchester, Massachusetts (1630), 14th in descent from Edward I.

In the pedigree of Douglas Vaughan Croker, of Ruxton, Maryland, a banker, the Crokers are traced through the marriage in the 15th century of Sir John Croker of Lineham with Elizabeth, the daughter of William Yeo, of Heanton Satchville, Devon, and by means of this union they descend through the families of Granville of Stow (later Earls of Bath) and the Courtenays, Earls of Devon, from Lady Margaret de Bohun, Countess of Devon, granddaughter (through her mother, Princess Elizabeth, Countess of Hereford and Essex) of King Edward I, by his first queen, Eleanor of Castile.

The Dakins of Massachusetts have a double royal descent. Amos Dakin, of Mason, New Hampshire, founder of the Congregational Church there, married in 1772, Sarah Thankful, who through her mother Sarah, daughter of Capt. Jonas Prescott, was descended by Margaret de Neville, wife of Sir William Harrington, from King Malcolm II of Scotland and from Alfred the Great. In addition the Dakins have a Norman royal descent. Amos Dakin's grandson, Samuel Dana Dakin, an editor and lawyer in New York and patentee of floating sectional drydocks, married Mary Pierce, the daughter of Thomas Mumford, of Cayuga, New York. She was a descendant of Lord Henry Percy (the famous Hotspur) who married Elizabeth, daughter of Edmund Mortimer, Earl of March, by Philippa, the daughter and heiress of Lionel, Duke of Clarence, second son of Edward III. There is thus a double Norman descent not only from the king, but also from the Percies who were Dukes of Northumberland. The modern Percies descend twice through the female line from the original Percy stock. Their real name is Smithson, though this name and the arms belonging to it have disappeared from the Northumberland escutcheon. The Dakins of America have as much claim to be Percies as the present ducal family.

Sometimes the somewhat ludicrous position arises in which a British family by marriage with an American acquires a royal Norman descent. The family of Sir Stuart Auchincloss Coats, second baronet, can be traced for several centuries in Scotland. Members of the Coats family held important offices at Glasgow in the 16th century; but the fleurs de lis in the chief of the family's arms are derived from the royal descent of the present baronet's grandmother, Sarah Ann, daughter of John Auchincloss of New York and Elizabeth Buck, his wife. A certificate signed by the former Windsor Herald, the late A.T. Butler, in 1934, states that the pedigree showing the descent of Sir Stuart Auchincloss Coats, Baronet, through the families of Auchincloss, Buck (i.e., the American link), Saltonstall, Gurdon, Sidley, Knyvett and Bourclim from Edward III, King of England, has been duly recorded in the College of Arms.

That there is an abundance of pedigrees of royal and therefore Norman descent to be found in America is clear even from a few of the many examples which could be produced. It may be asked, what is the value of this descent which is shared by so many? At one time, the degree of relationship between Queen Elizabeth the Queen Mother and George Washington had been worked out! An interesting curiosity of genealogical research like many other surprising discoveries in relationship, but did it mean very much?

I think that the matter is of some importance. All the claims to Norman ancestry from the royal family are in the female line and pass through many families. By contrast a male line descent from a son of King Harold II—if such a genealogical miracle could be substantiated—would have far greater interest.

The real significance of the enormous number of royal descents lies in the fact that Norman blood has been absorbed into the make-up of the English people and owing to the diffusion of the English-speaking race throughout the world, the Norman strain has become universal. But it is a strain completely submerged and lost, like a small stream which runs into an ocean. To compile a pedigree showing descent from Edward III (and ergo the Conqueror) one has to subtract everything except the essential link, generation by generation. In those 30 generations from 1066, numerous family lines come in, each contributing only one generation to the tale. All the other lines are neglected. In this way it is possible to build up a Norman royal pedigree, just as one can prove the Prince of Wales to be of Welsh descent. When numerous strains of ancestry have been blended over a long period there will inevitably have to be a screening off of elements unneeded for the particular purpose.

The Normans as a race have disappeared from the English-speaking world with the slight exception of the Channel Islands, the only relic of the former duchy of Normandy. They have been absorbed into the people whom they conquered. Like the Chinese, the English have had the ability to tame and naturalize their fiercest foes in the guise of both Vikings and Normans. Those who most loudly proclaim their Norman background are the most typically English.

In writing of royal descents above I have been referring to legitimate ancestry. As soon as royalty is mentioned as being present in a pedigree, the uninitiated raise the suggestion of bastardy. As already stated, William the Conqueror was credited with originating the Peverell family. The sexual delinquencies of British monarchs have not as a rule escaped notice, but they have not contributed much to the tales of royal descent, except for the 12 illegitimate offspring of Charles II, who are still well represented in the ducal peerage. Few are aware that a much earlier sovereign easily surpassed Charles in the extent of his extra-marital activities.

This was Henry I who had two legitimate children, and 19 or 20 or even more bastards. Grave authorities— the *Complete Peerage* and the *English Historical Documents* (Vol. II)—give the details of Henry's large family. He had eight bastard sons but of these only two received substantial lordships; Rainald of Dunsterville who was made Earl of Cornwall and Robert, Earl of Gloucester. Neither of these left male heirs. The rest of the royal brood disappeared into the population. Thus it could easily be that many persons now living have both Norman and royal descent from Henry I without any possibility of proving it.

CHAPTER EIGHT

The Normans at Hastings

HAVING dealt with the Norman families which are known to have existed in Normandy—the list given is of course not inclusive, but extends as far as our present knowledge —and the multitudinous descents from William I, we can now pass to the Normans who actually accompanied the Conqueror in 1066. Next to the assertion that their families are Norman or came over with the Conqueror, those who claim Normanity very often say that their progenitor was at Hastings in 1066. If they do not say this they imply or take it for granted.

Very, very few can show a male line descent from an ancestor who was actually present at Hastings. The fingers of one hand suffice to count the male lines who had a forbear at the battle. Malet, Gifford or Giffard, Gresley and possibly one or two others.

I must again emphasize that failure to prove presence at the battle does not mean denial of Norman blood. I have been at some pains to describe the pre-Conquest state of England and the course of the actual Conquest because I have hoped that this narrative would help to make clear the difficulties in finding the names of Normans who can be known to have been present in the Conqueror's expedition.

Something has been said earlier about the numbers of William's army. The figure of 60,000 Normans is actually a matter of contemporary evidence. It comes from the narrative of William of Poitiers, *Gesta Willelmi ducis Normanorum et Regis Anglorum* (The Deeds of William, Duke of the Normans and King of the English). This was written in, or soon after 1071. The author was a Norman, born near Pontaudemer. He studied at Poitiers, hence his surname, returned to Normandy as a soldier, but later became a priest, was made chaplain to William I and archdeacon of Lisieux. He is an extremely prejudiced writer, seeing his patron as a model of Christian virtue. He cannot discern any good in any Englishman, and refers to them as barbarians. Still, whatever else he may be, he is at least a contemporary of the Conquest, may have taken part in it, and wrote within five years of Hastings. The passage in which the numbers of William's army are mentioned occurs at the point in his narrative in which William, after having landed at Pevensey, finds himself unopposed, Harold being then in Yorkshire dealing with the Viking menace. "A rich inhabitant of the country who was a Norman by race, being Robert, son of Wimarc, a noble lady," sent a message to William in which he advised him to remain on the defensive because of the innumerable host which Harold was leading against him. To this William replied that he intended to give battle to Harold as soon as possible. "With the aid of God I would not hesitate to oppose him with my own brave men, even if I had only 10,000 of these instead of the 60,000 I now command." (E. H. D. Vol. II, p. 223, where the editors add a footnote, "The numbers of troops given here and elsewhere in this narrative should be read with caution.")

However, this is the origin of the numbers of William's army which was accepted by all historians from Dr. Lingard* right down to the present century but has now been generally given up in favor of a paltry 8,000.

Incidentally Robert, son of Wimarc, a genuine Sussex pre-Conquest Norman, seems to have been strangely neglected by the earnest seekers after Norman paternity. According to Round, Wimarc was a Breton name. I do not remember a pedigree made out from Robert, and I am certainly not suggesting that one should be, but it is a remarkable fact that this Norman, one of the small band whom we know to have been settled in England in Edward the Confessor's reign, should have been left unclaimed.†

What the truth may be about the numbers of William's host will never be known. There is great disparity between 60,000 and 8,000. The former number is obviously an exaggeration but it is interesting to see it quoted in a contemporary document, for it is to evidence of this nature rather than to real tradition that modern historical criticism appeals. It should also be observed that William of Poitiers attributed vast numbers to Harold, though this could have been done in order to magnify the skill and bravery of Willaim.

The size of the Norman host bears no relation to the numbers of Normans whose names are known to us as having been present at the battle. The highest estimate which can be gathered from the writings of those who can be regarded as authorities does not supply more than

---

* Note 38. Dr. Lingard.
† Note 39. Normans in England before the Conquest.

40 names. For convenience in reference I have numbered the names as follows:*

1. Robert de Beaumont, created Earl of Leicester by Henry I.
2. Eustace of Boulogne, who marred Godgifu, sister of the Confessor.
3. William of Evreux, great-grandson of Richard I of Normandy.
4. Geoffrey of Mortain, whose direct descendant, Philip, Count of Perche, was slain at battle of Lincoln, 1217, succ. by his uncle, William, Bishop of Chalons-sur-Marne, last of the line.
5. William FitzOsbern, 1st Earl of Hereford. His 2nd son, Roger, 2nd Earl of Hereford, lost his earldom for treason in 1075, but one of his two sons was ancestor of the baronial family of Ballon, which petered out about beginning of 14th century.
6. Aimery, IV Vicomte of Thouars, lived into reign of Rufus but this Poitevin family is of no interest to Anglo-Norman genealogy.
7. Hugh de Montfort (Hugh the Constable). Male line was extinct under Henry I; later Montforts descend from Hugh II's daughter, Alice.
8. Walter Giffard, from whose collateral descendants came the present Giffard family.
9. Ralf de Tosni, Lord of Conches. The heiress of the English line married Guy de Beauchamp, Earl of Warwick. From a cadet, Robert de Stafford, a great landowner in 1086, descended

---

* Note 40. Normans known to have been at Hastings; analysis of sources of information.

the barons of Stafford, who ended in the next century with an heiress Millicent, ancestress of the historic house of Stafford, Earls of Stafford and Dukes of Buckingham. It is from a member of this family that the descent of the Gresley baronets is often reckoned; the holder of their property at Drakelowe in 1086 being one Nigel, who is often reputed to have been brother of the Robert de Stafford mentioned above. It is noteworthy that both Round in *The Ancestor* (Vol. I, pp. 195–202) and Barron (Vol. X, pages 133–37), though such determined critics of the Norman ancestry claims of families, were yet very kind to this affiliation.

10. Hugh de Grandmesnil, whose eldest son Robert succeeded to the Norman honor of Grandmesnil which his granddaughter and heiress eventually carried to Robert, 3rd Earl of Leicester.

11. William de Warenne. His grandson, William 3rd Earl, left an heiress from whom descended the later family of Warenne, Earls of Surrey.

12. William Malet. Robert, his son, Master Chamberlain under Henry I, was deprived of his estate and banished in or before 1106. From him descended the family of the Malet baronets and the Mallets formerly of Ash, in *Burke's Landed Gentry*.

13. Turstin FitzRou, who seems to have left no issue.

14. Engenulf de Laigle. Killed at Hastings. His son was Gilbert de Aquila.

15. Odo, the famous Bishop of Bayeux, who had a bastard son from whom descended the great Norman house of Le Hommet, hereditary constables of Normandy.

16. Wadard.
17. Vitalis.
18. Geoffrey, Bishop of Coutances.
19. Taillefer.
20. *Pontivi nobilis haeres.*
21. Gulbert d'Auffay, a kinsman of the Conqueror.
22. Robert de Voitot.
23. Roger, son of Turold. Died in Hastings campaign.
24. Gerelmus of Panilleuse. Died in Hastings campaign.
25. Erchembald, son of Erchembald the Vicomte.
26. Robert FitzErneis, died at Hastings.
27. Gerard the Seneschal.
28. Ralf, or Rudolf Tancarville, the Chamberlain.
29. Hugh the Butler, i.e., Hugh d'Ivry.
30. Pons.
31. Richard FitzGilbert, i.e., Richard of Tonbridge and of Clare.
32. Humphrey of Tilleul.
33–34. Brian of Brittany and his brother Alan the Red.
35. Richard the Vicomte.
36. Ranulf.
37. Rolf Tesson.
38. Fulk of Aunon.*

The brevity of this ought to be explained. One of the greatest living writers about the Norman Conquest explains the position very clearly in a footnote to his *William the Conqueror* (David C. Douglas, 1964, p. 203): "Individuals who can, by express evidence, be shown to

---

* Note 41. Controversy regarding presence at Hastings of Adelolf de la Marck (Merc).

have been present in William's force at Hastings are not numerous." G. H. White [*op. cit.*—the reference is to *Complete Peerage,* of which Mr. White was editor—L.G. P.], also in *Genealogists' Magazine* (Vol. 4, 1932, pp. 51–53), lists 15 names. An independent investigation has led me to believe that it is reasonable to extend this list to 33 or 34 names ("Companions of the Conqueror," in *History,* Vol. 28, 1943, pp. 130–47). For a further comment see J. Mason, in *English Historical Review,* Vol. 71, 1956, p. 61. Such measure of difference as there is between Mr. White and myself on this matter may be contrasted with our emphatic agreement in repudiating the hundreds of names which have so often been cited. Could the excellent custodians of the castle of Falaise today be persuaded to revise their memorial tablets? To assert that a man "came over with the Conqueror" is hazardous. The army which sailed from Normandy to England in 1066 was of considerable size. The ascertainable "Companions of the Conqueror" are few.

The list given above contains a few names in addition to those originally set out by Prof. Douglas. One is from J. Mason.

The above details the main facts clearly but several points arise from it which need to be explained more fully for the purpose of our study. It is of the utmost importance to know the primary sources of authority concerning the Norman invasion and the battle of Hastings. Names of Normans which are found in these sources are obviously those on which we can rely. The principal authorities are the narrative of William of Poitiers, mentioned above, the Bayeux Tapestry, the history of Ordericus Vitalis, the narrative of William of Jumièges, and (with lesser authority now) the *Carmen de Hastingno Proelio,* formerly ascribed to Guy, Bishop of

Amiens, before 1068, but now thought to be later. There is the evidence also of charters. A full analysis of these sources is given in Note 40. The elaborate work of Vitalis, the *Ecclesiastical History,* gives an account of the life and death of William I. This man was born in England about 1075 and was the son of one of the Norman counsellors of the first Earl of Shrewsbury, Robert de Montgomery. He went to live in Normandy as a monk and wrote his work between 1123 and 1141.

It will be noticed that no previous mention has been made of Master Wace, the author of the *Roman de Rou,* which is a metrical history of the Duke of Normandy. Wace was born in Jersey at the beginning of Henry I's reign, went to Caen in Normandy when young and was made a prebend of Bayeux by Henry II. He died in England after 1174, having written his history some time before 1171. "He cannot have come to his account of the battle at the very earliest till 1171, 105 years after the event. For my part, I think that it was probably written even some years later. But imagine in any case an Englishman, ignorant of Belgium, writing an account of Waterloo, mainly from oral tradition, in 1920." (J. H. Round, *Feudal England,* 1909, p. 407), and he adds: "I venture to take my own case. Born within 40 years of Waterloo, I can say with Wace that I remember my father telling me, as a boy, stories of the battle. But he was born after it. The information was secondhand." Professor Douglas also demolishes the value of Wace as to testimony for Normans present at Hastings.

If then careful modern study has determined the value of the authorities on the Norman invasion, and if those authoritative sources no longer include Wace, then those who have built upon him and deduced Norman presences from his narrative are very likely to be at fault. The

uncertain, unreliable guide leading the would-be credulous
to a false conclusion explains why so many erroneous
Norman ascriptions are found even now in many pedigrees. "A reliable list of the principal personages who
actually accompanied William, duke of Normandy, to
England in 1066, and were present in the great battle
commonly called of Hastings, does not exist."(J. R. Planché, Somerset Herald, *The Conqueror and his Companions*,
1874, p. xiii) No roll call after Hastings has been preserved; the wildest ideas about such a document still
prevail, as in the case of the lady who said that her husband's family descended from the archer who shot Harold
in his eye. That archer whose arrow changed the course
of England's history remains for ever unknown, in the
company of that "certain man" who in the Book of Kings
"drew a bow at a venture" and mortally wounded King
Ahab. Immortal agents, altering the shape of history, yet
themselves for ever anonymous. Still such assertion is no
worse than the more sober seeming claims to an ancestor's
presence at Hastings. When Conan Doyle was writing his
romance, *Sir Nigel,* he made his hero, Sir Nigel Loring,
refer to the first Loring who had borne the Conqueror's
shield at Hastings. Modern philology shows that this
surname means "the man from Lorraine," so that at
least Loring is a continental-derived name. The romance
of the shield bearer is no worse than the ridiculous yarn of
the FitzWilliams,* about a scarf from the Conqueror's
arms which they had preserved. In their case, as their
family was of English origin, they had to presuppose an
ancestor who went from England to Normandy on an
embassy, became enchanted with William, and returned
to fight on his side, for which traitorous exploit he was

---

* Note 42. The FitzWilliams.

rewarded with the scarf and other more substantial gifts.

The reference to Planché above came from a work produced in the heyday of Victorian genealogy, when the giants of criticism were beginning their work, but when the gorgeous fables of the peerage writers still held full sway. Planché's work was very sober when compared to that of writers like his friend, Sir Bernard Burke, and the passage which I have quoted would lead one to suppose that Planché would apply a critique as severe as that of Round to Norman pedigrees. Indeed, compared with the prevailing 19th-century idea that the bulk of the English nobility were Norman descended, Planché was very restrained and sober. He made the mistake, however, of taking Wace's account of the invasion as the foundation of his work, "supplementing and illustrating it by the information directly or indirectly afforded me by writers who were actually living at the time of the Conquest." That is, an author who wrote a century after the event was to be supplemented from the works of those who were contemporaries of the Conquest.

In the result Planché lists 119 men in his catalogue of *The Conqueror and his Companions,* nearly four times as many as the best modern authorities but a great improvement upon the hundreds of names mentioned by Dr. Douglas as being given in many cases, especially in France. These hundreds of names are usually found in one of the lists of Companions beginning with the celebrated Battle Abbey Roll. Of this Planché remarked: "The Roll . . . formerly suspended in the building, consisted of no less than 645 names. Duchesne's list, derived from a charter formerly in the Abbey, contains 405 names. One of the lists printed in Leland's *Collectanea* gives 498 . . .; the rhyming catalogue, printed in *Brompton's Chronicle,* includes 245. Monsieur de Magny's catalogue contains 425, and that complied by Monsieur Leopold de Lisle, in the church at Dive, 485." (*op. cit.* pp. xiv–xv) As the name of the Dive Roll is mentioned, it is necessary to add Planché's later remarks on this and other lists compiled, not in England, but in France.

"The recently published lists of Messrs. de Magny and Delisle, while supplying some hundreds of names, are unfortunately unaccompanied by the evidence on which they have been recorded, and consequently cannot be confidently quoted either in corroboration or in contradiction of the older catalogues, varying as they do from them in many important instances and occasionally from each other." (Vol. II, p. 277)

Many books have been written on the Battle Abbey Roll, and far more have taken it for granted as an authentic record. The best work is that in three volumes by the Duchess of Cleveland in 1889. It was to her husband, the 4th and last Duke of Cleveland of the family of Vane (the title became extinct with his death in 1891) that Planché dedicated his *Companions of the Conqueror*. The full title of the Duchess's book is: *The Battle Abbey Roll With Some Account of the Norman Lineages*. In the preface she describes how her interest in the subject was quickened by having been resident at Battle Abbey, and how she went through many volumes in search of facts about the Normans. Unfortunately she accepted the anonymous work, *The Norman People*, as a guide, though at the same time using Planché's book. Her own good sense exposed for her such stupidities as the bearing of a name like that of Clement Cox by a nobleman before 1066, but she did take the roll as record of fact.

What is the truth about this roll? In the late 19th century an otherwise excellent account of Chaucer's life and works could refer to his surname as being on the roll of

Battle Abbey. The Duchess gives the explanation at the opening of her introduction (p. v): "The famous roll of Battle Abbey is believed to have been compiled in obedience to a clause in the Conqueror's foundation charter, that enjoined the monks to pray for the souls of those 'who by their labour and valour had helped to win the kingdom'. The great Sussex Abbey ... had been intended to be not only a memorial of his victory, but a chantry for the slain; and the names of his companions-in-arms, enshrined on this bede-roll, might thus be read out in the church on special occasions, and notably on the anniversary feast of St. Celict. It was most likely originally copied from the muster roll of the Norman knights, that had been prepared by the duke's orders before his embarkation, and was called over in his presence on the field of battle, the morning after it had been fought. The list, thus composed, was inscribed on a roll of parchment, and hung up in the Abbey Minster, with this superscription:

> *Dicitur a bello, 'BELLUM' locus hic quia bello*
> *Angligenae victi sunt in morte relicti*
> *Martyris in Christi festo cecidere Calixti*
> *Sexagenus erat sextus millesimus annus*
> *Cum pereunt Angli, stella monstrante cometa.*

"It is called Battle from the battle, the place where the English were left dead; they fell on the feast of the martyr Saint Calixtus. It was the year 1066 when the English fell, with the comet showing itself."

The Duchess goes on to state that only copies of the roll now remain, giving names of three, viz., that "published by Leland in his *Collectanea;* another in Holinshed's *Chronicle,* 1577; and a third printed a few years later by Stowe, who received it from Camden. There are at least ten—if not more—other lists of the Norman conquerors; but none of them even pretend to have any connection with the bede-roll of Battle Abbey." (*op. cit* p. vii) The Duchess then gives the Holinshed and Duchesne lists in parallel columns; Leland's Roll, alphabetically arranged; the Dives Roll; and a list of 49 names, "added to this list by M. de Magny in the *Nobiliaire de Normandie.*" The three volumes then consist of the names as given in the three principal lists, with an account of the family in question. Round remarked that there was much sound genealogy in the Duchess's book. Generally it can be followed as a fair exposition of the histories in each case. Thus Courtenay is viewed, rightly, as being very doubtfully included in the Roll. The Courtenays were an ancient French family, older than the Conquest, but not Norman, and not coming to England until the time of Henry II.

It would seem that the Duchess understood the facts about the Roll. In the passage which I have quoted from her book, the original Roll, if the account of its beginnings is accepted, was a cross between a muster Roll and a list of deceased for whom prayers and masses were to be said. William did found the Abbey at Battle— the place, some seven miles from Hastings, had no name until after the battle, and was not called Senlac. He filled it with monks from Marmoutier but it was not one of the greatest foundations in England, as perhaps might have been expected. Of the Roll, the Duchess stated: "As time went on, it became more and more an object of ambition to own an ancestor that had come over with the Conqueror; and the monks were always found willing to oblige a liberal patron by inserting his name." (p.vi)

If it were originally a list of the fallen it would in general be useless to those seeking Norman forbears. If it were a roll call it is hard to imagine any ecclesiastical foundation with a list running into thousands. In fact, as none of the copies runs to 700 names, such a roll call could only have been of the the knights.

The Roll is best summed up in the words of the Rev. Baring-Gould in the chapter which he gave to the subject in his book, *Family Names and Their Story*: "We cannot doubt that there was such a roll at Battle but at first it was a roll containing only the names of the dead, whose obits had to be observed and who had to be prayed for by name. But in process of time other names were added, successively, as paid for." Of the Duchess of Cleveland's book, he remarks: "The Duchess takes Holinshed's list as a basis for work, one of the most adulterated of all copies, and she lays some stress on the almost worthless Dives Roll as she calls it—a list drawn up by M. Leopold Delisle for the purpose of glorifying the French Norman gentry, and of no authority whatever."

Over 450 years passed between the founding of the abbey and its dissolution in the reign of Henry VIII. As usually happened with the monastic houses, the abbey was given to one of the king's favorites, Sir Anthony Browne, Henry's Master of the Horse, who was granted the abbey house and site in 1538. Sometimes the new lay owner of an abbey adapted it to his own use, but more frequently he used the stone from the old monastery to build himself a desirable modern residence. This was Sir Anthony Browne's procedure. Today the abbey lies in ruin, but with a fine house inside it. Sir Anthony's son, Viscount Montague, completed his father's building projects, but in 1717 the sixth viscount sold Battle to Sir Godfrey Webster in whose family it continues. The Duke of Cleveland was described in Planché's dedication of his book as the proprietor of the abbey, but he must have been a tenant.

The contents of the monastic houses were generally dispersed or destroyed and most of their manuscripts shared this fate. The monastic chartularies were preserved by the new owners, as they were useful in showing the landed rights possessed by the abbey, and which passed to the incoming proprietor. The Roll might have had some interest because it had little connection with religion, and certainly ministered to snobbery and family pride.*

Such then is the true description of this Roll, reference to which has figured in so many pedigrees. No one who has serious knowledge of the Norman period would think of quoting from as it an authoritative source. We have no knowledge of the original, the copies are discrepant, and even if we possessed a roll which could be proved genuinely to have come from the abbey, we should have no certainty that any name found upon it was that of a true Companion of the Conqueror.

Reference occurred above in Dr. Douglas's note to the Falaise memorial tablets—the Falaise Roll, so-called because in that place the Conqueror was born. A book was issued under the title *The Falaise Roll* recording Prominent Companions of William, Duke of Normandy, at the Conquest of England, by M. Jackson Crispin (of New York) and Léonce Macary, Professor of the College of Falaise, OI., printed in Great Britain in 1938. Some 315 names are given on a bronze tablet erected in the chapel of the chateau of William the Conqueror at Falaise, Normandy, 21 June 1931. A great deal of work went into the compilation of this list but it appears that it is based upon the *Roman de Rou* and the Battle Abbey Roll. This, in view of our conclusions above as to sources,

---

* Note 43. Charters of Battle Abbey.

puts the Falaise Roll at a low premium, being drawn up from materials at once late and unreliable. A sound genealogical scholar, T. R. Thompson, gives modern emphasis to Round's destructive criticisms of Wace: "Modern scholarship has found him to be grossly inaccurate and quite unreliable. Andresen in his standard edition proved that Wace did not begin Part III [of the *Roman* which deals with the invasion—L. G. P.] before 1170 and puts the earliest possible date for his birth at 1110. Upon Wace only are based many of the modern works so carefully considered by the committee." (*The Genealogists' Magazine*, December 1931, in an article, The Falaise Celebrations)

In the matter of celebrations, 1931 was neither the end nor the beginning. The Dives Roll was produced in 1866 for the eighth centenary of the Conquest celebrated in France. In 1931 I think that a steamer load of British Norman-born notables went to Normandy. In 1951 there was a fête for the rebuilding of Caen, severely damaged in World War II. At Caen, William and his wife were buried separately in two monastic establishments which they had founded, although only a thigh bone of the Conqueror remains in the grave which was ransacked at the French Revolution. A Festival of Caen was organized to take place in April 1951. Then the Mayor of Caen had the idea of inviting to the festival the British descendants of William's knights. Owing to the attraction of the idea for the press, a vast publicity arose, and large quantities of letters arrived at La Mairie of Caen asking for invitations to the festival because the writers were descendants of the Normans of 1066. A special clerical organization had to be set up in La Mairie to cope with the letters. The secretary of the committee sent to me lists of names of persons who were trying to get themselves invited to Caen. I dealt with 300 cases, and of the 300 few reached Caen on my recommendation. The French authorities for their part made a determined effort to prevent a recurrence of the Falaise farce.

Few invitations to descendants were sent out without good reason, although there were the usual gate crashers. At Caen one man whose Norman ancestry was diluted through some tortuous channels greeted me as the person who had failed to keep him from attending.

Of the less than 200 men and women from the British Isles who went to Caen invited by the municipality or by themselves, less than half a dozen could claim a direct line descent from a companion of William. The rest had either a devious female line Norman ancestry or a Norman name. In many cases even those who possessed the name were not able to affiliate themselves to the original Norman family from whom they claimed descent.

Many people may feel that the Battle Abbey and other rolls are quite inadequate to supply proof. They take refuge in references to the *Domesday Book*. Their ancestors were mentioned there. As *Domesday* is an enormously complex work, over which the most learned medievalists are often in dispute, it is hard to see how so many who are not specialists can know that a forbear of 30 generations back is in the record. Besides this consideration, there is the thought that *Domesday* was compiled 20 years after Hastings. Many who took part in the invasion were dead by 1086. Some, like the Normans who persuaded Waltheof into rebellion in 1075, were out of their estates in 1086. Then, too, the *Domesday* tenant is separated by a generation or more from the continuous record of land-holding in the Pipe Rolls. These begin in the later part of Henry I's reign but are not continuous until the time of Henry II, under whom there was in 1166 a fresh survey of the feudal tenures. *Domesday* is not primarily a genealogical record; only incidentally does it yield information about families. Its main purpose is to determine the value of the land and who dwelt in it. Putting aside the motives of William in making the survey, it is a wonderful landmark in English records. No other country has anything comparable to it. It was the last act of a conqueror, in rounding off his work, and it set the seal upon it.

The efficiency with which the *Domesday* survey was carried out is astonishing. It was ordered to be made in 1085. Within a year or slightly longer the commissioners appointed for the purpose had presented their reports. The information required was obtained by empanelling local men who had to answer a series of questions about their area. The returns when compiled were gathered into centers, whence they were taken to Winchester, still the old capital. The survey is contained in two volumes. Vol. I is of nearly 400 folios (800 pages) in double column on parchment, 15 × 11 inches. It records all England, county by county, apart from Essex, Suffolk and Norfolk. The survey did not include the counties of Northumberland, Durham, Westmorland and Cumberland, though portions of some of these are included in Yorkshire. The part of Lancashire, between Ribble and Mersey, is recorded at the end of Cheshire. Vol. I begins with Kent and ends with Yorkshire and Lincolnshire. Vol. II is of 450 folios 11 × 8 inches in single column and in varying scripts. It covers Essex, Suffolk and Norfolk and gives the full returns for these counties, not summarized as in Vol. I. The name given to Vol. II is *Little Domesday.*

Also we possess the *Exton* or *Exeter Domesday* which gives in 500 folios a record (but with gaps) for Wiltshire, Somerset, Dorset, Devon and Cornwall. It is thus similar to the *Little Domesday*. There is in addition the *Inquisitio Comitatus Cantabrigiensis,* listing the landowners of the county of Cambridge; and the *Inquisitio Eliensis,* a survey of the lands of the abbey of Ely. As a land and fiscal survey, the *Domesday* is unique in Europe of the 11th century. It was in effect what would be called in English income tax law a provision for Schedule A, since it provided the Crown with information as to the value of each piece of land T. R. E., i.e., *temporis regis Edwardi,* "in the day when King Edward (the Confessor) was alive and dead." Then follows the name of the owner in 1066, and of the owner in 1086 with the value at that date. Those who believe that the Norman Conquest was a necessity, or even that it was a good thing, may care to reflect that the value of the land in 1086 was often below what it had been 20 years earlier.

As to the change of land ownership by 1086, only about 8 per cent of the landholders bore names which were not continental. Many of the pre-Conquest tenants had been killed or gone into exile. There were English settlements in Ireland, Scotland, Scandinavia and the Greek Empire. Many other free landowners had been pushed down in the social scale by the imposition of what was known as a mesne tenant, one who came between the tenant-in-chief and the former English tenants. Prof. V. H. Galbraith, in *The Making of Domesday* (1961, p. 155), says that in reference to the actual farmer and tenant of Badlesmere in Kent, the manor has passed to Bishop Odo who had inserted a mesne tenant, Anfrid, over the head of the English freeholder. "If this is indeed what happened, and if such a practice was common, it suggests that we can easily exaggerate the severity of the tenurial upheaval caused by the Conquest. Behind Norman subtenants, in short, there may have been a great many unrecorded Saxons who continued actually to farm the land." But such farmers were likely to become villeins, no longer free men, and unable to leave their manor without their lord's permission.

The terms, owner and tenant, have been used above indiscriminately. In fact, even to this day English law knows no absolute ownership. The freehold owner in England is said to possess an estate in fee simple. *Domesday* reflected throughout a new theory of land law. On this the great legal historian, F. W. Maitland, remarks: "Now this theory that land in the last resort is held of the king becomes the theory of our law at the Norman Conquest. It is assumed in *Domesday Book*....On the other hand we can say with certainty that before the Conquest this was not the theory of English law. The process of confiscation gave the Conqueror abundant opportunity for making the theory true in fact." (*Constitutional History of England,* p. 155)*

In passing, some comment may be made on the speed and efficiency with which the *Domesday* survey was carried out. In 1969 in England it was announced that the *Domesday* record, with the various smaller surveys mentioned above, would be reprinted after a lapse of many years from the previous printing. The work is likely to take several years, perhaps a decade, a curious commentary on the slowness which afflicts modern printing and publishing, equipped though it be with all the aids without which William's staff had to survey a whole country. In July 1969 the Americans landed men on the moon and brought them safely back to earth. It is quite possible that they will have made a manned flight to, if

---

* See, however, Note 44, on ownership of English land, for criticism of this view.

not a landing on, Mars before the full printing of the *Domesday* records has been accomplished.

The explanation of William's ability to have England surveyed and catalogued in 12 months is that he inherited a competent civil administration. "After 20 years of Norman rule it seems likely that the old English administration had been rapidly developed but not transformed. In England, as elsewhere, the Normans appear as an open-minded, highly adaptable people, ready as we say, 'to try anything once' and to make it work. Coming from a small impoverished duchy which had suffered as much as England from bad government and internal strife, they took over a more highly developed system of government than anything they had known at home. In Normandy before the Conquest there is no clear evidence of the keeping of any central written records, and the duke did not even possess a seal. In England there had been some sort of Chancery department for nearly a century before the Conquest, which had used sealed writs, written in the vernacular, to convey the king's orders to the shire courts. There was also a well-established financial organization permanently located at Winchester." (V. H. Galbraith, *The Making of Domesday*, 1961, p. 45) Also on pages 55–58 of the same work there is an instructive note by Miss D. Clementi on the Norman Sicilian Surveys. In Sicily, as in England, the Normans conquered and inherited a country's administrative services. "The conclusion very reasonably drawn from the fact that the bulk of the survey was recorded in Arabic has been that it must have existed before the arrival of the Normans, who therefore merely adapted it." In England, the Old English government must have been used to making surveys or the *Domesday* could not have been made so quickly and efficiently. The name *Domesday* was given to the survey by the people because, like the Day of Doom, or Last Judgment, there was no appeal from it. *Domesday* is the basis of English land law.

The great change made by the Normans in English administration was the substitution of Latin for English in official documents, and the replacing of English by French as the language of the upper classes and also of Parliament as it developed out of the Great Council. Not for 300 years did English regain its position as the language of all in the realm. The use of Latin, for the writs and charters, was due to the influx of so many priests and monks from abroad who had of course as much sympathy with old English literature as Hilaire Belloc who in his studies of pre-Conquest England leaves his readers in total ignorance of the existence of *Beowulf, The Dream of the Rood,* and *The Battle of Maldon.* The Norman Conquest remains as Charles Kingsley described it, a great crime, aided and abetted by the Roman Church.* A later Protestant writer, Dean Inge, said of the Conquest that it was an almost unmitigated disaster.† We are often told that in the 11th century it was necessary for England to be drawn into either the Scandinavian or the western European sphere, and that the Conquest decided in favor of the latter. This statement is a good example of what can only be described as woolly thinking. England in 1066 was as much part of western Latin Christendom as France. The religious revival so-called of the post-Conquest period would have come about in any case as it has always done in the different parts of the Church by the working of the Holy Ghost. In any event we have only the testimony of the Normans that the English Church

* Note 45. Charles Kingsley.
† Note 46. Dean Inge.

was not in a good condition. As far as marriage of the clergy was concerned, it was not much different from other parts of the Latin Church before the time of the reformer Hildebrand, later to be Pope Gregory VII. The ensuing corruption which came after the imposition of the impossible rule of celibacy is surely less preferable than straightforward marriage of priests. Much is made of the fact that Stigand of Canterbury was a pluralist, for which he was deprived of the see four years after Hastings. Pluralism was soon to be a matter exercising the minds of Norman descended kings and nobles in England, and continual agitation developed in Parliament against the practice and that of presentation by the Pope of absentee foreigners to English benefices.

From the above, the reader will gather that I am not a great admirer of the Normans and am inclined to be a trifle amused at the desire for Norman blood.

In the quest for genuine companions of the Conqueror, it is instructive to look at the work of William of Poitiers. He wrote: "There were present in this battle [*scilicet* Hastings—L.G.P.]: Eustace, Count of Boulogne; William, son of Richard, Count of Evreux; Geoffrey, son of Rotrou, Count of Mortain; William FitzOsbern; Haimo, Vicomte of Thouars; Walter Giffard; Hugh of Montfort-sur-Risle; Rodulf of Tosny; Hugh of Grantmesnil; William of Warenne; and many other most renowned warriors whose names are worthy to be commemorated in histories among the bravest soldiers of all time." (E.H.D. Vol. II. pp. 227–28) Oh what a wealth of ancestry lies hidden in that last half sentence! How could anyone be so cruel as to leave in ignorance the scions yet unborn of these unknown warriors! Yet so it has been; the failure of William of Poitiers, that soldier turned priest, has deprived many an aspirant after Normanity of his or her due. As if to rub it in even more strongly the editors of the volume add the following comment: "The list which follows is, with the Bayeux Tapestry, the most important piece of testimony providing express evidence as to those individuals who were indubitably 'companions of the Conqueror.' Concerning it and the men mentioned therein, see D. C. Douglas in *History,* vol. xxviii, p. 129. Such express evidence, vouching for the presence of particular persons at Hastings, can be found in the case of less than 35 persons." In the Bayeux Tapestry in Plates XLVIII and XLIX we have (in England at the Norman invasion) one Wadard, later a tenant of Odo in Oxfordshire. In Plate LI, Bishop Odo, and Robert, Count of Mortain. Plates LVII-IX show Vital (Vitalis), later one of Odo's tenants in Kent. Odo appears again, and in Plate LXXIII is Eustace of Boulogne, distinguished by a pennon bearing some form of incipient heraldry.

Taking the full list can we trace any male line descendants at the present day? Giffard, Gresley and Malet are admitted; the addition of De Maris excites the fiercest controversy; the last-named family is of ancient record, and the argument rages over the statement that it had a first recorded ancestor at Hastings, a statement found in some heraldic sources. The matter is handled at length in some of the notes.*

Dealing for the moment with Giffard we have a very distinguished family. A former American ambassador to the Court of St. James stated on reaching England that he was a member of a notable Norman family. There are two main lines of Giffard in *Burke's Landed Gentry,* Giffard

---

* Note 47. Marris controversy.

of Chillington and Giffard of Rushall. These lines separated very early. Osbern de Bolebec, Sire de Longueville, living in the time of Richard the Fearless, Duke of Normandy (died 960), married Aveline, sister to Gunnora the second wife of the Duke Richard, and by her had three sons, Walter, Berenger and Osbern. Of these Walter Giffard was at Hastings and was one of the most favored of the Companions. He received 107 lordships and manors, 48 of which were in Buckinghamshire. This wealthy and powerful line were Earls of Buckingham until 1164 when the second Earl died issueless and his lands were shared among his relatives. The third son, Osbern, was the ancestor of the Giffards of Rushall, their earlier properties being at Brimsfield in Gloucestershire.

The second son, Berenger, was the ancestor of the Giffards who in 1966, when the English celebrated their greatest defeat, were represented by Thomas Arthur Giffard, the 27th squire of Chillington Hall, near Wolverhampton in Staffordshire. The two existing branches in England bear different coats of arms, a feature not by any means unknown in heraldry but which can be very misleading.

Mallet has to be distinguished from Malet. The latter is certainly Norman and derives its name from Carteret in Normandy; the full name and title is Malet de Carteret of St. Ouen's. St. Ouen is in the island of Jersey in the Channel Islands. One of the ancestors, Onfrey or Humphrey de Carteret, is described by Wace as having been present at Hastings. In this particular instance there may not be much cause for skepticism as this is incontestably a Norman family which did not settle in England but held its ancestral fief in the Channel Islands.

Of the Mallets in England we have two main lines. There are the Malet baronets and the untitled landed gentry family of Mallet, formerly of Ash and now of Curry Mallet in Somerset.

The baronetcy family starts its connected lineage with the William Malet who has been mentioned as present in England before the Conquest. He was also present at Hastings and held lands in both Normandy and England in Lincolnshire and at Eye in Suffolk. He died in 1071, having had children by his wife Hesilia Crispin who was alive at the time of the *Domesday* in 1086. The elder son was banished in 1105 in the troubles of the early part of Henry I's reign. The line continued through the younger son Gilbert to the present day. The family were seated at Curry Mallet and this juxtaposition of two place names is common in west country England after the Norman Conquest, with a few cases in other parts of the country.

In the course of the Middle Ages, the Malets settled at Enmore and at Ash. Many knighthoods were gained before 1500 and a baronetcy in 1791. The arms of the family are azure three escallops or, with the crest, out of a ducal coronet or an heraldic tiger's head ermine. There are however some more ancient arms, namely gules three buckles or. The Malets are entitled to use both these coats: the older coat is used by branches of the family in France and the Channel Islands.

According to the *Carmen de bello* formerly attributed to Guy of Amiens the original Malet in England had connections with the English nobility as well as being of Norman blood himself. In the words of this poem, he was *partim Normannus et Anglus*. Perhaps that was why he was entrusted by William with the task, it is said, of burying Harold's body on the seashore. Among the Mallets of Ash was Sir Claude Coventry Mallet, C.M.G. He served in the British consulate at Panama 1879–84, was present as British representative when Count de Lesseps inaugurated the work on the Panama Canal, and accompanied the first party which surveyed it. He was ambassador to several of the Central and South American republics and in 1892 he married Doña Matilde de Obarrio. She was the daughter of Don Gabriel Benjamin de Obarrio, and granddaughter of Don Pedro de Obarrio Guerrero Ponce de Leon, governor of Panama, 1824–30, a descendant of the ancient and noble Castilian family of Obarrio, which is said to have been settled at Guipzca as early as the 9th century. Their daughter was Matilde Dita Mallet du Cros. She married Philip du Cros, who succeeded to the baronetcy of du Cros. She later, after divorce, resumed her maiden name of Mallet and, according to a report in the *Sunday Telegraph* magazine (7 January 1966), she had given up the old Mallet manor house at Curry Mallet, which was to become a home for elderly people.

The Gresley baronets possess one of the most ancient baronetcies. The order of baronets was founded in 1611 and Sir George Gresley of Drakelowe was created the first baronet on 29 June of that year. The account in *Burke's Peerage* runs: "At the time of the Conquest, Nigel, son of Roger de Toeny, with his brothers, Robert, afterwards Lord Stafford and Ralph, the ancestor of the Cliffords, accompanied their kinsman, Duke William, to England, and was rewarded for his services by grants of numerous lordships in the counties of Derby, Leicester and Stafford. His son, William, fixed his residence at Castle Gresley, Co. Derby, and founded there the priory of SS. Mary and George. About three centuries afterwards they removed to Drakelowe, in the lordship of Gresley, which continued for centuries to be the family seat, having been in possession of the Gresleys from the time of the Conquest."

To which may be added the critical opinion of no less than Oswald Barron, who wrote of the Gresleys in Vol. 10 of *The Ancestor*** (pp. 133–37, 1904). After having said that the first baronet was preceded at Drakelowe and Gresley by 12 knights of his name and house, "for each of whom good proof is forthcoming"; that the Sir Geoffrey Gresley of the Barons' War (1264–66) was followed by five ancestors at Drakelowe, a manor in *Domesday* held by a great tenant, Niel of Stafford (Nigellus de Stafford), Barron goes on: "To the genealogist nothing can be more fascinating than the examination of those records which step by step carry the line of Sir Robert Gresley of Drakelowe, who was one of those representing his order at the crowning of King Edward VII, to Neel, who held Drakelowe under the Conqueror. With such a pedigree content might come, but the ingenious pleadings, which would derive Neel of Stafford from Roger de Toeni who bore the banner of the Dukes of Normandy before the Conquest, have not yet ended. The reasonings for this proud beginning to the genealogy of Gresley are not fully accepted by antiquaries, but disproof has not yet pushed them aside. When the last word has been said, it may be that the Gresley pedigree will dispute for place with the oldest line in England." (*op. cit.* p. 137)

The 12th baronet Sir Nigel Gresley is, I think, resident in Canada, but his brother lives in England.

What then of the many hundreds of Norman names which are found in England? As already explained, the possession of a Norman name does not necessarily mean Norman ancestry, but those surnames which are found in the annals of the peerage, baronetcies or landed gentry, in what were called quite rightly the county families, can

---

* Note 48. *The Ancestor.*

at least claim to have some amount of pedigree already worked out, or their histories would not be in the volumes mentioned. It is claimed for Viscount Morley, the politician and biographer of Gladstone, that he was the first nobleman to be shown in peerage volumes with a blank shield, because he had been ennobled, but had taken out no coat of arms. He has had a host of successors especially since 1945 with the advent of so many Labor peers, trade unionists and the like. Under the regime of Clement Attlee, prime minister from 1945–51, peerages created were still overwhelmingly of the hereditary variety. At the coming of the Harold Wilson Government in 1964, hereditary peerages ceased to be created. Life peers in full pack now crowd into the Upper House, minus armorial bearings and often dropping their h's. But in the period up to 1914 the upper classes in Britain were generally possessed of coats of arms and of pedigrees of at least a few generations in length.

Taking the first volume of the Duchess of Cleveland's book, and selecting some of the names, readers may at first sight be surprised to hear that they are Norman. It should in fairness to the Duchess be stated that the bulk of her genealogy is good; the only error of magnitude is the initial fault of relying on the Battle Abbey Roll and on such other doubtful sources as *The Norman People*, and Wace. As examples of discernment, the Duchess looks upon a surname such as Audley as being without doubt an interpolation into the Roll. The habit of forgery was known and practiced among the monks all through the medieval period. Earnest ecclesiastics did not scruple to forge the Decretals* (letters and other documents alleged to be written by early popes); similarly with the famous

---

* Note 49. The Decretals.

Donation of Constantine, purporting to be a grant of the
western empire to a pope of the 4th century.* Forgeries
in favor of benefactors to a monastery were among the
contents of every monastic chartulary.

The name of Arundell is a curious puzzle. It cannot be
that the name was given to the place in Sussex, seat of the
Dukes of Norfolk, from a Norman settler. There is
supposed to have been a family of the name in Normandy.
On this subject Dr. Reaney remarks: "The earliest
bearer of the name, Roger Arundel, the *Domesday* tenant-
in-chief, has left his name in Sampford Arundell in
Somerset which he held in 1086. His by-name cannot
derive from the Sussex place but must be a nickname from
Old French *arondel* 'little swallow'." (P. H. Reaney,
Dictionary of British Surnames, 1961, p. 12) It seems that
there were two separate names. Arundel the place name
in Sussex came from the old English *harhundell* "hoar-
hound valley," and early lost the initial 'h'. The French
word soon became *hirondelle.* Thus there are two origins for
the surname of Arundel or Arundale, Arundell, etc. Most
likely they come from the place and have no necessary
Norman connotation since the various Normans known as
de Arundel, 'of Arundel,' did not leave recognizable descendants. Incidentally the play on the name of Arundel,
hirondelle, is reflected in the martlets or feetless birds in the
Sussex coat of arms.

Archer sounds at first very much an occupational name,
and so it probably was in the overwhelming majority of
cases. It is, however, of French origin and appears in the
1166 survey as Archier or Larchier. Cleveland here is
led astray in a manner to be encountered later in connection with the Grosvenors. "This family took its name

---

* Note 50. Donation of Constantine.

from the office it held under the Dukes of Normandy before the Conquest. Its derivation is rather uncertain but a family of L'Archer, still flourishing in Brittany, bears the same three arrows that were borne by the English Archers, differenced in tincture. The latter claim as their ancestor Fulbert L'Archer, the father of Robert to whom the Conqueror entrusted the charge of his son, afterwards Henry I. But Robert the tutor was the son of William and not of Fulbert, who is found neither in *Domesday* nor in any list now extant of the Conqueror's companions. According to the habit of those times, Robert only took the name of Archer after his father's death, and was the undoubted progenitor of the Barons Archer— Recherches sur le Domesday." (Cleveland, *The Battle Abbey Roll,* 1889, p. 22) I reproduce the above as a warning. Nearly every statement in it is either wrong or to be taken with great reserve. The idea of hereditary officers at the Norman court which turns up again with the Grosvenor family can be forgotten except in four instances which do not include Archer.*

Bardolf which is known to be a name of old German origin is boldly ascribed to a Norman foundation by Cleveland. The medieval Lords Bardolf have their pedigree in *Burke's Extinct Peerage,* a work which is still very much extant and is unlikely ever to be revised so that it remains the joy of all who like to study early Victorian genealogy.

Browne appears in the Duchess's list but fortunately with the note: "Yet it would be presumptuous to pronounce all the Brownes to be of Norman origin, for they are so preponderant that in one single year (1838) 5,585 births, marriages and deaths were registered among them;

---

* Note 51. Hereditary officers at Norman court.

and 21 different families have received from the sovereign hereditary titles of nobility." (p. 114)

Of Barrett we are told that it is written in *Domesday*, and indeed modern research shows the name Bared, or Baret in the survey in Yorkshire and Lincolnshire. The origin of the surname is not easy to determine, but in the form Barat which is the commonest, it comes from old French *barat*, with middle English *barrat* or *barrette*. The forms of the name are Barratt, Barrett, Barritt, Barrott.

The above considerations will, I hope, demonstrate the impossibility of claiming with any chance of success an ancestor at Hastings for the very great majority of families. To have Norman ancestry is another matter and I think that there are probably some 200 known families in Britain who are of Norman origin, apart from the many female line descents. Such families have many offshoots in America, grown now to large trees, and my next chapter is devoted to dealing with these families.

CHAPTER NINE

Normans in the British Peerage and Landed Gentry

I have been quoted as saying that there are probably not more than 20 members of the British peerage who can claim Norman male line descent. Very many British peers possess a female line Norman ancestry, as do many other people. Considerations of history render it unlikely that today the Normans would be strongly represented in the peerage. Vicissitudes over 900 years bring many changes in fortune's wheel. The nobility of England fought like the proverbial Kilkenny cats in the Wars of the Roses. Many were killed in battle or executed soon afterward, although the common saying that only three noble houses survived the civil war which ended in 1485 with the battle of Bosworth is not correct. It was rather the Tudor period which ended the old nobility. A new peerage dates from the time of the Tudor sovereigns; men who had served them were rewarded. These men, like the Cecils, Russells, Cavendishes and Wriothesleys, might strain after a Norman connection but they were emphatically *novi homines*, 'new men.' While they prospered exceedingly, the older nobility tended to perish through conspiracies or framed charges of treason. The Tudor dynasty itself had come to the throne through a very devious claim and felt more at ease with new lords of its own creation than with a Norman-descended aristocracy. The last male Plantagenet, Edward, Earl of Warwick, the nephew of Edward IV, was beheaded in 1499, simply because his existence was a reminder that Henry VII's presence on the throne could not overcome the fact that he was not the rightful heir. This was the last known male Plantagenet. Even Edward's sister, Margaret, Countess of Salisbury, shared his fate in 1541.

With the Plantagenets removed thus drastically, is it any wonder that other old Norman lines in the peerage died out? Under the Stuart kings there began the practice of selling peerages which was only ended with the passing of the Honours (Prevention of Abuses) Act in 1925. Not length of lineage but repletion of banking account brought ennoblement of blood to many during the 300 years from James I to Lloyd George.*

If anyone seeks for Norman blood, it is probably to be found in the lower ranks of English society, though owing to the obscurity of earlier records, it may not be possible to trace. Often the only evidence will be a Norman or French name possessed by a family but this is an exceedingly dubious witness to Norman origins. The surname Russell comes from the old French, *rousel,* a diminutive of *rous* (red), which may have been a nickname and also a personal name. It occurs in England in 1095 at Bury in Suffolk but attempts to provide the Duke of Bedford, the head of the house of Russell, with a medieval ancestry have not succeeded.

There are 27 non-royal dukedoms out of which not more than 12 can be classed as Norman. Of these, four— Richmond, Grafton, St. Albans and Buccleuch—have a

---

* Note 52. Sale of Honours.

female line descent through the liaisons of their ances-
tresses with Charles II. These four should not therefore
be included at all; otherwise the Duke of Norfolk would
be reckoned of Norman ancestry, as indeed he is by the
royal descent which he has from his family's alliance with
the Plantagenets. It is incidentally an interesting possibility that the Howards who stand at the head of the
British peerage are of English origin. The sources of their
surname are very involved, and no clear indication of
racial origin can be drawn from them, but it seems unlikely that the surname would have been borne by a
person of Norman descent.

Of the other dukedoms remaining for consideration,
that of Northumberland, like those just mentioned, is
Norman only through the female line, for as already
stated, the Percy male line died out very early. The male
stock ended before 1200 when the descendants of Agnes
de Percy became heirs of the family. She married Joceline
de Louvain, the brother of Queen Adela, the young
second wife of Henry I. There were two sons of this
marriage both of whom took the name of Percy. The
family continued in greatness down to the death of
Joceline, the 11th Earl of Northumberland, when in
1670 the male line again ended. The heiress, Lady
Elizabeth Percy, was married three times. By her first
husband, heir to the dukedom of Newcastle, who assumed
the name of Percy, she had no issue. Her second husband,
Thomas Thynne, of Longleat, a member of the Marquess
of Bath's family, gave her no children. He was murdered
in London's Pall Mall in 1682, while in his coach, an
event which is shown on his memorial in Westminster
Abbey. At last by her third husband, the 6th Duke of
Somerset, Charles Seymour, she had issue. The eldest of
her children was Algernon Seymour who was the 7th

Duke of Somerset, and was created Earl of Northumberland with special remainder to his son-in-law, Sir Hugh Smithson, a baronet who later became Duke of Northumberland, the first of the present creation. Thus the male line of Percy has died out as long ago as the 12th century and has been continued four times through female stocks.

What of the Dukes of Somerset? Their pedigree begins in the reign of Henry III (1216–72) with Sir Richard St. Mauro, a knight who acquired some estates in Monmouthshire at Woundy and Penhow. It is curious that the pedigree is not traced further back in this source for the surname Seymour does derive from St. Maur, or *Sancto Mauro*, there being a place called Saint Maur-des-Fossés in the Dept. of Seine. Here it should be noted that the name in its Anglicized spelling can be derived from a place called Seamer in Yorkshire. Perhaps the reason for the lack of exact pedigree before the 13th century is the old story of want of evidence, though modern surname experts trace the name as early as 1159. The 6th Duke of Somerset mentioned above may have found his Norman blood an ingredient in his inordinate pride which has been described on all sides as so extreme as almost to amount to madness. He "was a man who from his extravagant eccentricities, might . . . run the risk of being considered insane. His pride of birth and rank was nothing short of a mania. He had an almost overwhelming sense of his own dignity; and aping the seclusion observed by oriental monarchs, shunned to expose himself to the profanation of vulgar eyes. When he took the air in his state coach, running footmen preceded him to warn everyone else off the road. His daughters never sat down in his presence; and when, suddenly aroused from an after dinner nap, he found that one of them had been guilty of this gross breach of etiquette, the offense never passed out of his mind, and he remembered it against her even in his will. Again, when his second wife, Lady Charlotte Finch, once tapped him familiarly on the shoulder, he was amazed beyond measure, and severely rebuked her for her forwardness. 'Madam,' said he, 'my first duchess was a Percy, yet she never dared to allow herself such a liberty.' " (The Duchess of Cleveland, *The Battle Abbey Roll,* pp. 378–79) The same author goes on to observe that this maniacally proud man, "not content with the old manor house of the Percies at Petworth . . . transformed it into a palatial mansion, built on a scale of grandeur proportioned to his aspiration." His first duchess, the Percy, was only 16 or 17 when she married him, her first two husbands having died in rapid succession as related above. The Duke of Somerset was compelled by the marriage settlement to take her name and arms, but when she came of age he induced her to release him from this condition and was able to revert to Seymour. He must indeed have been greatly taken with the renown of the Percy name for him to have made so great a sacrifice. The mansion at Petworth which he erected was later termed "princely Petworth." It remains a monument of 18th-century grandeur, made over now to the National Trust; but the monument to the duke in the chapel is apt to make one wonder to what deity it is dedicated. One enters a fairly plain and simple chapel of a great house, and then turning around beholds a vast canopy setting forth the heraldic magnificence of the 6th Duke.

The dangers of assuming from a surname that one can surmise Norman, or other ancestry, are proved by the fact that the Dukes of Manchester are Montagus, a Norman name. The older form of the name was Montacute (i.e., *de monte acuto*), hence the three lozenges in fess on their shield, as if to represent the crests of jagged mountains. The Norman family is found in *Domesday* and came from Montaigu-le-bois, or from Montaigu. The place name is found in Somerset where there is a great house called Montacute. In some cases this place must have given a surname to families which may be deluding themselves that they are Normans. It should also be remembered that the name of Montagu is one now often assumed in England by expatriate continental Jews.

There was a considerable Norman family of Montagu in medieval England. How far the new people in the Tudor period were connected with them is not clear; had they been, it must surely have been proclaimed from the loudest organ of family pride. The Dukes of Manchester stem from one Richard Montagu, alias Ladde, of Hanging Houghton in the parish of Lamport, in Northamptonshire, who was the son of William Ladde of Lamport. It could be that these Laddes who became Montagus were descended from the old Norman house. The modern peerage Montagus have the arms of the medieval family, within a bordure sable, one of the indications that the linkup has not been entirely proved. Lord Swaythling's family name is Montagu, changed from Samuel; the supporters of his shield are soldiers of ancient Judea, not of Normandy.

The family surname of the Duke of Rutland is Manners, from Mesnières in Seine Inf., yet here too the pedigree begins in the 14th century. If the antecedents could be traced to the Norman settlement why not show them?

The Dukes of Newcastle, the Clintons, found a champion in the great destroyer of Norman pedigrees, John

Horace Round. The Clinton surname derives from Glympton in Oxfordshire, and their origins come from Saint Pierre-de-Semilly in Manche. Geoffrey de Clinton was Chamberlain to Henry I and one of the early Norman chroniclers, Ordericus Vitalis, refers to him as being raised from the dust of the earth. Both Round and Lewis Loyd are sure of the Clintons' Normanity.

Among the Scots dukes those of Roxburgh (Kerr), Hamilton (Douglas Hamilton), and Montrose (Graham) have alliances with royalty and thus Norman line descents. In Ireland, the Dukes of Leinster descend from Walter FitzOther, a tenant-in-chief in Berkshire and other counties. With the Clintons these form almost the only certain male line descents from Normans among the British dukes.

Among the marquesses, Norman descents, except in the sense in which we all have them through the female line, are not common. The Marquess of Ailesbury has a very interesting descent, female line none the less. His surname is Brudenell-Bruce and through these two families and the earlier lines of Seymour and Estormit he traces his ancestry from a Norman, Richard Estormit or "the wary," who was appointed by William I as warden of Savernake Forest in Wiltshire which was a royal preserve more than a century before the Conquest, being mentioned in a charter of King Athelstan in 934. The wardenship became hereditary in the Estormit family and on the death in 1427 of Sir William Esturmy, passed to his grandson, Sir John Seymour, of the Duke of Somerset's family. On the 4th Duke's death in 1675 it went to his niece and so by marriage into the Bruce family and thus it came to Thomas Brudenell, Lord Bruce in 1747, the ancestor of the present marquess. The last-named is the 29th Hereditary Warden of Savernake Forest, a true instance of holding an office from the time of the Conquest.*

Two great Norman houses are those of the Hays (the Marquess of Tweeddale, and the Countess of Erroll), and the Nevilles, the Marquess of Abergavenny. The origins of both these families in Normandy have been given in chapter five. The Nevilles have one thing in common with the Berkeleys; there is a mixture early in their history of Norman and English. In both cases the surname adopted was that of the Norman line. With the Nevilles, as with the Percies, a great heiress, Isabel, succeeded her brother Henry de Neville in 1227 and was married to Robert FitzMaldred, the lord of Raby in the county of Durham. In the view of modern researchers he is regarded as having come from the Saxon Earls of Northumbria through the wife of the Scottish Prince Maldred Mac Crinan. He was a brother of Duncan I, King of Scots (reigned 1034–40) and married Aldgyth, the daughter of Uchtred, Earl of Northumbria, who was killed in 1016. His ancestry also joined on to that of the Scottish Swinton family previously mentioned.

The Nevilles held many peerages and were a most powerful medieval family. Nearly everyone must have heard of Warwick the Kingmaker. He was Richard Neville, Earl of Warwick and of Salisbury who alternately set up or pulled down Henry VI and Edward IV. At last he was defeated and killed at Barnet in 1471, and no other nobleman in England ever again possessed power such as his. There must be many branches of this great family still in existence, although there is only one, that of the Marquess of Abergavenny, to represent it in the modern peerage.

---

* Note 53. Marquess of Ailesbury.

Passing to the de la Poer family, of the Marquess of Waterford, they are a line of Norman knights who went from England to Ireland to better their fortunes by invading the latter country. It is often said in literary reference works that Edgar Allen Poe was a distant scion of the de la Poers.

The Cholmondeleys, the head of whom is the Marquess of Cholmondeley, descend from Norman stock. William le Belward received the property which gave the family its surname and title, Calmundelai (or Cholmondeley, pronounced Chumley) in Cheshire, when he married Beatrice, the daughter of the famous Hugh Kevelioc, the palatine Earl of Chester. This family by virtue of descent from the de Veres, the Earls of Oxford, has another distinction. The de Veres were Hereditary Lords Great Chamberlain from the Conquest. When the 20th Earl died in 1702, the title was supposed to have become extinct. The rights of the office of Lord Great Chamberlain are shared by Lord Cholmondeley with the Earl of Ancaster and Lord Carrington, so that they hold the position in turn.

The Marquess of Ormonde, the Butler family, are of the most distinguished and illustrious of the Anglo-Norman nobility who invaded Ireland. The original ancestor is said to have been a relative of William Malet mentioned earlier. The surname of Butler comes from their appointment as Hereditary Chief Butler of Ireland, hence too the covered cups in their coat of arms. These seemingly menial offices were much coveted by the noble families. In days when the sovereign really ruled, it was highly important to be able to gain the royal ear, and what more useful opportunity than when pouring the royal draught of wine?

Among the few families who can trace a descent from a

tenant recorded in the *Domesday Book* is that of the Earl of Shrewsbury, whose ancestor was Richard Talebot. He is mentioned as holding nine hides of land from Walter Giffard, Earl of Buckingham. The surname is not from a place name and its derivation is very obscure, one possible origin being the old French *talebot,* meaning a bandit. However, in Normandy the Talebots were considerable under tenants, of Giffard, Count of Eu, and of Gournay. This was in the Dept. of Seine Inf., and as we find Geoffrey Talebot in England as under tenant of Hugh de Gournay in Essex and Richard Talebot of Walter Giffard in Bedfordshire, it is clear that the Talebots came from the Norman district mentioned. In the Conquest settlement the lord and vassal relationship which had existed in Normandy was continued in England.

In the case of another under tenant in England, the family was destined to become far greater than its overlord. The Curzons (Curson is another and more frequent transatlantic spelling) held West Lockinge in Berkshire of Henry de Ferrers, in the *Domesday* record, together with other fiefs of the same lord. The family came from Notre Dame de Courson in Calvados, and in 1223 Herbert de Courson was seigneur of Courson. One of the knights' fees held by Curzon from Ferrers was at Kedleston in Derbyshire. That is the seat of the head of the family, Viscount Scarsdale, and there the Curzon family has lived since the reign of Henry I, in the early 1100s at least. In a French work, *Recherches Historiques sur la Maison de Courson* (1881), some details are given of the Norman and Breton lines of the family. The arms of the French stock show the three popinjays which are the chief charge of the English branch. Since heraldry originated about the middle of the 12th century, the fact that on both sides of the English Channel the Curzons bore the same arms would argue a regular communication between the French and English cousins; otherwise the origin of the Curzon arms must have preceded the Norman Conquest, which is contrary to our knowledge of heraldic beginnings. The Curzon pedigree in the College of Arms, in the Visitation of Derbyshire in 1611, shows a connected line to the reign of Henry VI (1422–71) after which there are some disconnected notes which remind one of the preparations to draft a formal pedigree. Three and a half centuries ago! Fortunately we do not have to depend on these items. One Curzon branch was at Croxall in Staffordshire and a pedigree of this line made by the heralds in 1635 is at Knole in Kent; from a copy of this pedigree at Kedleston, from ancient documents in Viscount Scarsdale's muniment room, and from old Curzon pedigree books, the descent is shown. From the Norman founder Robert de Curzon descent is traced generation by generation to Sir John Curzon, of Kedleston, whose grandson John "with the white head" was High Sheriff of the counties of Nottingham and Derby in 1437.

The Ferrers who have been mentioned more than once were among the great tenants of the Crown at the *Domesday*. They have long ceased to hold the Earldom of Derby, nor are they any longer represented in the peerage, but the family of Ferrers of Baddesley Clinton in Warwickshire is still very much in existence among the untitled aristocracy of England.

In an earlier chapter I mentioned the pedigree of John Farrow, the film producer, husband of Maureen O'Sullivan and father of Mia Farrow. Others of note in the annals of Hollywood are Olivia de Havilland and her sister Joan Fontaine. They are members of the ancient Norman family of de Havilland which took its name from the fiefs of Haverland, situated near Valogne in Normandy, where they were lords in 1050. They settled in Guernsey as early as 1176, but the manner of their settlement in England exemplifies the social habits of notable families in late medieval times. Thomas, seigneur de Havilland, fought at the siege of Mount Orgueil Castle in Jersey in 1467. As a reward for his services he was granted a patent conferring some commercial privileges. To avail himself of these he set up his second son, James, at Poole in Dorset, where he became mayor in 1494. The present de Havilland line descends from James' elder brother Thomas, but there was a branch, the Havellands of Wilkswood House, in the Isle of Purbeck (really a peninsula) in Dorset, the last-mentioned family being now extinct. In earlier times there was no objection to a family of gentry participating in trade. The silly snobbery of looking down on an honest occupation appears to have originated in the 18th century. Also among Channel Island families is that of Lord de Sausmarez, of whom it can be said that they descend from the Norman family of St. Hilaire du Harcouet, who held a castle built on the borders of Britanny by William I. The name variously spelled as Sausmarais, Samares and Samarez, was derived from the fief de Saumareys, i.e., salt marsh, situated in low-lying land by the sea in the parish of St. Clement, Jersey, which is said to have been given to Ralph de Saint Hilaire by William Rufus (William II) in 1096. The family went from Jersey in 1333, but has long been associated with Guernsey.

A distinguished family which is probably of Norman origin is that of Lord Keyes. The first peer was the famous seaman, Admiral of the Fleet, Sir Roger Keyes, later Lord Keyes. His brother, Sir Terence Keyes, himself a distinguished soldier, traced the genealogy of the family to Thomas Keyes, Sergeant Porter at the court of Queen Elizabeth I and the biggest man there, who dared to espouse the smallest woman at court, Lady Mary Grey, who was in the line of succession to the throne. He had three children by his first wife which was fortunate for him as he was never again allowed to see Lady Mary, for once the Queen had discovered his marriage she had him arrested and kept in close custody. Before this, the descent was traced to Richard Keyes who fought in France in 1373. There was a collateral ancestor who was a priest and who helped to build All Souls College at Oxford for Archbishop Chichele, and to complete Eton College for Henry VI. The latter in 1449 granted arms to the priest, with extension of the grant to Roger Keyes' brother Thomas and his descendants. This grant which is extant is very un-usual, not only because the existence of grants from the 15th century is rare, but also because this particular patent confers nobility without a summons to parliament as a baron, probably because the recipient was in Holy Orders. In earlier periods before 1373, the name occurs frequently in the Lancastrian records, the Exchequer Rolls, and the Rolls of Knights Banneret (Edward I, 1272–1307) under the following spellings: Keyes, Kys, Cays, Cauis, Guiz, Guise, Guyz, Gyse, Gyz and Goyz. It is thought that there is a line of descent from the Norman house of Guiz or Gyes, akin to the old family of Guise, now baronets.

The Sackvilles, headed by Lord Sackville of Knole, Kent, are of Norman origin, though like many other peerage families the Norman ancestry is through the female line, the family surname being Sackville-West. At Knole, one of the most beautiful mansions in England, there is a stained glass window which purports to show the martial features and stout mailed form of the original

Herbrand de Sauqeville, *qui venit in Anglia cum Gulielmo Conquistore.* Whether he was at Hastings we do not know but in 1074 he was holding land in England. The Knole property came into the possession of the Sackvilles in the time of Elizabeth I. The name is undoubtedly derived from Sauqeville, Seine Inf. In England the family flourished mightily, becoming Dukes of Dorset, but the male line became extinct in 1843.

In dealing with the British peerage, it is impossible to avoid female lines of descent, as can be seen from the modern family of Sackville. In the history of Lord Harberton we have on the contrary a male line Norman descent. The family name is Pomeroy which reached England from La Pommeraye in Calvados near Falaise, the birthplace of William I. The old seat of the family in England was at Berry Pomeroy in Devon, where as often happened in the west country the settlers added their name to the already existing Saxon place name. The historian of the *Worthies of Devon,* John Prince (edition of 1701), writes of "this great progeny who had their dwelling at the Castle of Berry Pomeroy from the Norman Conquest unto the days of King Edward VI which is upwards of 500 years. The name in several ages was severally written, as de Pomerio, de Pomeri, de la Pomerai, and then Pomeroy. The first so called in England was Ralph de la Pomerai, who came in with William the Conqueror, and was greatly assistant to him in obtaining this kingdom; for which reason he conferred upon him a noble estate, no less than 58 lordships in Devonshire, as Sir William Dugdale tells us in his *Baronage of England,* Vol. I, p. 498." Modern historians confirm the Norman ancestry. Prof. Edward B. Powley in *The House of de la Pomerai* (1943) traced the descent of the family through its several branches. Lewis Loyd gives details of Ralf de Pomaria holding land in Devon and Cornwall under the Count of Mortain (1086).

Another place in the west country, Stoke Courcy in Somerset, is named after the Norman lords of Courcy who settled there. The great antiquarian scholar, Sir Henry Maxwell Lyte, proved that John de Courcy, the conqueror of Ulster in the reign of Henry II, was a junior member of the Somersetshire house. No one has proved the connection of the Courcys, Lords Kingsale, with the Stoke Courcy family, or with John de Courcy for that matter, as he left only illegitimate children. It can be shown that in 1221 Patrick de Courcy is mentioned as one of the nobles of Ireland and there is no reason to suppose that he was not a member of the family in England, though no proof can be obtained for this.

The old baronies by writ of summons which can be transmitted through the female line contain some Norman ancestors. De Ros, Mowbray, Hastings, Furnivall, Clinton, etc., all have Norman progenitors but are connected with the present representatives through the several female lines. With the Beaumonts, their descent is from Henry de Beaumont, *circa* 1300, the younger son of Louis de Brienne who was *jure uxoris*, Vicomte de Beaumont in Maine, and grandson of John de Brienne, King of Jerusalem. The name of the family now is Fitzalan-Howard, and their descent is on the female side. The male line of Beaumont is represented by a baronet with a very long pedigree going back to the French Counts of Brienne before the Norman Conquest.

Again, D'Arcy de Knayth, another old peerage, has an ancestry from Norman de Areci, a *Domesday* tenant who held 33 lordships in Lincolnshire, but it is through female lines, the surname of the present head being Ingram. Finally, before leaving the baronies, I cannot forego mentioning the family of the Lords Cromwell, who are supposed to be of Norman origin, and more significant to be the kinsfolk of Oliver Cromwell himself. It may be so. Many great families have had lesser lines, and so it could have been that the Putney blacksmith, the father of Thomas Cromwell, Minister of Henry VIII and ancestor of Oliver's line, was of Norman blood.

Coming to the baronets, we have one undoubted example already mentioned, Gresley. Mordaunt is supposed to be Norman and has a pedigree of father to son descent which begins with Osbert of Radwell in Bedfordshire in the 1100s.

Bacon, the name of the premier baronet on the roll, is undoubtedly Norman, and used early in our records of Norman knights, yet the baronetcy pedigree begins in the Tudor period. De Hoghton, another very historic family of the baronets' Roll, has a common origin with the Marquess of Ormonde from Hervey Walter. Some baronetcies are held by peers. That of Molyneux, possessed by the Earl of Sefton, is almost certainly Norman. The Traffords of Trafford are probably Norman though they have the legend or tradition of a Saxon origin. The earliest names in their pedigree are foreign, but as French Christian names were speedily adopted by the English, we cannot be sure of the true origin of the Traffords.

Both Hoghton and Trafford adopted in the 19th century the use of "de" before their surnames, under the belief that in so doing they were reverting to medieval usage. The latter was only a scribe's way of writing that the bearer of the name was the tenant of the place. The use of "de" in England had nothing in common with the French *de* which is often part of the surname.

Over the Wake baronets' ancestry a fierce controversy has raged. One traditional belief held by the family is that they descend from the great English hero, Hereward the Wake, the last man in England to resist the Normans. On the contrary they are known to descend from a Norman, Hugh Wac (later Anglicized into Wake), who held Bourne in Lincolnshire in 1142. According to Round, Hugh Wac's father was Geoffrey Wac, who held lands in the Bessin in Normandy and in Guernsey in the Channel Islands. I have been told that he was manufactured or produced to spite the 12th Wake baronet! I can sympathize with the Wakes, for who would not want to descend from such a hero? For long he holds out against William in the Isle of Ely and is only overcome in the end by the treachery of the Ely monks. Hereward is received into the Conqueror's favor, and his lands at Bourne are restored to him. But Norman treachery does not let him rest. At last his foes surprise him. Accompanied by his foster brother Winter, he falls, but only after he has stood in a ring of a dozen Norman corpses.

When I was editing *Burke's Peerage,* I was sorry to remove this story from the Wake pedigree, for I had from boyhood loved the romance of Charles Kingsley, *Hereward the Wake.* After long correspondence with the head of the family I added a footnote to the pedigree. Hugh Wac married Emma, the daughter and heiress of Baldwin FitzGilbert. My note ran: "On this marriage the family bases its claim of descent from Hereward. Controversy has raged over this claim. See E. A. Freeman, *Norman Conquest* and J. H. Round, *Feudal England.*" Since then a new champion of the Wake has appeared, a Scottish historian, Sir Iain Moncreiffe. Hereward had a daughter Turfrida who was married to Hugh of Envermeu, brother of Turold, the Bishop of Bayeux. This Hugh held Deeping (in the neighbourhood of Bourne) under Peterborough Abbey. They had a daughter Godiva, married to Richard de Rullos (brother of William de Rullos, lord of Bourne), a chamberlain to Henry I. Their daughter, Adeline, married Baldwin FitzGilbert de Clare, and the child of this union, Emma, became the wife of Hugh Wac, Baron of Negreville in the Cotentin, and lord of Bourne. Sir Iain supports his argument with much documentation (*The Genealogists' Magazine,* June 1967) and I very much hope that he is right.

Of the large number of baronets—there are 1,250 without counting another 250 titles of this kind held by peers—only a few need mention on account of their Normanity. Of Cave-Brown-Cave, we read "A pedigree, collected and certified by Sir William Segar, Garter King of Arms, 1632, derives it from Jordan de Cave, who inherited the lordships of North and South Cave, co. York, at the death of his brother Wymarus." The latter had received it from William I in 1080, according to this same pedigree. I am not very impressed with the authority of these old college certificates, but the pedigree does at least show a generation-to-generation descent from the Norman period, instead of some vague general statement at the beginning of the account, e.g., "this family is of Norman origin," followed by a connected pedigree beginning 600 years after the Conquest.

Salisbury Trelawny derives from Hamelin who held Treoloen in Cornwall on feudal tenure from the Count of Mortain. The Paston Bedingfelds have been owners of Bedingfield in Suffolk from the early 12th century. Francis Blomefield in his nine volume *History of Norfolk* where this family was mainly seated, said (Vol. vi, p. 175) that their pedigree began with Ogerus de Pugys. He is unknown outside Blomefield's pages and is, I fear, one of those linking figures brought forward to join the land-holder of 1100 with a fighter at Hastings. The family figures early in the Roll of Baronets and the first baronet had suffered grievously for Charles I. "After the Restoration he laid before Charles II an estimate of the losses sustained by the family, amounting to £47,194–18–8; he was answered by the monarch, that it was too great a sum for him to recompense: to which Mr. Bedingfeld answered that all he begged of his majesty was that he might hope for the future to enjoy in tranquillity the small remnant of his fortune. To soften, however, the asperity of this unmerited refusal, the dignity of baronet was conferred upon him." (article on the family in *Burke's Peerage*)

The Wallers of Braywick Lodge have a pedigree in the archives of the College of Arms which begins with Thomas Waller of South Lambeth who died in 1731. The Waller coat of arms, however, indicates a much more distant history, for on their crest of a walnut tree they have the fleur-de-lis which is said to have been granted to Sir Richard Waller for his part in capturing Charles, Duke of Orleans, at the battle of Agincourt in 1415. In all probability the medieval Wallers were of Norman origin but there are 300–400 years between the famous battle and the date of registration of the arms with the fleur-de-lis in the College of Arms. I made some investigations in order to extend the pedigree. In the church of St. Mary the Virgin at Speldhurst, near Tonbridge Wells, Kent, is a mural tablet which I have seen and which was put up by the first baronet, Sir Jonathan Wathen Waller, Groom of the Bedchamber to William IV. This tablet was to perpetuate the memory of his ancestors whose monuments and memorials were destroyed with the church in 1791. On this tablet it is stated that the Wallers descend from Alured de Waller, of Newark, Notts, who died in 1183, and that they were settled at Groombridge Place in

Speldhurst parish from 1360 to 1604. Twenty names with dates are given on this memorial, including the Thomas Waller of 1731 mentioned above.

After leaving the titled aristocracy we come to the untitled, known in Britain as the landed gentry or the county families. The well-known Gloucestershire family of Poyntz descends from Simon, youngest son of one Pons, or Poinz, who gave three hides in the manor of Eaton Hastings, near Farringdon, Berkshire, to Westminster Abbey, and who died before 1086. Through Simon's elder brothers the Poyntz family was connected with the Giffards and one line obtained Clifford Castle in Herefordshire. They became the de Cliffords and one of them was the Fair Rosamund of legend, the mistress of Henry II. Other Norman lines in the landed gentry are Tremlett from Les Trois Minettes, a hamlet of St. Germain Largot, near La Pommeraye in Calvados. The name was Latinized to *De Tribus Minetis*. The family still flourishes in England where for centuries the knightly Tremletts lived in Devonshire. The Constantines of Yorkshire are a Norman family whose ancestry has been traced by the College of Arms. The original form of the name is often spelled as Cosentine. As far back as 1150–61, a Josceline Constantine received a conveyance of his father's land in Coney Street, York, from the abbot of St. Mary's York. The family was found in many counties in medieval England.

Martin can be a Norman surname and is commemorated, as with so many other places, in the name of an original Norman settler's fief, Combe Martin in Devonshire. A foreigner from Tours in Normandy came into England in the reign of William (Rufus) II, conquered Cameys in South Wales, and settled in North Devon. A long line of descendants through the Martins of Athelhampton and of Seaborough, in Dorset, come from this invader.

As was pointed out under FitzWilliam, possession of French Christian names at the start of a pedigree does not always betoken Norman ancestry. The Kingscotes of Kingscote in Gloucestershire begin their pedigree in the second great survey in 1166, when Nigel FitzArthur married Adela, the youngest daughter of Robert Fitzhardinge. Nigel and Arthur are not native English names, but who can say that Arthur was not a Saxon's son?

The Bassets of Tehidy, Cornwall, and the Barnardistons of Durham are of continental origin; so too the Muschamps whose name is said to derive from the field or house fly (Latin *musca*), obviously a nickname, and they have flies or bees in their arms. The Muschamps became a powerful family in Durham and Northumberland.

Many descents of Norman blood connect with William de Warenne, Earl of Surrey, and his countess Gundreda, who was for long thought to have been the daughter of William I. Expert opinion is now of the view that she was not his daughter but a close kinswoman. It might give pause to those who are enamored of Norman ancestry to reflect that if we cannot be sure of the paternity of one of William's alleged daughters, married to one of his greatest nobles, we are likely to be lacking evidence for the genealogy of many lesser folk. Another very important warning arises in the case of the name Warren, which can indeed be derived from the powerful Earl de Warenne but is also derived from the occupation of one who looked after his rabbit warren. The Normans introduced rabbits into England, where they were at first kept in rabbit warrens under the care of a warrener. Still, if this underling were a Norman, perhaps he will do as well as a more exalted forbear. A genuine descent from the Earl de

Warenne was that of the Leckys of Beardeville, Cloyfin, co. Antrim, Northern Ireland. Both Hugh Lecky and his wife, who had been Miss Frances Dimsdale, were descended from de Warenne, his line coming through the Scottish kings and hers through the families of Plantagenet, FitzWilliam, Musgrave and Thornburgh.

The Normans penetrated into Wales, Scotland and Ireland. Like their Viking forbears they had the urge to expand overseas, though their widespread conquests did not, like those of the Norsemen, extend across the Atlantic to Iceland, Greenland and Vineland. Many intermarriages took place in Ireland, Scotland and Wales, as in England, and the Normans were eventually absorbed, leaving in a few instances the fact of their presence at the base of family trees. Some of the cases of Normanity in these countries I have dealt with. There are others which have considerable interest, if only because their surnames are so widely used.

Few names are better known than that of Haig. The origin is in the district of La Hague. The founder of the Scottish line was Peter de la Haga who appears to have been an under-tenant of the Moreville family. This was between 1150 and 1200, and Bemersyde on the Tweed was the Scottish property held by the Haigs. As with other families whom we have noticed, the Haigs were under-tenants of the Morevilles in their Norman homeland, in Dorset, England, and in Scotland. In the 200 years between the Norman Conquest and the attempt by Edward I to conquer Scotland, many great nobles held lands of the crown in both countries.

Another Norman line settled in Scotland was that of Haldane. The stem begins with Roger de Haldane, a cadet of the house of Haldane on the English border, who is believed to have settled in Strathearn, Perthshire, where he acquired lands which were later incorporated in the barony of Gleneagles. He was probably a nephew of Bernard, son of Brien, who was given the manor of Hauden by William the Lion and granted a carucate of land to the monks of Kelso Abbey between 1165 and 1171. The family has been of continuous distinction down the centuries to our time.

Hamilton is a great Norman house with many branches in Scotland. The Duke of Abercorn and the Duke of Hamilton and Brandon are chiefs of the line. Of the Hamiltons, the immediate ancestor, Gilbert de Hamilton, is described as descended from the ancient Norman race of de Bellomont or Beaumont, Earls of Leicester. This Gilbert lived in the reign of Alexander II, King of Scotland.

The head of the house of Sinclair, or St. Clair, is the Earl of Caithness. The name comes from Saint Clair-sur-Elle in Manche. Sir William Sinclair of Roslin, Midlothian, was the second son of Robert de Saint Clair of Normandy by his wife, Eleanor, the daughter of the Comte de Dreux and thus cousin of Yolande de Dreux, second wife of Alexander III of Scotland, from whom Sir William had a charter of the barony of Roslin, 14 September 1280.

The family of Montgomery was founded in Scotland by Robert de Montgomery, in the second part of the 12th century when he obtained the lands of Eaglesham in Renfrewshire. The family is that of the Earls of Eglinton and Winton.

Some of the great Irish families of Anglo-Norman origin have been mentioned. That such a common name as Burke should be derived from the baronial de Burgo shows how far the Normans were assimilated in Ireland. Not all Burkes are de Burgos in blood! Most of the names must have come about either through servants who adopted the surname or from simple imitation. One other Irish family can be mentioned, that of the Segraves of Cabragh in county Dublin. They descend from Thomas de Segrave, who is mentioned in *Domesday* as the holder of Segrave in Leicestershire. They were great barons in England and one of them is mentioned in the poem, *The Siege of Caerlaverock** at the end of Edward I's reign. In Ireland the family settled in county Meath.

The de Burgos were Earls and Marquesses of Clanricarde, and descended from William FitzAdelm, sent by Henry II to receive the submission of Roderick O'Conor, King of Connaught.

In more than one of my books I have written of the famous case of *Scrope v. Grosvenor*,† so important in the law and practice of heraldry. With its heraldic aspects I am not here concerned, but only with the fact that both the contenders claimed Norman blood. This was in 1385, so that nearly 600 years ago the concept of the superior quality of Norman ancestry was ingrained in English nobility. The dispute gathered interest from the genealogical point of view because in later times the Grosvenors were very exalted in the social sphere and became Dukes of Westminster. At the time of the dispute both the parties were knights, but whereas Sir Robert Grosvenor was a simple Cheshire gentleman, Sir Richard le Scrope belonged to one of the most powerful families of the time, and was high in the king's favor, being soon to enter the House of Lords. Today the Scropes are represented by a Yorkshire squire, Mr. Scrope of Danby, while the Grosvenor chief is the Duke of Westminster. In fact, the

---

* Note 54. *The Siege of Caerlaverock.*
† Note 55. *Scrope v. Grosvenor.*

change in their respective positions is the perfect illustration in the turns of fortune's wheel which so delighted medieval poets and moralists.

What is the truth of the claims of Scrope and Grosvenor? Neither genealogy can be traced earlier than the 12th century. Both names are of foreign origin. Scrope is said to mean a crab and to be Norse. If this etymology is correct then the surname must be ultimately a nickname possibly with reference to the sidelong walk of a remote ancestor. The meaning of Grosvenor is simply "chief huntsman" and on this basis a splendid myth was built in less critical days. The first of the Grosvenors was the Chief Huntsman of Normandy. There is nothing to support this belief but the derivation of the name from the French, *gros veneur*. There are instances of the occurrence of the name from 1200 onward; thus Robert le gros-Venour in the Coucher Book of Whalley Abbey in Lancashire; again, Warin le Grovenour in 1259 in the Assize Rolls for Cheshire. These two counties adjoin and the Grosvenors begin their pedigree in the latter in 1160. Here then is the origin of the name, a head game keeper as he would now be called, or chief hunter on an estate. From these humble beginnings the mighty house of Grosvenor arose, and not from a great functionary of the Duke of Normandy. The Grosvenor story is not a legend, for a legend contains a factual basis as do most traditions. It is plainly and simply a myth. The first bearers of the name may not even have been of Norman French descent but Englishmen employed by the Norman lords. There is in America a probable branch of the Grosvenors whose name was early spelt Gravenor. Their pedigree is given in *Burke's Landed Gentry American Supplement,* 1939.

CHAPTER TEN

The Invasion of America

IN many respects the English settlements which developed into the original Thirteen Colonies and the U.S.A. bore strong resemblances to the settlement 11 centuries before of the English in Britain. The one essential difference lay in the fact of government sponsorship behind some of the colonies, and the certainty of government interference after settlement. Most of the colonies, however, originated from the desires of English people to leave England and to find a home for themselves in what was then an undeveloped land, striving against nature and the native inhabitants. Political and religious ideas supplemented the economic reasons which we surmise—and it is only a sensible surmise—lay behind the removal of Angles and Saxons from the continent to Britain.* One interesting feature in each case was the use of the sea, and then largely its abandonment. The original Germanic and Nordic settlers in England were much more skilled seamen and shipbuilders than the Romans, but they soon abandoned their shipping in favor of land-lubbing once they had begun to farm good

---

* Note 56. Original English settlements.

soil in Britain. The sea tradition did not die off at once in the new land of England, but persisted as something pertaining to the lives of the kings and great men. Thus in *Beowulf* * there are two burials described, one being that of a hero whose ship is made ready for the deep; the prototype Viking funeral. This poem was brought from abroad to England, possibly from southern Sweden, kept alive by bardic recitals like the Homeric poems, and written down by English Christian scribes about A.D. 700. Now the interesting thing is that in 1938–39 at Sutton Hoo in Suffolk a ship of the sea-going kind, 80 feet in length, was found; it had been hauled half a mile over the land from the Deben estuary and dragged up a hundred feet to the top of an escarpment. Here it was buried in a trench which had been dug to receive it. No body was buried in the grave, but otherwise all the objects which the dead hero might need in his journey to the next world were placed in the vessel. The whole was covered over to a height of nine feet and it formed one of 11 barrows which despite an attempt by thieves in the 17th century remained inviolate until opened by modern experts. The contents of the burial ship showed the rich craftmanship of the early English settlers. It has been conjectured that the great man who received this elaborate tribute to his memory was Ethelhere, King of the East Angles who was killed in a battle on 15 November 655 fighting on the side of the old pagan King of Mercia, Penda. Ethelhere's brother was a Christian and if the ship was a memorial to Ethelhere, then this was a broad-minded act, and also the last of the pagan ship burials. I cite it here merely to illustrate the old English cessation in the use of shipping when they no longer required it. In

---

* Note 57. *Beowulf.*

the time of Alfred the Great, it was necessary to train Englishmen in the use of warships, although English trading vessels were very much employed during the 8th–10th centuries.

The Germans in their pre-war Nazi propaganda made out that English folk had a strictly utilitarian view of the sea, being unconcerned with it until it proved profitable to them. This seems a sensible attitude, though the Germans forgot the existence during medieval times of English shipping, which voyaged from Iceland to the Mediterranean. The English who settled in America used the sea as their highway to a New England and then largely forgot it.

In carving homesteads from the wilderness in New England, the parallel with the long past settlements in the old country holds good. The natives were hostile. The burden of civilization had shifted. The Romano-British provincials had belonged to a high civilization in decay, which was wiped out by the less civilized invaders. In New England the literate and sometimes cultured settlers came against the primitive societies of the Indians. Their treatment of these savages, as they called them, often with justification, was not less cruel than that which their remote pagan forbears gave to the Romano-Britons. It was probably worse, for no Indian tribes exist on reserves in New England, whereas the persistence of Celtic blood in the English people is proof that not all the natives were exterminated in the 5th–6th century.*

In hewing farms, villages and towns from the American wilderness the New Englanders had yet another feature resembling the English settlements of Britain. The Roman province had many towns, with well made roads inter-

---

* Note 58. English treatment of Roman Province.

secting the carefully organized department of empire, but the population does not seem to have pressed on the subsistence level. Certainly when the English landed there were huge areas of forest land. The newcomers did not, at least at first, inhabit the towns and cities, but preferred to make their homes in open country where they gradually cleared the forest and built up their farms. This process could almost be said to have persisted to our own time.

In America, the steady, unremitting efforts of the settlers, and not any government prodding, spread the white race across the entire continent, especially after the severance from England.

Where were the Normans in all this? Long before the settlement began in New England, the Normans along with the Vikings had been absorbed in the English who were of course related to the Scandinavians by racial connections and by linguistic affinities. The unfortunate verse written by Daniel Defoe about the true-born Englishman has encouraged all sorts of wrong ideas about racial mixtures in England.* After the Norman Conquest, there were for a period of some 200 years infiltrations of persons from continental Europe, not only the Normans, whose leaders at any rate traced descent from the Norsemen, but Angevins, Poitevins, Bretons and men from the southwest of France. There were also, during the Middle Ages, small settlements of Flemings. On the other hand Norse or Danish settlement ceased abruptly after 1066, and it had never in all probability been very large, and the Jewish community was expelled in 1291. When the 16th century arrived, the English were a close-packed homogeneous, stock.

---

* Note 59. Daniel Defoe.

The next considerable arrival, that of the Huguenots, did not come in any size until the second half of the 17th century. In 1655 the Jews were allowed to settle in England, but did not mingle much with the natives until the 19th century when unions between British nobility and Jewish women became an increasing feature in English social life.* The Huguenots like the Normans have been completely absorbed in the English population, though naturally the knowledge of their French origin is remembered. Not only French but sometimes Norman as well, so that Norman ancestry can truthfully be claimed by some whose families arrived 300 and not 900 years ago. It was Charles Kingsley who said of a character in one of his novels that he boasted of ancestors who had come over with William I, but who had in reality arrived with William III (of Orange).

Apart from the Huguenots and the Jews no further racial elements of any but minute size arrived in England until World War II and after. In the past 30 years there have been very large additions of non-English stock, from central Europe and more particularly from the non-white lands of the former British Empire. There are now some 2 millions of such people in Britain. The great cities of the country all possess communities whose language, color, religion and social habits are alien to the make-up and traditions of England. Unthinking persons, including many ecclesiastics, talk glibly about integration. Britian is not now in any position to judge critically or caustically about the United States and its racial problems. Before 1939 there was no color problem in England. One has been deliberately created by the insanity of bringing in large numbers of West Indian, African and Pakistani elements

---

* Note 60. Jewish settlement in England.

who can never fuse with the native population. This is all part of the weakening of Britain which has lost its former high international standing and is rapidly declining into the position of a third or fourth-rate country.

In consequence of the merging of the Normans with the English, the Norman strain definitely invaded America. Here is one American's account of the process and of how its knowledge has been treasured. "All descendants of Laurence Wilkinson of Rhode Island descended from the following 17 sureties for the Magna Carta of 1215:*

William d'Albini	William Malet
Hugh Bigod	William de Mowbray
Roger Bigod	Saher de Quincy
Henry de Bohun	Robert de Roos
Gilbert de Clare	Geoffrey de Saye
Richard de Clare	Robert de Vere
John FitzRobert	Robert FitzWalter
John de Lacy	William de Huntingfield
William de Lanvallei	

"The lineage of Roger Bigod goes to the de Grey line and Darcy to Conyers thence to Wilkinson." (with acknowledgments to Mrs. Louis Toté)

Next there is a case of descent through the Blakiston, Whitby, Wingate and Davis families from William the Conqueror. Taking the start of this genealogy from the first Blakiston to land in America we have the following generations:

1.   Geoge Blakiston, *b. ca.* 1616; *d.* 30 Sept. 1669; *m.* 16 Oct. 1638, Barbara, *d.* 1672. dau. of Henry Lawson and Catherine Warmouth.

---

* Note 61. Magna Carta sureties.

2. Marmaduke Blakiston, *bur.* 3 Sept. 1639; *m.* 30 June 1595, Margaret James, *bur.* 10 Mar. 1636.
3. John Blakiston, *b.* 1535, *bur.* 7 Feb. 1586/7; *m.* Elizabeth, eldest dau. of Sir George Bowes, 1517–46.
4. George Bowes, *b.* 1517, *d.* 1546; *m.* Muriel, dau. of William Eure, of Witton.
5. Ralph Bowes, *b.* 1516, *m.* Elizabeth (or Joan), dau. of Henry Clifford.
6. Henry Clifford, *b.* 1455, *d.* 1523, *m.* before 1493 Ann, dau. of Sir John St. John.
7. John Clifford, *b.* 1435, *d.* 1461, *m.* Margaret, dau. of Henry de Bromflete, Baron de Vesci.
8. Thomas Clifford, *b.* 1414, *d.* 1455, *m.* 1424 (?) Joan, dau. of Thomas Dacre, of Gillesland.
9. John Clifford, *b.* 1388, *d.* 1422, *m.* 1412, Elizabeth, *d.* 1437, dau. of Henry Percy.
10. Henry Percy, "Hotspur," *b.* 1364, *d.* 1403, *m.* 1376, Elizabeth, living 1407, dau. of Edmund de Mortimer.
11. Edmund de Mortimer, *b.* 1352, *d.* 1387; *m.* 1368, Philippa Plantagenet, *b.* 1355, *d.* 1394, dau. of Lionel of Antwerp.
12. Lionel of Antwerp, *b.* 1338, *d.* 1368; *m.* 1352, Elizabeth, *d.* 1363, dau. of William de Burgh.
13. Edward III, etc. The next eight generations are of course those of the English royal line back to William I. (with acknowledgments to Mrs. C. Raymond Cummins)

In the two cases of Norman descent given above we have the well-known royal connection from Edward III. These lines of descent also illustrate the very considerable interaction of English medieval royalty with the families of the great nobles and theirs in turn with the lesser gentry and the rest of the Norman people.

Now we have a Norman male line descent given in the papers of the Hartwell family in America. The details below are described as taken from *The History of the Family of Hartwell*, a ms. book of the 4th baronet Hartwell, now in possession of the 5th baronet, Sir Brodrick Hartwell, of Lavendon, Bucks. It is stated from this source that at the Norman Conquest the manor of Hartwell (or Hertwells), in Northamptonshire, was granted to Odo, half brother to William I, whose sub-tenant was William Peverel, who enfeoffed a family, whose surname was eventually taken from the place. The pedigree goes thus: Geoffrey de Hartwell had issue three sons, Simon, William and Henry. The eldest had a son, Geoffrey of Hartwell, and from him the line is traced to the 17th century, when Hartwell ceased to belong to the family. According to a note in *Burke's Peerage* the family was then scattered and some members served in the Irish wars of the period. It is from soldiers of that time that the descent of the present baronets is traced. There is a considerable Hartwell Family Association in America, The Hartwells of America, and it is to their useful production, *The Beetle Gazette*, that I am obliged for the above information.

What was the proportion of Norman ancestry in these early settlers? Possibly, if not probably, higher than in the present-day English population, for many Norman-descended families sent their scions to the colonies but have since become extinct or obscured so as to be unknown in modern England. An American scholar has written: "From a considerable investigation (i.e., of the early settlers) I should say that in New England they were rather a cross section of the middle classes. The smaller upper crust of the settlers was made up of cadets of the Puritan county families, well-to-do merchants, and clothiers and the Puritan clergy, while the bulk of the emigrants were substantial yeomen. Of the lower classes there was little emigration, which was quite costly in those days."

There is much force in this view. It was the embracing of Protestant beliefs at the time of the Reformation by the higher classes which turned the scale in England in favor of Protestantism. The propertied men at the end of Henry VIII's reign or Edward VI's had made a substantial profit out of the dissolution of the monasteries and this rendered the attempted return to Catholicism under Mary very difficult. In every country which adhered permanently to Protestantism, the monasteries were abolished, and always the wealthier classes owed much of their new property to the former monastic lands. England was no exception and out of this Protestant upper class came many of the most determined Puritan leaders, like the wealthy Cromwell family. Even when the lower social ranks provided Puritan recruits they were, as remarked above, frequently from the class of the substantial yeomen. Often these yeomen families were offshoots of older baronial lines of Norman stock. The emigrant from England may not always have known of his Normanity but the researches of his 10th, 11th or 12th generation American descendants have ferretted out the noble blood.

"Among the early settlers were Throckmortons, Wentworths, Bulkeleys, etc. Isaac Johnson and John Humphrey came with their wives, the ladies Arabella and Susanna, daughters of the Earl of Lincoln. Jeremy Clarke, who belonged to the Clarkes of Ford in Kent, was a nephew of Richard Weston, Earl of Portland, the lord treasurer under King James, and was named for his maternal grandfather, Sir Jeremy Weston, chief baron of the exchequer under Elizabeth. One of the Mildmays was an early undergraduate at Harvard, and Herbert Pelham, first treasurer of Harvard, belonged to the Pelhams and was a grandson of Lord de la Warr. Sir Richard Saltonstall and John Winthrop belonged to the new rich, whose families rose in the social revolution of the 16th century. Brewster of Plymouth had been secretary to Davidson, Elizabeth's secretary of state, and went with him in the embassy to the Netherlands, long before he sailed in the *Mayflower*. The bulk of Plymouth Colony (*Mayflower*) settlers were rather humble folk, more so than those at the Bay, but there were some gentlefolk among them, such as Standish, whose descendants still flourish among us, Winslow, Richard Warren, the London merchant, and a few others. Bradford, the historian of the colony, came of a family of very well-to-do yeomen in Yorkshire which have been traced to the early 16th century. The Massachusetts rulers were particular in not allowing the dregs of society to be sent over to them. Before 1640 there were 104 graduates of Cambridge and 22 of Oxford, mostly Puritan clergy and quite a few members of the London Livery Companies. In the non-Puritan colony of Virginia, the situation was somewhat different. The percentage of the Tudor and Stuart gentry, Throckmortons, Skipwiths, Berkeleys, Culpeppers, Digges, etc., was higher than in New England, but they also had a goodly number of the dregs of society, the sweepings of the London streets, sent out as indentured servants."*

Among the names mentioned above some will at once be remembered as borne by Norman-descended folk, others as those of people sharing in the royal blood. The American Throckmortons were given a special place in

---

* Information supplied to author by correspondent.

Burke's Peerage after the article on their English cousins. The Standish family became extinct in the male line, in England, though the female line descendants assumed the name and arms. The latter are a play on the name, being three dishes or standing plates. The surname is from a place in Lancashire, and as can be seen from the above quotation the male line is still known in America. Shades of Miles Standish! So here is one instance of a family of ancient, possibly Norman, lineage, extinct in England, save through female line descendants, but known in the U.S.A. The Earldom of Lincoln to which reference was made is now a title of the Dukes of Newcastle, the Clintons, again Normans through the female line, so that any American descendants are on a par with their British relations.

The colony of Maryland, as everyone knows, was founded by George Calvert, who was made Lord Baltimore of Baltimore, in the county of Longford in Ireland, by James I in 1624. He had from Charles I a patent of Maryland as a lord proprietor. It was his son, the 2nd Lord, who founded the colony, the patent being made out in his name in 1632, his father having died before he could complete it. It would have been strange if in settling the colony this nobleman had not been careful as to his colonists and their quality. The system of lords proprietors was much used in what may be called the second wave of colony founding and it must have had an effect upon the social quality of the settlers and hence their share of Norman blood.

Thus the stage was set in the Thirteen Colonies for families of the better classes to settle in New England. A fair percentage of these were of Norman descent in the male line and I have been careful to indicate many cases throughout this book. Nearly all must have a mixture of

Norman blood owing to the way in which that strain has pervaded our population. Large numbers of the immigrants have been discovered by subsequent research as of Norman descent through royal and noble ancestors.

American interest in and literature on genealogy is very great and one cannot read far in the published works on the subject of family history without coming upon references to the Norman progenitors. In *The American Genealogist* (July 1952) the editor, Donald Line Jacobus, wrote of the royal ancestry of Alice Tomes Welles: "The discovery made by Col. Charles E. Banks that the wife of Gov. Thomas Welles of Connecticut was Alice Tomes, of an English county or gentry family, was published in 1926 in *The New England Historical and Genealogical Register* (Vol. 80, p. 279 ff.). This was, of course, followed by the attempts of amateurs to discover, by use of English printed sources, some line of ancestry for her which would go back to royalty. Such a line appeared in print and was widely copied, going from the Tomes family through the Fulwood and Milton families to the wife of one of the Miltons who was daughter of Sir Adam Peshall by his wife who belonged to the baronial house of Botetourt and had undoubtedly royal ancestry."

In a volume issued by Mr. Wurts, descents are shown at great length from the Magna Carta barons which would yield the high prize of Normanity through the links which most of these barons had with the Conqueror's knights and the Plantagenets.

It is often said that America has little history compared with England's 2,000 years of documented record. It is not 200 years since the U.S.A. began; not much over 350 since the first colonies were founded. Americans nevertheless have this great advantage: Their settlements were made in a literate and civilized age. Arthur Meredith

Burke, one of Sir Bernard Burke's sons, wrote: "In this respect the United States of America stands alone among the great nations of the world. The first history of the nation as representing a civilized country is known intimately and decisively with full, reliable and accurate records, dating as it were from the beginning of time." (*The Prominent Families of America*, Vol. I, 1908, containing 500 pages and many American pedigrees very carefully worked out; unfortunately no other volume came out to complete the work.) Among the Virginia settlers the author noted Washington, Carter, Randolph, Lee, Byrd, Page, Fairfax, Harrison, Bolling, Claiborne, Digges, Conway, Cabell, Ashton, FitzHugh, Fowke, Gordon, Henry, Pendleton, Slaughter, Tyler and Chichester—all as being still represented in America. Among individuals there were also Sir George Somers, Sir George Yardley, of an ancient family, and Sir Ferdinando Gorges, whose Norman ancestors have already been mentioned.

Another prolific source of Norman descents is to be found in the lists of armigerous persons issued by the Committee on Heraldry of the New England Historic Genealogical Society. I can only quote a selection here, without room for comment: Bracey, Bulkeley, Cranston, Davenport, Fenwick, Fitch, Manwaring, Marshall, Mason, Pelham, Pole, Saltonstall, Thorold, Throckmorton, Washington, Wentworth, Willoughby, Clinton, Channey, Dudley, Gorges, Livingston, Colpeper, Josselyn, Standish, Carteret, Hooke, Barclay, Champernoune, Crispin, Skipwith, Reade, Randolph, Percy, Delafield, Winslow, Bellingham, Chetwood, Eden, Kyle, Lisle, Rodney, Baskerville, de Courcy, Daubeny, Isham, Montague, Washbourne, Zouch. Here is a glimpse of the widespread nature of American participation in Norman blood. In many cases the American scion has a surer line of descent than the present-day British family which bears the same surname. If the modern American has his descent to the original immigrant ancestor and if that ancestor is known to have been a member of the old English family, then the present-day scion in the U.S. is 300 or more years nearer to a Norman pedigree than someone bearing a Norman name but who has not traced his ancestry in England before 1800.

It is hard to know where to stop in writing of American Normans. The name of Disney was anciently written de Isney or D'Eisney and was, according to the family genealogy, originally derived from the town of Isigny, near Bayeux in Normandy, whence it was brought into England. At the end of the 11th century the first member of the family settled in England was Lambert de Isney, who made his home at Norton, hence called Norton d'Isney in the wapentake of Boothby Graffoe, in the parts of Kesteven in Lincolnshire, and from him descend the main line of Disney of the Hyde in Essex, and the junior lines outside England, which included Walter Elias Disney, of Hollywood, the creator of Mickey Mouse and Donald Duck.

From Lincolnshire also there went the New Jersey family of Kyme (in America spelled Kime). One account attributed their origin to the Saxons; but it is certain that they derived their name from Kyme in Kesteven, where from early Norman times they are found as landowners, always bearing Norman Christian names. They were formerly holders of the great barony of Kyme, in which William de Kyme was summoned to Parliament from 1323 to 1336. This barony is one of those still in abeyance and which could be called out of vacuity in favor of a descendant of the old lords.

The Norman origin of Bassett has been mentioned so

that it is not surprising to read in the genealogy of William Busnet Kinney Bassett, of Pottersville, New Jersey, that his surname was brought into England by the Normans; and that few families in the early annals of England can boast of a more eminent progenitor. The descendants of few of the Anglo-Norman nobles attained a higher degree of power.

William Ashmead Dyer, of Ardmore, Pennsylvania, had a Graham ancestry from Malise Graham, Earl of Menteth, son of Patrick Graham, Earl of Strathern, by Euphemia, Countess of Strathern, the latter being connected with the Norman Muschamp family.

I have mentioned the Grosvenors and their American relatives whose name is spelled Gravenor. A large branch of the family settled in America, e.g., in 1939, Grahame Bethune Grosvenor, a director of Pan American Airways, was living on Long Island. His middle name recalls another ancient race, celebrated by Sir Walter Scott: "Bethune's line of Picardy." In the early records of Cheshire the names Grosvenor and Gravenor are frequently interchangeable. In 1663 Leicester Grosvenor, or Gravenor, of the Friars, Bridgnorth, Salop, entered the pedigree at the Heralds' Visitation. Commencing from his grandfather, William Grosvenor of Bridgnorth, he claimed descent from the Grosvenors of Cheshire; and there is reason to suppose that Adam de Grosvenor, from whom the American line can show descent and who lived in the reign of Edward I, was descended from the Duke of Westminster's family before that period (1272–1307).

The Birches claim descent, with some good reason, from the Birch family of Ardwick and of Birch in Lancashire. The Binghams are traditionally sprung from the Binghams of Melcombe in Dorset; the Hydes from a branch of the same family as the Earls of Clarendon. The name of William Henry de Courcy Wright enshrines the memory of a descent from the de Courcys. Norman lineage is indeed very much to be found in the great and the lesser names of America. One revealing example occurs in connection with Elihu Yale. He was a member of the Honourable East India Company and Governor of Madras. Being a great benefactor of the collegiate school of Connecticut, his name was adopted for Yale University. He belonged to the same branch as the Yales of Plas-yn-ial, in Carmarthenshire. They like other ancient Welsh houses, the Wynnes of Glyn and the Wynnes of Penarth, descend from Osbern called Wyddel or "foreigner" by the Welsh because he had emigrated from Ireland to Wales. His original name was Osborn FitzGerald, one of the Norman invaders of Ireland.

From my numerous correspondents I have received a great deal of information which is not in books, but in their family papers. The following account from a member of the Bayne family is of considerable interest because it shows the ramifications of Norman and royal ancestry. After mentioning the Baynes of Westmoreland County, Virginia, and later of New York and of Georgia, the writer goes on:

"My grandfather, Col. Thomas Levingston Bayne, C.S.A., married a dau. of the Hon. John Gayle, Governor of Alabama (of the family of Gale, of Whitehaven, Cumberland, England). My father bore . . . the arms . . . azure a wolf's head erased or armed and langued gules. My mother was descended from Col. Robert Carter, of Corotoman, in Virginia, known as King Carter (1663–1732). According to his obituary in the *Gentleman's Magazine*, London, he left an estate of 300,000 acres. As president of the King's Council, he was for a year acting Governor of Virginia and had filled most of the high positions in the colony.

"The Carters were connected with most of the prominent families of colonial Virginia, the recognized ruling aristocracy of the colony. Among my mother's ancestry were Armestead Carys (a cadet of the Bristol Carys, now represented by Cary-Elwes) and others. All these Virginians bore arms. Considering their social status when they came to Virginia, I presume that the arms that appear upon their early 18th century tombs were arms they brought with them. 'King' Carter's mother was Sarah Ludlow, dau. of Gabriel Ludlow, of Dinton, Wiltshire, England, a grandson of George Ludlow, of Hill Deverell in the same country who married Edith, dau. of Sir Andrew Windsor, K.B., Baron Windsor, of Stanwell, Middlesex (d. 1543), by Elizabeth, granddau. of Sir Walter Blount, K.G., Baron Mountjoy (d. 1474). The evidence for the descent of Lord Windsor from Edward I through the families of Bohun, Courtenay, Luttrell, Stratton and Andrews is handled in a very thorough manner in *The American Genealogist,* Vol. XV, No, 3, Jan. 1939. The arms of Cary of Devon were carved on the altar tomb of Col. Miles Cary (1623–67). His grandfathers were both mayors of Bristol (William Cary and Henry Hobson). These arms were confirmed to the Bristol Carys (with the usual differences) in 1699. In Virginia their kinsmen continued to bear them undifferenced. At the time of the confirmation Baron Hunsdon and Cary, of Torre Abbey, Devon, deposed to the effect that the Carys of Bristol were kinsmen. In Bristol, the family has now died out and is represented by Cary-Elwes. I have many Cary cousins in Virginia. The sister of Ann Cary (my great-great-great-grandmother) married the 8th Baron Fairfax, then a resident of Virginia. The present Lord Fairfax descends from them."

In another case, an American of unimpeachable English ancestry, was desirous of obtaining a grant of arms from the English College to whom he wrote in the following terms:

"My mother was a Howard whose family, allegedly connected with the Duke of Norfolk's family, came to Virginia and was prominent in colonial government circles there in the early 18th century. Her mother was a Lewis, the family having been founded in America by one John Lewis who came from Northern Ireland in 1737, a friend of Lord Dunraven and settled Stainton, Virginia, after receiving a grant of 1,000,000 acres of land in the Shenandoah Valley from King George II. My father's original ancestor came from England to Massachusetts between 1620 and 1639, and helped John Davenport found the new colony of New Haven in 1639. My father's family also included John Howland who came over in the *Mayflower,* and other English families, including Denisons, Chesebroughs and Washburns."

Another of my correspondents sends me the following information with regard to descent through a line of the Mumford family. Thomas Mumford of Newport, Rhode Island, m. Sarah Sherman, 1655; in 1657 joined others in buying great Pettaquamscutt purchase (Narrangansett country), now north and south Kingston; was Constable; member of the first Episcopal Church in South Kingston and Wickford; active in civic affairs. The Mumford family has two ancient seals, the shields are similar, but the crests are different. Dr. James Mumford states that authorities date the oldest of these as of Elizabethan times (in possession some time ago of Edward Winslow Paige, of New York City). The crest is a talbot's head. The later seal, owned by G. D. Mumford, of New York City, has a demi-cat for crest. According to the present Garter King of Arms, Sir Anthony Wagner, there was a Mumford family in Sussex about 1570 who were allowed by the heralds arms closely resembling those of the Montforts of Warwickshire who go back to very early days.

I am obliged to Mrs. Richard Hartung for sending me some notes with regard to the well-known Irish surname of Woulfe, which like that of Burke would appear to have been adopted widespread throughout Ireland from a non-Irish original. Mrs. Hartung has sent me various details, including some references to Dr. MacLysaght's book, *Irish Families: Their Names, Arms and Origins*. In this appears the following passage: "The Woulfes, or Wolfes, are a family of Norman origin, who first came to Ireland at the time of the invasion at the end of the twelfth century. In Irish the name is usually written *de Bhulbh* but *le* would be more fitting than *de* since the Norman form is Le Woulf (the wolf). Though both influential and fairly numerous they never actually formed a sept on the Irish model, as did several of the Anglo-Norman invading families. From the beginning they settled in two widely separated areas. In co. Killdare they became so well established that their territory near Athy was known as Woulfe's Country. The Wolfes of Forenaughts, co. Kildare were still extensive landowners in that county and also in co. Limerick in 1880."

To conclude this study it may not be inappropriate to refer to the fact that many of the presidents of the United States are related in the ramifications of genealogy and that these connections often stem from English and ancient Norman roots. In fact so close is the connection between the presidential families that an American scholar has not scrupled to refer to the presidential dynasty of the U.S.A. He refers to 12 families, all interrelated who can be singled out to form the interlocking presidential dynasty. "These 12, the families of Adams, Bayard, Breckinridge, Harrison, Kennedy, Lee, Livingston, Lodge, Randolph, Roosevelt, Taft and Tucker are the core of our dynasty."*

As so many presidents' families are connected, there is naturally a very wide inclusion of men holding high office, so that from a study of these genealogies, one can speak of a ruling class in America. Looking through the several tables of descent one is struck by the recurrence of names which earlier in this study we have associated with the Normans. Thus we have names such as Isham, Tailboys, Dymoke, and in the ancestry of Gen. George Washington a carefully traced descent from Edward I. The Livingstons descend from James IV of Scotland by his mistress Isabel Stuart. President Taft's ancestry includes the old Cheney family of England.

In considering the numerous lines of Norman descent there is need for great caution before conclusions are taken for granted. As I have pointed out earlier, most if not all people of English descent must have Norman blood. Research continues to prove that an increasing number of us are of royal stock, legitimate at that. From these established facts, to assume that the possession of a Norman surname guarantees Norman descent or affiliation to another family of the same name, is to repeat the mistakes of 18th and 19th century genealogists without their excuses. Since their time immense research has been given to the subject and many conclusions established

---

* Note 62. Presidential dynasty of the U.S.A.

which render a too facile connection with desirable ancestors unlikely.

The advice then which must be given to the aspirant after Normanity is that he or she should prove every step of the pedigree, never allowing that contradiction in terms, a gap in the family tree. Even when research has reached medieval times, the seeker must remember that the paucity of records at crucial points such as the period from 1086 to 1135 may leave him in the position that he cannot be positive. Tantalizing no doubt, but all pedigrees must end somewhere, and truth must be the main consideration. We strive at times to pierce the darkness of unrecorded time. There is a fascination in wondering what the people were like who were responsible for our presence in the 20th century. When we reflect that sometimes we come upon a bundle of old letters written perhaps 100 to 200 years ago, and that then people whose names have been merely entries of birth, marriage and death, become for a few brief moments, people of flesh and blood—when we think in this vein we wish that some similar discoveries could enrich our knowledge of all our predecessors. Carlyle reproached the monkish chronicler who had actually seen King John on a visit to his abbey, and had allowed him no more mention than to record his exactions from the abbot. He had had John Lackland there before his very eyes and he left succeeding ages no picture.

We can then use our imagination provided that we distinguish between its productions and the records of proven facts. Foremost in the imagination of all English descended folk must be that day, 14 October, over 900 years ago, when the destinies of the English-speaking race, and so of the world, took a new and revolutionary course. The late afternoon of a bright October day; a grimly contested battle on a hill in Sussex, framed on three sides by the deep forest; the issue very much in doubt. Then a great leader in one of those split-second decisions which change the fate of battles, ordered his archers so to shoot that their arrows fell as though directly from the sky above the opposing host. The result was victory for the invader, and the entry into the English nation of a new strain, giving a new direction to England, so that it would never be the same again. Everyone who belongs to the Anglo-Saxon or English race has participated in that remote event for it has vitally affected everyone of us.

English Counties

Most of the references in this book to counties concern those of England. There are 40 counties in England; 12 in Wales; 32 in Ireland (6 in Northern Ireland or Ulster, and 26 in Eire); and 33 in Scotland. English county divisions are often very old, many of them going back to Saxon times. They are called shires, the Old English name, while the word 'county' refers more to the administrative term introduced by the Normans, with their counts who ruled over an area equivalent to the English shire. Both shire and county are used to designate the same areas in modern English. The list given below shows the full name of a shire, then its abbreviation:

Bedfordshire (Beds)
Berkshire (Berks)
Buckinghamshire (Bucks)
Cambridgeshire (Cambs)
Cheshire
Cornwall
Cumberland
Derbyshire
Devonshire (usually put as Devon)
Dorsetshire (usually Dorset)

Durham (sometimes Durhamshire)
Essex
Gloucestershire (Glos)
Hampshire (Hants)
Herefordshire (Herefs)
Hertfordshire (Herts)
Huntingdonshire (Hunts)
Kent
Lancashire (Lancs)
Leicestershire (Leics)
Lincolnshire (Lincs)
Middlesex
Monmouthshire (Mon)
Norfolk
Northamptonshire (Northants)
Northumberland
Nottinghamshire (Notts)
Oxfordshire (Oxon)
Rutland (sometimes Rutlandshire)
Shropshire (Salop)
Somerset (sometimes Somersetshire)
Staffordshire (Staffs)
Suffolk (an east and west div.)
Surrey
Sussex (an east and west div.)
Warwickshire (Warwicks)
Westmorland
Wiltshire (Wilts)
Worcestershire (Worcs)
Yorkshire (Yorks)

The above are the names of the famous 40 shires of England. The Isle of Wight is part of Hampshire, but administratively separate. London is of course an administrative county. The Isle of Ely is in Cambridgeshire; the Soke of Peterborough in Northamptonshire. Lincolnshire has three very ancient divisions, Lindsey,

Kesteven and Holland. There are three divisions of Yorkshire—West Riding, East Riding, and North Riding. Sussex has six Rapes, another ancient term of division.

Kings of England from Earliest Times

Old English or Saxon Kings
> Egbert regnal years, as King of Wessex, 802–839.
> Ethelwulf, 839–58.
> Ethelbald, 858–60.
> Ethelbert, 860–65.
> Ethelred I, 865–71.
> Alfred the Great, 871–99 (in older books date given as 901).
> Edward I, the Elder, 899–924.
> Athelstan, 924–39.
> Edmund I, 939–46.
> Edred, 946–55.
> Edwy, 955–59.
> Edgar, 959–75.
> Edward II, the Martyr, 975–78.
> Ethelred II, the Unready, 978–1016.
> Edmund II, Ironside, 1016.

Danish Kings
> Sweyn Forkbeard, king of part of England, 1014.
> Canute, 1016–35.
> Harthacnut or Hardicanute, 1040–42.
> Harold I, 1035–40.

English line restored
>   Edward III (the Confessor), 1042–66.
>   Harold II, 1066.

Norman line
>   William I (the Conqueror), 1066–87.
>   William II (Rufus), 1087–1100.
>   Henry I, 1100–35.
>   Stephen, 1135–54.

Plantagenet or Angevin dynasty
>   Henry II, 1154–89.
>   Richard I, 1189–99.
>   John, 1199–1216.
>   Henry III, 1216–72.
>   Edward I (i.e., post-Conquest), 1272–1307.
>   Edward II, 1307–27.
>   Edward III, 1327–77.
>   Richard II, 1377–99.

House of Lancaster (Plantagenet)
>   Henry IV, 1399–1413.
>   Henry V, 1413–22.
>   Henry VI, 1422–61.

House of York (Plantagenet)
>   Edward IV, 1461–83.
>   Edward V, 1483.
>   Richard III, 1483–85.

House of Tudor
>   Henry VII, 1485–1509.
>   Henry VIII, 1509–47.
>   Edward VI, 1547–53.
>   Lady Jane Grey, reigned 9 days, 1553
>   Mary I, 1553–58.
>   Elizabeth I, 1558–1603.

House of Stuart
>James I (James VI of Scotland), 1603–25.
>Charles I, 1625–49.

Republic of England (Commonwealth), 1649–60.
>Oliver Cromwell, Protector, 1654–58.
>Richard Cromwell, 1658.

House of Stuart restored
>Charles II, 1660–85.
>James II, 1685–88.
>Mary II and William III of Orange (Mary, 1689–94, William, 1689–1702).
>Anne, 1702–14.

House of Hanover, or Brunswick (Guelph)
>George I, 1714–27.
>George II, 1727–60.
>George III, 1760–1820.
>George IV, 1820–30.
>William IV, 1830–37.
>Victoria, 1837–1901.
>Edward VII, 1901–10.

House of Windsor (name taken 1917)
>George V, 1910–36.
>Edward VIII, 1936.
>George VI, 1936–52.
>Elizabeth II, 1952—

Glossary

Armed—a term applied to the horns, hoofs, beaks and talons of an animal when they differ from the color of the rest of the body, in heraldic drawings and pictures.

Azure—blue.

Bretwalda—literally, ruler of Britain, a term given to an English king when he gained supremacy over the neighboring kingdoms in Saxon times.

Charge—(or ordinary), any figure borne on the field or ground of a coat of arms.

Commendation—a technical term in the Middle Ages when a man placed himself in vassalage to another.

Commoners—persons who are not peers. In England only a peer and his wife are noble.

Confirmation—a term used to denote the acceptance by an heraldic authority of arms in use. Confirmation is usually accompanied by the addition of a difference mark to the arms.

County families—a term used in older literature in England to denote as a rule families who do not possess titles but who are of the same social class as the titled.

Couped—cut off by a straight line (contrast *erased*), applied to the head or limbs of an animal.

Crest—object shown on top of helmet in a coat of arms. Term often used wrongly in place of coat of arms.

Erased—in contrast to *couped,* means forcibly torn off the body, leaving the severed part jagged.

Ermine—white fur with black spots.

Ermines—black fur with white spots.

Erminois—gold fur with black spots.

Fess—a charge or ordinary formed by two horizontal lines across the shield, taking up one-third of the area.

Feudal system—a term invented by historians of the Middle Ages to denote the system of land tenure by which a vassal held land from his overlord. There is still much discussion among scholars as to the exact meaning of the term.

Fiefs—name given to lands held of a feudal superior.

Fine—a sum levied by the English Crown for the performance of certain acts.

Fyrd—the levée of the Old English kingdom, bound to serve when summoned by the king.

Generation—length of, is reckoned by genealogists as 30 years; in older days, sometimes as 40 years, but in 20th century likely to be less than 25.

Gules—red.

Homage—the act by which the vassal gave promise of fealty or obedience to his lord, in which the vassal put his hands between those of his lord and said, "je suis votre homme."

Honor—a term used to include a number of manors, a large fief.

Hundred—originally an area sufficient to support 100 families.

Inquisitio post mortem—inquiry made by the Crown on the death of an estate owner in the Middle Ages, as to sums due before the heir could enter upon his inheritance.

Knights' fees—the amount of land capable of supporting a mounted knight and his retinue; about two carucates or 240 acres.

Landed gentry—another term for the county families. The peers and baronets are the titled aristocracy; the landed gentry, the untitled.

Langued—when the tongue of an animal is of a different tincture from that of the rest of the body.

Lozenge—a charge shaped like a diamond and four sided.

Modern and ancient—coats of arms. Some families have acquired two coats of arms, because in ignorance of their existing coat, they have obtained a new one. When the existence of the earlier coat is discovered, the two can be quartered, 1 and 4 being ancient, 2 and 3 modern.

Ogam script—name of the earliest inscriptions in Ireland before the introduction of letters.

Or—gold.

Ordinary—an heraldic charge, a term very frequently used.

Pipe Rolls—or Great Rolls of the Pipe, or of the Exchequer, so-called because the documents were rolled round a rod or pipe. They are largely financial records which give the findings of the Exchequer officials on specific questions of revenue.

Popinjays—parrots in heraldry.

Quarterings—when two or more coats of arms are shown in the same shield. Thus the royal arms of England: 1 and 4, England; 2, Scotland, and 3, Ireland.

Runic inscriptions—found in the Scandinavian countries in use before the introduction of letters.

Tiger—heraldic, different from real tiger which in

heraldry is called a Bengal tiger. The heraldic tiger has a lion's tufted tail and mane, no stripes on body and a head perhaps closest to that of a wolf.

Undifferenced—said of the bearing of arms without any change being made to them, e.g., a chief of a Scottish Highland clan bears undifferenced arms; the heads of the junior branches of the clan must have differenced arms.

Vassal—Low Latin, *vassus,* from Celtic *gwas,* a boy. The term used for a man who holds land from an overlord. E.g., William the Conqueror as King of England was a lord, with vassals under him; as Duke of Normandy he was a vassal of the French King.

Notes

NOTE 1. p. 18. Irish pedigrees. The best account of the latter is found in Prof. David Greene's article, *The Irish Genealogies,* at the beginning of the 1958 edition of *Burke's Landed Gentry of Ireland.* The latter work contains numerous examples of traditional Irish genealogies as viewed by modern scholarship.

NOTE 2. p. 19. Welsh history. For information on Welsh history and tradition, Sir Edward Lloyd's *History of Wales,* to 1284 (the time of conquest by Edward I) is the best. As to the present state of research on King Arthur, the best book is *The Quest for Arthur's Britain* (1968) by Geoffrey Ashe, Leslie Alcock, C. A. Raleigh Radford, Philip Rahtz, and Jill Racy. This work gives a full account of the Arthurian literature and the excavations at Cadbury in Somerset.

NOTE 3. p. 21. Highland Clans. Lord Macaulay's *History of England* (Everyman edition, 1953, Vol. II, p. 617). "Soon the vulgar imagination was so completely occupied by plaids, targets and claymores, that by most Englishmen, Scotchman and Highlander were regarded as synonymous words. Few people seemed to be aware that, at no remote period, a Macdonald or a Macgregor in his tartan was to a citizen of Edinburgh or Glasgow what an Indian hunter in his war paint was to an inhabitant of

241

Philadelphia or Boston. Artists and actors represented Bruce and Douglas in striped petticoats. They might as well have represented Washington brandishing a toma-hawk and girt with a string of scalps."

NOTE 4. p. 22. English royal pedigrees. The *Anglo-Saxon Chronicle* (Everyman's Library, 1953, p. 66) gives the descent under the record for the year 855, of King Ethelwulf, son of King Egbert of Wessex from Adam, the first man. It is from Egbert that Her Majesty, Elizabeth II, descends.

NOTE 5. p. 24. Hereward the Wake. A long account of the information respecting this celebrated hero is given in E. A. Freeman's *Norman Conquest,* Vol. IV. Appendix 00, p. 804. In the opening of Charles Kingsley's novel, *Hereward the Wake,* there is a good summing up of the details known about Hereward, together with the author's views as to his parentage. A less known work is *de Gestis Herewardi Saxonis,* transcribed by S. H. Miller from an original manuscript in the possession of the Dean and Chapter of Peterborough (1895), and translated by the Rev. W. D. Sweeting, with the Latin and English in parallel columns.

NOTE 6. p. 27. *Domesday Book.* An immense amount of study has been given to the subject by both English and foreign scholars. One of the best modern studies is *The Making of Domesday Book,* by V. H. Galbraith (1961); other and earlier views are given in *Domesday Book and After* (1897, reprinted 1965), by F. W. Maitland; *The Constitutional History of England* (1908), by F. W. Mait-land; *Feudal England,* by J. H. Round (1909), has a large amount on *Domesday.* The fifth volume of E. A. Free-man's *Norman Conquest* gives much detail. Two later works of value are *The Governance of Medieval England from the Conquest to Magna Carta* (1963), by H. G. Richardson and G. O. Sayles and *The Medieval Foundations of England,* by G. O. Sayles (1948). The subject of the *Domesday*

Book, like that of the Norman settlement in England of which it formed a part has been discussed at much length. Most of the expositors of the subject have spent at least half their space combatting the views of other writers.

NOTE 7. p. 30. Attitudes toward the Normans. A very interesting account is in Christopher Hill's *Puritanism and Revolution* (1962), which has a chapter (3) entitled "The Norman Yoke" (pp. 50–123). This traces the course of English attitudes toward the Conquest from the end of the 13th century to 1954. On the whole, English sentiment has been anti-Norman.

NOTE 8. p. 32. Use of French in England. The speech of the upper classes up to the 13th century was French, though their understanding and use of English must have been considerable. The language of heraldry was taken from France. Attempts to render French heraldic terms in English about 1400 failed. In the Parliament, French was used until 1362 when a statute was passed that English was to be the language of the courts. (J. Enoch Powell & Keith Wallis, *The House of Lords in the Middle Ages* [1968], where many details are given. Cf. also O. Hood Phillips, *The Principles of English Law and the Constitution* [1939].) From the reign of Henry VII all acts are in English though much Norman French lingered in the law courts until 1735.

NOTE 9. p. 36. Old English poetry can be studied in *Anglo-Saxon Poetry,* selected and translated by Prof. R. K. Gordon (1954). This work contains 34 poems dating from 650 to 1000 A.D. They are varied in content ranging from *Beowulf* to the *Battle of Maldon,* and include many religious poems, apart from *The Dream of the Rood,* mentioned in the text.

NOTE 10. p. 37. Norman military ability. Some modern authorities do not allow the Normans military superiority.

Thus Richardson and Sayles in *The Governance of Medieval England,* remark on p. 27: "The Normans had very little to teach, even in the art of war." Also, p. 61: "There was no evolution in the art of war."

NOTE 11. p. 40. Hilaire Belloc's *History of England,* in 4 vols., Vol. I. (1925) p. 237: "The doubtful new borderland . . . but lately broken into Christian order, by the blows of Charlemagne's French armies."

NOTE 12. p. 49. *English Historical Documents* is a series of books giving the sources of English History from *circa* A.D. 500 to 1914. The two volumes which principally concern students of the Norman Conquest are Vol. I (500–1042) and Vol. II (1042–1189). Out of the 12 volumes planned, 8 have been published to date.

NOTE 13. p. 50. Ethelred's invasion of Normandy. Whatever the truth behind this story there was animosity between Normandy and England. "By the summer of 990 the English and Norman courts had become openly hostile to each other." Sir Frank Stenton, *Anglo-Saxon England,* (1943) p. 370. A negotiation was followed by a treaty between Ethelred and the Duke in 991.

NOTE 14. p. 52. Norse sagas. An easily accessible work is the translation of Samuel Laing: *Heimskringla: The Norse King Sagas,* (Everyman's edition, 1951). Very valuable is *A History of the Vikings,* by Prof. Gwyn Jones, (1968) in which not only the sagas but every aspect of Norse history is handled.

NOTE 15. p. 54. Lord Lytton's novel, *Harold,* in many respects a most romantic departure from the truth, does illustrate well the slight persistence of Norse speech in the Bayeux area.

NOTE 16. p. 50. The late Earl of Onslow's book which has been quoted in the text is the best account of the Norman rulers. *The Dukes of Normandy and their Origins*

(1945). Those who consult the modern editions of
Burke's Peerage will also find an account of the Dukes of
Normandy in the section before the royal lineage.

NOTE 17. p. 64. Historians of the Conquest are numerous,
and include E. A. Freeman and Sir Frank Stenton. The
former produced a monumental work in 6 vols., mentioned above. The first volume appeared in 1870. It was
given a great deal of criticism by J. H. Round, but remains a source of information on every person and event
of the period. Stenton's *Anglo-Saxon England* in the *Oxford
History of England* is of great service. The modern standard
work on the life of William is by Prof. David C. Douglas:
William the Conqueror, The Norman Impact upon England
(1964).

NOTE 18. p. 69. Lives of the Confessor are collected in
a volume of the *Rerum Britannicarum medii aevi scriptores,*
or Chronicles and Memorials of Great Britain and Ireland
during the Middle Ages, a volume in the Rolls Series,
so-called because the Master of the Rolls in London in
1857 proposed that there should be published materials
for the history of England. *The Lives of Edward the Confessor*
(1858) was edited by H. R. Luard. Included in the
volume were three works: a history of King Edward,
written about 1269 but supposedly based on earlier
work; an abridged life based on Aelred of Rievaulx, and
a contemporary Latin life written between 1066–74 for
Queen Edith.

NOTE 19. p. 72. The title of Confessor. In the *Acta
Sanctorum,* the lives of the saints produced by the Bol-
landists, there is an entry (*Januari tomus primus xi priores
dies complectens,* p. 300) which gives the text of the Bull for
the canonization of St. Edward the Confessor in 1163.
The relevant passage simply refers to the Saint as the
Confessor without giving any reason for the use of the title.
In translation, it reads: "On the common counsel of our

brethren and in accord with the wish and desire of our beloved son the king and yours, we determine that just as the Lord has glorified the said Confessor by his grace in heaven, so we consider that the body of the Confessor should be glorified and honoured in accordance with his merits on earth. Hence let it be understood that for the rest he is to be numbered among the Confessors who thus himself deserved to obtain the like honor with God for his merits and virtues."

NOTE 20. p. 74. Plato—in the *Republic*, Bk. V, p. 473, "Unless it happens either that philosophers acquire the kingly power in states or that those who are now called kings and potentates be imbued with a sufficient measure of genuine philosophy . . . there will be no deliverance for the human race."

NOTE 21. p. 74. Marcus Aurelius. Edward Gibbon in the 4th chapter of *The Decline and Fall of the Roman Empire* says of Marcus Aurelius: "His excellent understanding was often deceived by the unsuspecting goodness of his heart" and again, referring to the licentious conduct of Aurelius's wife, Faustina, "Marcus was the only man in the empire who seemed unaware or insensible of the irregularities of Faustina."

NOTE 22. p. 75. Duke William's visit to England in 1051. There is considerable difficulty in the matter of the visit which Duke William is said, by one of the old chroniclers (AS. 'D' 1052), to have paid to Edward the Confessor in England. The only time when this could have taken place would have been in 1051–52 when the Godwinsons were in exile, and when Edward fully controlled his kingdom. This was a time of great unrest in the Norman duchy. One of the modern authorities, Dr. Sayles (*The Medieval Foundations of England*, ch. 13), accepts William's visit as likely. Dr. David Douglas (*William the Conqueror*, p. 169) thinks it unlikely and feels it more probable that emissaries were sent by Edward to William to give him the nomination to the succession.

NOTE 23. p. 76. Election of British monarch. This feature of the Coronation Service is known as the Recognition. I quote from the *Form and Order of the Coronation of George VI and Queen Elizabeth (1937)* p. 13:

"The King and Queen being so placed, the Archbishop and after, together with the Lord Chancellor, Lord Great Chamberlain, Lord High Constable, and Earl Marshal (Garter King of Arms preceding them) shall go to the East side of the Theatre and after shall go to the other three sides in this order, South, West and North, and at every of the four sides the Archbishop shall with a loud voice speak to the People: and the King in the meanwhile standing up by his chair, shall turn and shew himself unto the People at every of the four sides of the Theatre as the Archbishop is at every of them, the Archbishop saying;

"Sirs, I here present unto you King George your undoubted King: Wherefore all you who are come this day to do your homage and service, are you willing to do the same?

"The People signify their willingness and joy, by loud and repeated acclamations, all with one voice, crying out, God save King George. Then the trumpets shall sound."

This ceremony follows the entrance of the sovereign into Westminster Abbey. The Theatre referred to is the platform on which the Coronation is performed. The English Coronation service or *ordo* dates from approximately 960–973 when King Edgar was crowned by Dunstan, Archbishop of Canterbury, and certainly the ceremony retains its essential elements after 1,000 years. The question put to those in Westminster Abbey at William the Conqueror's coronation was basically the same as that quoted above. The best historical study of coronation is by a German, Percy Ernst Schramm, *A History of the English Coronation,* (English translation, 1937).

NOTE 24. p. 80. Bayeux Tapestry. A good short study of the tapestry was by Sir Eric MacLagan (1949) in which the whole is illustrated. A longer account with a commentary and illustration of the whole is in *English Historical Documents*, Vol. II, pp. 232–78. In this it is pointed out that the tapestry represents 623 persons, 202 horses and mules, 55 dogs, 505 other animals, 37 buildings, 41 ships and boats and 49 trees. Modern scholarly opinion holds that the tapestry was made within living memory of the Conquest; the traditional story is that it was wrought by the ladies of Matilda, the Conqueror's wife. As English embroidery was famous at the time of the Conquest, it is possible that those who made the tapestry were English. From at least as early as 1476 the tapestry has been kept in the Cathedral at Bayeux. There is a diorama of the tapestry in the Victoria and Albert Museum, London.

NOTE 25. p. 81. Edward's building of Westminster Abbey. Dean A. P. Stanley, Dean of Westminster, gave a full account in his *Historical Memorials of Westminster Abbey* (1868): "The Abbey had been 15 years in building. The king had spent upon it one-tenth of the property of the kingdom. . . . It was the first cruciform church in England. . . . Its very size—occupying, as it did, almost the whole area of the present building—was in itself portentous." (pp. 26–27)

NOTE 26. p. 81. The king's deathbed visions. For an account of these see the book, *The War and the Prophets* (1915), by Fr. Herbert Thurston, S.J., pp. 173–75: "Contemporary evidence makes it practically certain that St. Edward on his death bed did narrate some such vision to those who stood around."

NOTE 27. p. 82. Reference to the Atheling. There is a long discussion on the latter in Freeman's *Norman Conquest*, Vol. III, pp. 766–67, Note 00. The Atheling Edgar.

"An election . . . followed by an abdication of the King-elect before the day of coronation came." p. 528

NOTE 28. p. 87. Numbers at Hastings. Dr. John Lingard, a Roman Catholic priest, wrote a *History of England*, 3rd edition, 1825. In Vol. I, p. 441, he quoted some of the original authorities for the numbers of William's host, as being 50,000 to 60,000. Thus, Ordericus Vitalis, p. 174. *Quinquaginta milia militum cum copia peditum*. Freeman wisely refused to go beyond the statement that Harold's numbers were adequate. Belloc inclines to a large number of English, because of the nature of the ridge at Hastings, which in his view would demand large numbers to hold it for any length of time.

NOTE 29. p. 95. Papal Bull on Ireland. *In Irish Historical Documents, 1172–1922*, edited by E. Curtis and R. B. McDowell (1968), the first place is given to the Bull *Laudabiliter*, Pope Adrian's grant of Ireland to Henry II. In this the Pope—the only Englishman ever to occupy St. Peter's chair—refers to the king's purpose "to enlarge the boundaries of the Church, to proclaim the truths of the Christian religion to a rude and ignorant people, and to root out the growths of vice from the field of the Lord." The Pope goes on: "There is no doubt that Ireland and all islands on which Christ, the sun of righteousness has shone, and which have accepted the doctrines of the Christian faith, belong to the jurisdiction of the blessed Peter and the holy Roman Church. ... Whereas then well-beloved son in Christ, you have expressed to us your desire to enter the island of Ireland in order to subject its people to law and to root out from them the weeds of vice, and your willingness to pay an annual tribute to the blessed Peter of one penny from every house," etc.

The whole is worth reading. The editors remark: "The original Latin text of this famous document is found in Giraldus Cambrensis, *Expugnatio Hibernica*, II, chap. VI.

It was granted during the pontificate of the English pope, Adrian IV (1154–59), probably in 1155 but was not acted upon until 1172 (*op. cit.* p. 18)." For a forthright commentary on the Bull, the reader may note the following quotation from Charles Kingsley's *The Hermits* (1905 edition, p. 253): ". . . all the miseries, deserved or undeserved, which have fallen upon the Irish since Pope Adrian IV (the true author of all the woes of Ireland), in the year 1155, commissioned Henry II to conquer Ireland, and destroy its primeval church, on consideration of receiving his share of the booty in the shape of Peter's Pence."

NOTE 30. p. 97. Coulthart of Coulthart. On this strange pedigree, see *The Ancestor,* Vol. IV, January 1903: "The Bonny House of Coulthart" by Oswald Barron.

NOTE 31. p. 98. The ancestry of Barclay. The descent of the Scottish Barclays is given in *Burke's Landed Gentry,* 1952, where Roger, mentioned in *Domesday* as provost of the manor of Berkeley, had a son, John, who went to Scotland in the train of the future Queen Margaret *ca.* 1069 and became laird of Towie in the parish of Turiff, Aberdeenshire. Lineal descent of the Scottish Barclays is traced from 1165. There are difficulties in accepting the traditional origin 100 years earlier, i.e., it seems unlikely that a Norman would travel with the Atheling's sister but the tradition points to the Barclays being sprung from the Norman side of the Berkeley complex.

NOTE 32. p. 107. Surnames: sources of information. Useful books are: C. W. Bardsley, *English Surnames* (reprinted 1969). P. H. Reaney, *A Dictionary of British Surnames* (1966). Dr. George F. Black, *The Surnames of Scotland* (New York Public Library, 1962). Dr. Edward MacLysaght, *A Guide to Irish Surnames* (1964). Also the last named author's three books on Irish families.

NOTE 33. p. 107. Change of surname and legality thereof.

See *Change of Name* by J. F. Josling, Solicitor, 1962. "It has always been recognized by the common law that a man may take any surname he pleases, provided he does not do so for any fraudulent purpose, or in order to deceive and inflict pecuniary loss on another."

NOTE 34. p. 109. Biscop genealogy. A correspondent has sent me some very interesting notes regarding the subject of English folk coming to take French names, including surnames. While the Norman family of St. Hilaire du Harcouet is undisputed, there may have been another family of the same name but of English origin. The name Bishop is derived from Old English bisc(e)op, possibly a nickname for one whose bearing resembled that of a bishop, etc. In *Domesday* the lord of Harpole in Northants was one Biscop. He had held it in the Confessor's time, and managed to keep it 20 years later. In accordance with the usual arrangements he found himself with a Norman overlord, William Peverel, and by 1155 the de Albinis had become overlords of Harpole and many villages around it. It would appear that descendants of Biscop entered into the service of the de Albinis. They held lands under them in Northants and neighboring counties. They held under the name of de Bisege for five generations Baddesley Clinton in Warwickshire. One of the later holders (in 1240) of Harpole is called either Peter de Harpole or Peter de St. Hilary de Harpole in various documents. The theory has been advanced that as one of the de Albinis took part in Henry I's victory at Tinchebrai, when many English soldiers served in Normandy, and was rewarded with grants of land there, some of his vassals may have been given posts under him in Normandy. Later when John lost Normandy, these English holders would perforce be compelled to reside solely in England. This may account for the use of de Harpole and St. Hilary as names of the same man, and thus it could come about that a family bearing the name of St. Hilaire or Hilary could be not of Norman but of English origin. This is purely a theory; an alternative theory is that the English-descended lord of Harpole may have taken the surname of one of his overlord's territorial fiefs in Normandy.

NOTE 35. p. 123. Queen's Champion. The descent of the Dymoke family is in *Burke's Landed Gentry*, 1952. Up to the time of George IV, the Sovereign's Champion rode into Westminster Hall at the banquet which followed the Coronation. The Champion was clad in armor and mounted on a powerful horse. He flung down his glove and offered to do battle with anyone who dared to deny that the newly crowned monarch was the lawful sovereign. It is a great pity that this colorful ceremony has been allowed to drop out and become obsolete. It was last used at the coronation of George IV. His successor William IV was obsessed with the need for economy, and even wished to dispense with a coronation. When William IV died and was succeeded by his niece, a young girl of 18, it was thought hardly suitable for her age, to be the principal figure at a great banquet. She reigned so long that all memory of customs connected with the coronation had vanished when her son and successor Edward VII came to the throne. The horse used for the ceremony had to be a strong animal and well used to backing in a crowd. So when the Champion rode into the Hall for the last time, he was mounted on a horse from Astley's Circus. For a romantic version of the challenge at the coronation of George III, no one should miss the story in Sir Walter Scott's *Redgauntlet*, though the account is of course imaginary.

The title of Champion is still borne by the head of the Dymoke family and he is also styled Standard Bearer of England. At the coronation in 1953 he bore the standard in the procession in the Abbey. In *Coronation*

Claims, Sir G. W. Wollaston tells of the records of a claim put forward by Frank Scaman Dymoke, the grandfather of the present Champion.

NOTE 36. p. 123. Incidents of Grand Serjeanty. "Coke tells us that 'tenure by Grand Serjeanty is, where a man holds his lands or tenements of our Sovereign Lord the King by such services as he ought to do in his proper person to the King, as to carry the banner of the King, or his lance, or to lead his army, or to be his marshall, or to carry his sword before him at his Coronation, or to be his Sewer at his Coronation, or his Carver, or his Butler, or to be one of his Chamberlaines of the receipt of his Exchequer, or to do other like services.' " (Sir G. W. Wollaston, *Coronation Claims,* 1910, pp. 17–18) The Coke referred to was Sir Edward Coke, one of the most learned judges ever to live in England. The claims to which reference was made still exist in England, and consequently before a coronation it is necessary for the Court of Claims to sit and hear the various claims adduced before it. Sir G. W. Wollaston's book is a very interesting account of this type of claim, at the coronations of Edward VII and George V.

NOTE 37. p. 136. William of Poitiers. "The insignia of royalty became him as well as the quality of his rule, and his sons and grandsons by a just succession will reign over the English land." The reference is to William I. The quotation comes from the extracts in *English Historical Documents,* Vol. IV, p. 231, from William of Poitiers, "The Deeds of William, Duke of the Normans and King of the English."

NOTE 38. p. 154. Dr. Lingard. John Lingard (1771–1851), Roman Catholic priest and historian. He was created a D.D. and a doctor of civil law by Pius VII in 1821, and was a pioneer in the writing of history as he refused to give any statements not based on authentic sources. His work is still well worth reading. A good analysis of his *History of England* was given in *History Today*, April 1951, by Philip Hughes.

NOTE 39. p. 154. Normans in England before the Conquest. In J. H. Round's *Feudal England* (1909), pp. 317–31, there is a study of this subject "The Normans under Edward the Confessor." The latter seems to have put various places on the coast, or a little inland, under the Normans, e.g., Winchilsea, Rye, Steyning, the last being then a place accessible by sea. Bosham King Edward gave to his Norman chaplain, Osbern. He favored the Normans in London. There was Richard, son of Scrob, who built a castle in Herefordshire, and was succeeded there by his son Osbern; and Osbern Pentecost, who had to go into exile when Godwin returned in 1052. According to Round, Alfred was a name known in Brittany before the Norman Conquest and he found an Alfred and a Jukel of Lincoln, the latter at least being a Breton settled in England under the Confessor. In addition there was William Malet, already mentioned, and Robert Fitz-Wimarc, claimed by Round as a Breton. He was a kinsman of Edward the Confessor and of William. Of this list only Malet is of use as a forbear.

NOTE 40. p. 155. Normans known to have been at Hastings; analysis of sources of information. In the first place we have the list given by Geoffrey H. White in the *Genealogists' Magazine,* Vol. VI, 1932, pp. 50–57. He gave as the only reliable authorities, William of Poitiers, Orderic Vitalis and the Bayeux Tapestry. He then gave a list of 15 persons, as in the text from 1 to 15, i.e., Robert de Beaumont to Odo. White then concluded with naming a few remaining families which traced a male line descent from a *Domesday* tenant, notably Fitz-Gerald, Carew, Gresley, and possibly St. John from tenants-in-chief, and Shirley and Wrottesley from sub-tenants. As has been emphasized in the text, mention in *Domesday* is evidence very frequently of Norman or

French origin, but not of presence at the actual battle in 1066, 20 years earlier. The chairman of the meeting at which White spoke then remarked that there are now no descents in the male line from any of the warriors mentioned—a statement difficult to reconcile with facts—and that besides the Conqueror himself, descents existed in the female line from perhaps 10 of the known Companions. Anyone who could show a descent from the medieval English baronage could probably show a descent from all of these. This list was greatly extended by Prof. David Douglas in *History*, Vol. xxviii, 1943, pp. 129–47. He demolished the authority of Wace, on whom writers like Planché and the Duchess of Cleveland had relied. The basis of Douglas's statements he gives as coming from the sources named above, Bayeux Tapestry, William of Poitiers, Vitalis and also from the poem *Carmen de bello,* formerly attributed to Guy, Bishop of Amiens, 1058–76; also from grants and charters. G. H. White commented on the enlarged list in 1944 (*Genealogists' Magazine,* IX, pp. 417–24); the *Complete Peerage,* (XII, part 1, new edition, 1953, pp. 47–48 of appendix) also gave a list of Companions of William. The name added by Mr. J. F. A. Mason was that of Humphrey de Tilleul, custodian of Hastings. It appears that the latter had been in England in the Confessor's time. Some of the later names mentioned by Prof. Douglas, i.e., nos. 33 to 38, are put by him as only possibles. It seems that another name can be gleaned from his earlier lists, however, that of Robert, Count of Mortaigne.

NOTE 41. p. 157. Controversy regarding presence at Hastings of Adelolf de la Marck (Merc). In *Burke's Landed Gentry* for 1952 there are included three articles of Marris, de Marris, and this family claims a Norman descent from an ancestor who was at Hastings. The pedigree was severely criticized by the present Garter King of Arms, Sir Anthony Wagner, then Richmond Herald, in the

Genealogists' Magazine for June 1954. A similar article, but not giving any reasons, was to the same upshot, in the December issue of the magazine, 1954, by the late Brig. B. C. Trappes-Lomax. J. F. A. Mason, in *English Historical Review*, Vol. lxxi, 1956, commented in a note: "There is no need to discuss here the attempt made to add the name of Adelolf de Merc to the list by L. G. Pine in *They Came with the Conqueror* (London, 1954). Adelolf's claims were demolished in the pages of *The Times Literary Supplement, Sunday Times* and *Observer*, during May, June and July, 1954 (p. 203)." The quotation from J. F. A. Mason gives references to three British periodicals, the back numbers of which are not likely to be accessible even in Britain unless one can examine the editorial files of the publications or visit the British Museum Library, Newspaper Section, at Colindale. There was much more to the controversy over my book, *They Came with the Conqueror*, than any demolition of a claim for Adelolf's presence at Hastings. For full details, I refer readers to Note 47 on the Marris controversy and to my preface to the present work.

NOTE 42 p. 160. The FitzWilliams. *Burke's Extinct Peerage* gives the story which is worth telling if only for its hilarious value. The barony of FitzWilliam created by writ of summons in 1327 petered out in the 14th century but the Earldom of FitzWilliam still exists and the holder is descended from the same stock. In the *Extinct Peerage* (1962 facsimile reprint, p. 215), the account is: "William FitzGodric is stated to have been cousin in blood to King Edward the Confessor, and to have been deputed upon an embassy by that monarch to William, Duke of Normandy, at whose court he remained until he returned with the expedition in 1066 as marshal of the invading army, and it is added that the Conqueror bestowed upon him a scarf from his own arms, for the gallantry he had displayed at Hastings." The true account of the rise of the FitzWilliams is given in the modern editions of *Burke's Peerage.* Those who can obtain a copy of *The Ancestor,* Vol. 12, pp. 111–17, can enjoy Oswald Barron's criticism of the hotchpotch of nonsense which I have quoted. That such a story could ever have been accepted goes far to demonstrate the low esteem in which early Victorian writers held genealogy. Also that so eminent a writer as Sir Bernard Burke should have given countenance to it. Incidentally, Barron mentions that "For this legendary beginning and for each and all of its details, the signatures and seals of three Elizabethan kings of arms stand for all proof, William Harvey, Clarenceux, testifying that the descent 'is sufficient to satisfy any judge.' " (p. 112)

NOTE 43. p. 166. Charters of Battle Abbey. A Descriptive Catalogue of the original charters, royal grants and donations of Battle Abbey was made and set up for sale by Thomas Thorpe, of London, in 1835.

NOTE 44. p. 171. Ownership of English land. "Let us agree that after the conquest all land in England was, in some sense, held directly of the king (as indeed it was until 1925)." A note is added: "The rule (i.e., that all land was owned by the Crown) was abrogated by the Administration of Estates Act, 1925, s. 45 (i) (d)." This is from *The Governance of Medieval England from the Conquest to Magna Carta,* by H. G. Richardson and G. O. Sayles (1963), p. 116. The section of the Act quoted reads: Abolition of descent to heir, curtsey, dower and escheat. S. (i) (d) (Abolished) "Escheat to the Crown, or the Duchy of Lancaster, or the Duke of Cornwall, or to a mesne lord for want of heirs."

It is suggested, however, that the above ruling does not really abolish the theory that the Crown owns the whole land of England, and that absolute ownership of land is unknown to English law.

NOTE 45. p. 173. Charles Kingsley. I cannot find this exact quotation in Kingsley's works, but the sense is undoubtedly in his writings, e. g., in the introduction to his *Hereward the Wake*.

NOTE 46. p. 173. Dean Inge. "The Norman Conquest, which may have depended on the accident that Harold, and not William, was killed at the battle of Hastings, was probably an almost unmitigated misfortune to England. Two hundred years of foreign rule never yet did a nation anything but harm, and our long entanglement with France was disastrous to both." W. R. Inge, *England* (1926), p. 27.

NOTE 47. p. 175. Marris controversy. The full story is given on pp. 263–70 of this book.

NOTE 48 p. 179. *The Ancestor* has been mentioned more than once, so that it may interest readers to have have some details about it. It began in April 1902, as a Quarterly Review of County and Family History, Heraldry and Antiquities. The editor was the noted heraldic scholar, Oswald Barron, and among the distinguished contributors were Sir George Sitwell, Sir Henry Maxwell Lyte, J. H. Round and W. St. John Hope. The work ran to 12 vols. ending in January 1905. Anyone who can acquire a set is advised to do so.

NOTE 49. p. 180. The Decretals or the Forged Decretals as they are often called were published in 850 under the name of Isodore Mercator to suggest that they were the work of St. Isodore, Bishop of Seville. "They consisted of authentic canons, and papal decretals, interspersed with others purporting to have been issued by the popes from the earliest times, which were in fact fabricated by the author. They were accepted in good faith. Doubt was cast upon them by Nicholas of Cusa in the 15th century and by Erasmus and others in the 16th but it was not until the 17th that they were given up by the Roman Church."

C. P. S. Clarke, *Short History of the Christian Church From the Earliest Times to the Present Day* (1929). The aim of the author was to protect ecclesiastics and church property from violence and spoliation. According to the Decretals, the clergy were supreme in their property, in church government and in church courts. The emperor was not, like Charlemagne, to summon synods. The metropolitan was not the final court of appeal for oppressed bishops. They were to appeal to the Pope. The immediate effect of the Decretals was negligible. "But in the 10th and 11th centuries they were a potent weapon in the hands of the theocratic Popes from Hildebrand to Boniface VIII." (*op. cit.*)

NOTE 50. p. 181. Donation of Constantine. Lord Bryce in *The Holy Roman Empire* (edition 1912) p. 43, wrote: "For this is probably the very time, although neither the exact date nor the complicity of any pope can be established, to which must be assigned the extraordinary forgery of the Donation of Constantine, whereby it was pretended that power over Italy and the whole west had been granted by the first Christian emperor to Pope Sylvester and his successors... in the singular document most stupendous of all the medieval forgeries, which under the name of the Donation of Constantine commanded for seven centuries the almost unquestioning belief of mankind. Itself a portentious fabrication, it is unimpeachable evidence of the thoughts and beliefs of the priesthood which framed it some time between the middle of the 8th and the end of the 9th century." (pp. 99–100) In Note IV (p. 509) part of the document is given in the original Latin as found in Gratian's *Corpus Juris Canonici*, Dist. XCVI., cc. 13, 14. Bryce adds: "The spurious nature of the Donation of Constantine was proved by Laurentius Valla in 1440."

NOTE 51. p. 182. Hereditary officers at Norman court. Dr. Douglas gives details about great officers at the ducal court. The steward (William FitzOsbern); Chamberlain (Ralph, son of Gerald, lord of Tancarville); Butler (Hugh of Ivry), and Constable (Robert of Ver). *William the Conqueror*, p. 146.

NOTE 52. p. 185. Sale of Honours. This subject is treated at length in *Honours for Sale, The Strange Story of Maundy Gregory* (1954), by Gerald Macmillan. The person concerned, Maundy Gregory, was the only person ever to be prosecuted under the Honours (Prevention of Abuses) Act, 1925, mentioned in the text. The history of the sale of honours from James I's time up to 1932 is given in Appendix II to Macmillan's book. For the end of the Gregory episode, the latest account is in *Memoirs of a Conservative*, by R. H. James (1969), pp. 278–82 and p. 288.

NOTE 53. p. 190. Marquess of Ailesbury. The present marquess is author of a very interesting book, *The Wardens of Savernake Forest*, written before he succeeded to the marquessate, when he was known by the courtesy title of Earl of Cardigan. In this he tells of the descent of the wardens, he being the 29th hereditary Warden.

NOTE 54. p. 207. *The Siege of Caerlaverock* is a poem written in French which relates the siege and capture in 36 hours of a small castle in Dumfrieshire, Scotland, in 1300 during the July campaign of Edward I in that year. The author's main purpose was to describe the armorial bearings of those present. He describes 87 or 88 banners and more than 100 coats of arms. It has been conjectured that he was a herald in the train of King Edward I, and the lists of arms are known as the Roll of Caerlaverock. The manuscript of the poem was translated and printed by Sir Harris Nicolas in 1828 with copious notes; again translated in blank verse and published in 1864 by Thomas Wright.

NOTE 55. p. 207. *Scrope v. Grosvenor*. The proceedings in this case are contained in two large volumes published in

1832 by Sir Harris Nicolas under the title, *The Controversy between Sir Richard Scrope and Sir Robert Grosvenor in the Court of Chivalry,* 1386–90. The original documents consisting mainly of depositions of witnesses were in French.

NOTE 56. p. 209. Original English settlements. The best sources for the study of this subject are in the first two volumes of the *Oxford History of England:* I *Roman Britain and the English Settlements,* by R. G. Collingwood and J. N. L. Myres (1937); II *Anglo-Saxon England,* by F. M. Stenton (1943). For contrast, see Vol. I. of Hilaire Belloc's *History of England* (1925), and for the older view, Green's *Short History of the English People.* Some of the original sources are fairly easy of access: *de Excidio Britanniae,* by St. Gildas with Latin and English text and many notes (Cymmrodorion Record Series), and the *Historia Ecclesiastica* or *Ecclesiastical History of the English Nation,* by the Venerable Bede (Everyman's Edition).

NOTE 57. p. 210. *Beowulf.* The latest translation of this poem has been in prose by David Wright (Penguin Books, 1957), with an introduction, notes and appendices. The translator wrote (p. 9): "Almost everyone has heard of *Beowulf,* which is one of the earliest and indeed the most impressive of the Anglo-Saxon or Old English poems that have come down to us. The whole body of Old English poetry known to be in existence comes to no more than about 30,000 lines."

NOTE 58. p. 211. English treatment of Roman province. Argument never ceases as to the degree of extermination or driving out of the native inhabitants by the English. Perhaps the most useful guides are found in archaeology which shows few British cities taken by storm; and in place names. The elaborate work by Eilert Ekwall, *The Oxford Dictionary of English Place Names,* records the survival of many British place names.

NOTE 59. p. 212. Daniel Defoe. His verses, *The True*

Born Englishman (1701), are directed against the objections to William III as being a foreigner and set out to show the idea of the English as a mixed race. For a corrective, see, *An Essay on the Nature of Contemporary England* (1937) by Hilaire Belloc, where the homogeneous nature of the British population is stressed. Also, the opinion of a noted authority, Sir Arthur Keith, who wrote: "Do people . . . of the Romano-British type occur in our modern population? I would answer that inquiry with a confident yes–in very considerable numbers, particularly amongst the English middle classes." (Quoted in R. G. Collingwood's and J. N. L. Myres's *Roman Britain and the English Settlements,* p. 18) The import of these views would be to endorse the view that there is a basic British population which has received in the period of the 11 centuries before the Norman Conquest waves of invaders, who became a ruling caste until displaced by the next body of invaders. This would make the newcomers small in numbers, while the basic population remained in the majority. It does appear that in the course of the 5th and 6th centuries there were large migrations into Britain of Germanic peoples, who pushed the Britons back into the western side of the island. There can hardly be a question that the Celts— Welsh, Highland Scots, and Cornish—differ greatly from the English, even though much Celtic blood has been mixed with English. The later Scandinavians were closely akin to the English and the Norman leaders themselves were often of Scandinavian descent. Moreover, the Norman and French elements, like the Scandinavian before them, were not too large to be mingled with the English, with whom they were three parts of the same blood. Instead of a mixed race we have a reasonably homogeneous people derived from closely related stocks.

NOTE 60. p. 213. Jewish settlement in England. For Jewish communities in England in previous times, the reader should consult, *The Rise of Provincial Jewry, The*

Early History of the Jewish Communities in the English Countryside, 1740–1940, by Prof. Cecil Roth (1950).

NOTE 61. p. 214. Magna Carta sureties. The names of these were:

William d'Aubigny (de Albini)
Hugh Bigod
Roger Bigod
Henry de Bohun
Gilbert de Clare
John FitzRobert
Richard de Clare
Robert FitzWalter
William de Huntingfield
John de Lacy
William de Lanvallei.
William Malet
William de Mowbray
Saher de Quincy
Robert de Roos
Geoffrey de Saye
Robert de Vere
The Mayor of London
William Marshall
Richard de Percy
William de Fortibus
Geoffrey de Mandeville
Eustace de Vesci
Richard de Montfichet
Roger de Montbegon.
(also) Stephen Langton, Archbishop of Canterbury, from whom of course no descent is traced.

Note 40, with regard to descent from the English baronage of the Middle Ages, applies here. How far this ancestry is found in the U.S.A. can be gauged by the existence of the Baronial Order of Magna Carta, the members of which usually have a banner of the arms of their distinguished baronial ancestors.

NOTE 62. p. 228. Presidential dynasty of the U.S.A. The article on this subject is in *The Augustan*, by Robert W. Formhals, Vol. X, no. 4, April–May 1967.

*   *   *

Marris controversy. The full story of this controversy is as follows. In the records of Ulster Office (now the Genealogical Office), Dublin Castle, Ireland, a pedigree for Marris was entered. It begins with:

Osbert de Marc, who held lands in Northamptonshire in 1086 (*Domesday* Survey). He had a son.

Adelolf, alias Athelwulf, alias Aluf, alias Alan de Marc, who held land in Essex, 1086, and inherited the Northamptonshire lands. He *m*. the daughter and heiress of de la Launde and had issue,

Jordan de Marrisco, alias de Insula, who *m*. Hadwissa, the daughter of Baldwin Redvers, of the Isle of Wight and of Devon. They had issue,

Geoffrey de Marrisco, who held a half fee in Huntspill, Somerset, and of the manor of Bampton, in 1166 (*Liber Niger*). He *m*. the dau. of FitzAzor of the Isle of Wight family and had issue,

Robert de Marisco, mentioned in Devon Pipe Roll, 1175–80, and *m*. a sister of Archbishop Comyns who *d. circa* 1220. They had issue,

1. William de Marisco, son and heir, *b*. before 1162, of Huntspill, Cameby and Lundy, *d*. 1194–1229–30. He *m*. Lucy, dau. of Alexander de Alneto, Lord of Cameby. She was *bur*. at Bath Abbey. They had issue,

   (1) Jordan de Marisco of Huntspill, Cameby, Lundy Corkeduffeney, *b*. before 1189, *suc*. by 1233, *d*. 1234 and *bur*. at Bath Abbey. He had issue,

   1a. William de Marisco, of Huntspill, Cameby, East Rasen (now Middle Rasen), Lincolnshire, Lundy, Weyperous, Corkeduffeney and Latteragh, *b*. before 1213, *d*. 1284, *bur*. at Bath Abbey. He *m*. 1st Margery, mentioned as being in Devon with her husband 1242, in Lincolnshire with him, 1268, (Pipe Rolls) and *m*. 2nd Matilda, widow of William Fukeram, of Wyke, Somerset, who *d*. 1257.

   2a. Richard, of Balylymasty and Balyrigan.

   3a. Jordan, 1258. In Lincolnshire 1271–72 (Assize Roll).

(2) Three other sons, probably named Adam, Robert and Elias.

(1) Agnes, by 1211 *m.* William de Hanton, Lord of Bridgeworth, Somerset.

(2) and (3) two other daus. living 1217 and 1220.

2. Walter *d.* by 1192.

3. Jordan, *d. circa* 1192.

4. Geoffrey, *b.* before 1171. Justiciar, *d.* 1245. His 1st wife was dau. of . . . Esserby and his 2nd, Eva de Bermingham. By his 1st wife he had issue,

(1) William, 1242. *m.* Matilda de Londres, niece of Henry de Londres, Archbishop of Dublin.

(2) John.

(1) Joan, *d.* 1225, *m.* Theobald, Walter II, who *d.* 1230.

By his 2nd wife, Geoffrey had

(3) Robert.

5. . . . *m.* . . . Travers, and had issue,

(1) Robert Travers, Bishop of Killaloe, deposed 1221.

(2) John Travers, *d.* 1234.

It should be noted (i) that various spellings of the same name occur above, as in most old pedigrees; (ii) there are mentions of places in Ireland, since this family took part in the Anglo-Norman Conquest of Ireland; (iii) numberings of sons and daughters of the same generation are in different sequences.

The above is of course only the beginning of the registered pedigree, but on its basis were written the three articles on the Marris family in the 1952 edition of *Burke's Landed Gentry,* namely, *Marris of Burton Corner, Marris of Clinton House,* and *Winston-Davisde Marris of Pattyndenne Manor.* The first and second derive the beginnings of their genealogy from the third. The pedigree as recorded in Ulster Office has been much enlarged and in some parts of the narrative altered, but the main point in dispute, i.e., the descent from Adelolf, remains the same. In the registered pedigree it should also be noticed that although there is no mention of Adelolf having been present at Hastings, both he and his father, Osbert, are described as *Domesday* tenants, and from other references shown below, they appear as having been among the invaders and settlers in England.

When the pedigree was printed in *Burke*, it began with the statement, "The early part of this pedigree is taken from a pedigree recorded in Ulster's Office." In this connection it is of interest to see that the first of the Marris articles, *Marris of Burton Corner,* has an arms illustration which is unusual, except in the case of a family which has been traced for a long period. It is quarterly of 12, and has 1st and 12th quarters, Marris Modern, 2nd Marris Ancient, 3rd de la Launde, 4th de la Haye, 5th Camville, 6th Hansard, 7th Harcourt, 8th Brignell, 9th Neville, 10th Conyers and 11th de Vesci. For those not familiar with heraldic usage it should be explained that the difference between Marris Modern and Marris Ancient occurs when a family is found to have two coats of arms, possibly because the existence of the older coat has been overlooked or forgotten, a new coat granted and then the old one rediscovered.

Not only was the Marris pedigree registered in the Ulster Office by the Deputy Ulster, T. Ulick Sadleir, but the bulk of the pedigree was accepted in 1944 by the then Garter King of Arms, Sir Algar Howard. He requested to see the recorded pedigree. In a letter to Mr. H. C. Marris, of Burton Corner, Sir Algar wrote (8 Sept. 1944): "I told your cousin that I would be prepared to allow the quarterings of the ancient coat of Herbert de Maresco as borne by him at the Dunstable Tournament." The tournament occurred in 1308. In a letter of 11 Sept. 1944, Sir Algar again wrote to Mr. H. C. Marris: "In reply to your letter I propose making a painting of the 12 quarterings repeating the Marris one at the end to make it an even number. The cost of this, somewhat about the size on your confirmation, would be £21–0–0. Below, I would nominate the quarterings, giving a special description to Marris Ancient, and I will then certify it as being extracted from the records of Ulster Office and the College of Arms. Please let me know if you approve this."

In 1966 when England was preparing to celebrate the 9th centenary of the Norman Conquest, the *Daily Telegraph* produced its weekend color magazine under the title "1066 The Invasion, The Battle, The Families, etc." Among the families with a claimed ancestor at Hastings was Marris. [The others were Pomeroy, Curzon, Mallet and Giffard.] Mr. H. Marris was interviewed by the newspaper and quoted as saying: "All my work on the pedigree seems worthwhile. .... I have a steel filing cabinet filled with documents. This is the coat of arms that I have had approved. Ten quarterings, you see, apart from my own. I am delighted that the College of Arms granted me it. A Marris bore it at the Dunstable Tournament in 1308" (*Daily Telegraph, Weekend Telegraph*, no. 67, 7 Jan. 1966).

The Marris family had good reason to be pleased. Registered in Ulster Office (one of the three official heraldic offices in the British Isles, the others being the Heralds' College, London, and the Lyon Office, Edinburgh). Accepted by the principal of the three Kings of Arms, the Garter King, in the Heralds' College. The confirmation of the quarterings included arms borne by a Marris in 1308. This Marris was summoned in 1302 as a baron to the Irish Parliament. He was unlikely to have been a parvenu. He is described as holding family properties which were held by his ancestors in 1166. It is to be noted also that the quartering of de la Launde is accepted and given in the list of quarterings which Sir Algar Howard was willing to illustrate. This coat of de la Launde must have been that ascribed to the de la Launde who married the second man on the pedigree, Adelolf de Merc. In addition, many of the families mentioned in the list of quarterings were of Norman origin, so that the

Marris line have Norman ancestry through females, apart from the male line descent which is claimed and which has twice been accepted by heraldic officers.

Why then the doubts on this pedigree? They were set forth in 1954 by the then Richmond Herald, now Sir Anthony Wagner, Garter King of Arms, after the publication of my book, *They Came with the Conqueror*. In an article in the June issue (1954) of the *Genealogists' Magazine,* Sir Anthony went over the various parts of the earlier Marris pedigree. He said nothing about Sir Algar Howard's acceptance of the formal pedigree registered in Ulster Office, but of the Deputy Ulster's acceptance of the Norman or *Domesday* origins of Marris he had this to say, in a letter to me dated 20 Ausgust 1954: "I should much prefer not to bring Sadleir into this if you could see your way to avoid it because though he has made a bad mistake in this matter and is no authority on Anglo-Norman Genealogy, he has always been a very kind and helpful person and is now old and has had misfortune, nor has he for a long time held any official position."

It should be explained that two years before the publication of my book, the Marris pedigree with the reference at the beginning to Ulster Office, had been published in *Burke's Landed Gentry*. Also in an article on English pedigrees in that 1952 edition, I had written (p. xli) after giving a list of companions of the Conqueror, "to this list I would add the name of Adelolf de Merc, ancestor of the Marris family."

For those unfamiliar with the old Ulster Office, the last Ulster King of Arms was Sir Nevile Rodwell Wilkinson, who died in 1940. From 1921–43 Thomas Ulick Sadleir was Deputy Ulster and he acted after Wilkinson's death until the office of Ulster King was united with that of Norroy at the College of Arms. The Genealogical Office was then set up in Dublin Castle under the Chief Herald of Ireland, an official of the Irish Republican Government.

The crux of the matter is that a herald was criticizing two others of his own order, one of them the principal King of Arms in his own office. Thus by criticizing the pedigree, Sir Anthony was implicitly criticizing the decision of Sir Algar Howard, one of his predecessors in the high office which he now holds, for having accepted the earlier portion (and of course the whole) of the pedigree, this being inevitable in view of the entry of de la Launde in the list of quarterings.

There appear to be two elements in the Marris pedigree which arouse criticism. There is the critique of the descent prior to 1166. Apart from this is the argument that Adelolf de Merc was not at Hastings, a matter which assumes more importance with some critics than a religious or scientific dogma. Now, even if the Marris pedigree is incorrect, there remains the subject of his presence at Hastings.

In his *Norman Conquest*, Vol. iii, p. 313 and Appendix Y, Freeman mentions the story of Arnold of Ardres who with his brother Geoffrey went from the county of Guines to fight for William. The brothers were well rewarded with lands which they held of Count Eustace of Boulogne, in Essex and East Anglia. Freeman remarks that "Arnold and Arnulf are names whose various forms are often and easily confounded" (p. 714), and he gives Ernulfus and Arnulfus as forms of Arnold. J. H. Round in *Feudal England* (pp. 462–64) goes further and in a paper, "The Lords of Ardres," refers to a paper by Freeman, "The Lords of Ardres," later than the latter's *Norman Conquest*. Round makes several interesting points: (i) The brothers, Arnold and Geoffrey, were not as Freeman thought the sons of Geoffrey, an officer of Saint Bertin's Abbey at St. Omer, but of Arnold, Lord of Ardres; (ii) the Count of Guines, the heir of Arnold of Ardres, held lands in Bedfordshire, Cambridgeshire, and Essex; (iii) Adelolf de Merk (Merc) is found in *Domesday* holding many manors direct from Eustace of Boulogne and later these manors were divided between his descendants Simon and Henry de Merk; (iv) "It is therefore possible that he [i.e., Adelolf de Merc,—L.G.P.] held the three Essex Manors in 1086, not directly from Count Eustace, but like his descendants from their under-tenant."(Arnold, pp. 463–64) Round also quotes from Freeman's Essay on "The Lords of Ardres" in which Freeman says "The local writer seems to have mixed up the possessions of Arnold with those of a less famous adventurer from the same region, Adelolf—our Athelwulf—of Merck." (Round, *ibidem*, p. 463)

Bearing in mind my own caution against assuming presence at Hastings from a mention in *Domesday*, there does still seem some good reason for thinking that Adelolf de Merc was present at the battle. I leave it to readers to judge whether my statements regarding this man have been demolished. The curious spectacle of one herald demolishing the pedigree accepted by two others is quite another matter.

Index